★ ARIZONA

Enjoy Arizona!

Jim Turner

A Celebration of

MAYNARD DIXON

ARIZONA
the Grand Canyon State

Jim Turner

GIBBS SMITH
TO ENRICH AND INSPIRE HUMANKIND

First Edition
15 14 13 12   7 6 5 4 3

Published by
Gibbs Smith
P.O. Box 667
Layton, Utah 84041
1.800.835.4993 orders
www.gibbs-smith.com

Image Credits:
Title Page: Cloud Banks and Shadows (1944–45),
Arizona, by Maynard Dixon. Courtesy of Mark
Sublette, Medicine Man Gallery, Tucson, Arizona.

Designed and produced by Kurt Wahlner
Printed and bound in China

Gibbs Smith books are printed on either recycled,
100% post-consumer waste or on FSC-certified
papers or on paper produced from a 100% certified
sustainable forest/controlled wood source.

Library of Congress Cataloging-in-Publication Data

Turner, Jim.
  Arizona : a celebration of the Grand
Canyon State / Jim Turner. — 1st ed.
     p. cm.
  Includes bibliographical references and index.
  ISBN 978-1-4236-0742-7 (alk. paper)
  1. Arizona—History. 2. Arizona. I. Title.
  F811.T79 2011
  979.1—dc22
                                    2011013861

 # CONTENTS

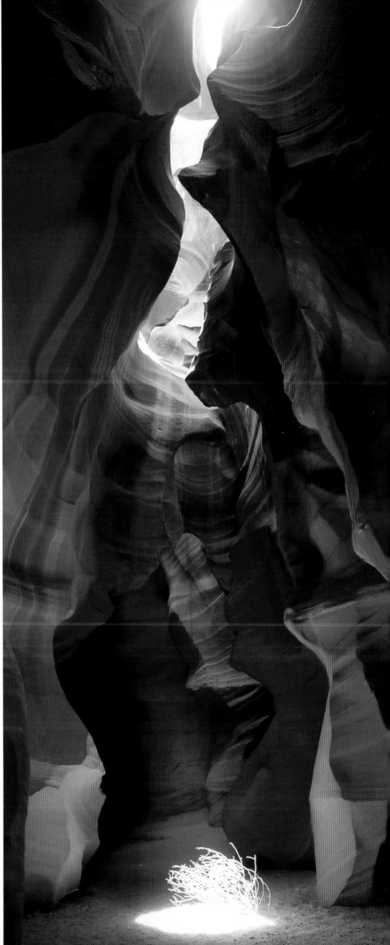

*The Corkscrew, Antelope
Canyon near Page, Arizona.
© Jerry Jacka, 2011.*

To Ed and Mary Turner—
dedicated and supportive parents who
passed on their passion for Arizona

*Gamblers liked to be known as
"Knights of the Green Felt."
Courtesy of the Arizona
Historical Society (B409).*

★ ACKNOWLEDGMENTS

I want to thank every history professor, classmate, student, friend, and colleague who helped me accumulate the smattering of Arizona history I've absorbed over the past forty years. I especially appreciate all the staff and volunteers from more than seventy history museums in every corner of the state that I had the privilege to work with while serving as Community Outreach Historian for the Arizona Historical Society.

Those who were especially helpful with the images for this book include the following:

Bill and Lynn Haak, Gila County Historical Society Museum;

Hal Herbert and Mel Jones, Graham County Historical Society;

Bill Porter and Shannon Rossiter, Mohave County Museum of History and Arts;

Maria Hernandez, Phoenix Public Library;

Pat Faux, H. Christine Reid, and Lynn Smith, Pinal County Historical Society Museum;

Cheryl Mammano and Stan Benjamin, San Pedro Valley Arts and Historical Society;

Janeen Trevillyan, Sedona Historical Society;

Melanie Hefner, Show Low Historical Society;

Kathy Klump, Sulphur Springs Historical Society;

Jim McMeekin, Verde Historical Society.

Arizona Historical Society staff members Dr. Bruce Dinges, Kim Frontz, Jill McCleary, and Kate Reeve were of invaluable assistance and support.

Fellow historians and authors Jan Cleere, L. Boyd Finch, Bernard Fontana, James S. "Big Jim" Griffith, Jeff Guinn, Diana Hadley, Charles Herner, William D. Kalt III, Richard Jones, Alan Kruse, Jack Lasseter, Dr. James McBride, Joseph Meehan, Dr. Lydia Otero, Dr. Robert Smith, Jon Talton, Dr. Andrew Wallace, and William Wilson shared their experience, strength, and hope.

And many thanks to publisher Gibbs Smith and his staff, who encouraged and supported me from start to finish, especially Kurt Wahlner for his stunning design.

Without you all, this book would not be here.

The night-blooming cereus is in flower for just one night, but it has a beautiful fragrance.

⭐ INTRODUCTION

> The trip across Arizona is just one oasis after another.
> You can just throw anything out and it will grow there;
> I like Arizona.
>
> —Will Rogers

Almost everyone in the world knows something about Arizona, and some of it is even true. The Grand Canyon State is famous for Geronimo, Tombstone, the Petrified Forest, Zane Grey, Barry Goldwater, and—later—John McCain. From ancient cliff dwellings to cutting-edge bio-tech industries, Arizona's history is unique and often misunderstood. Even before the railroad closed the great American frontier, dime novels and Wild West shows made up their own history of the Southwest. It was always more "fakelore" than fact, but the public couldn't get enough gunfights and Apache raids. They make for great reading, and some of them are based on true stories—or at least they were before the editors and directors got their hands on them.

Those legends are great, and we never tire of them, but there's always more to learn; and when it comes to Arizona history, the truth is still stranger and more interesting than fiction. For instance, we all love the idea of a town named Tombstone, but whatever happened to Ed Schieffelin, the man who found a rich silver vein instead of his tombstone? How did Arizona wind up with the most misunderstood name of any of the fifty states? The standard cowboys and Indians tales are just the tip of the sand dune when it comes to Arizona's fascinating realities.

Nicknamed the "Baby State" because it was the last of the contiguous

FACING: Totem Pole [*right*] and Yei-bi-chai Rocks, Monument Valley, Arizona. © *Jerry Jacka, 2011. ABOVE: Climate and location brought World War II training bases to Arizona. Courtesy of the Mohave County Historical Society.*

states to join the Union, its admission in 1912 created the 48-star American flag that flew until Alaska and Hawaii rounded it out to 50 stars in 1959. Arizona may be a latecomer to statehood, but it's the home of the first Republican Party presidential candidate and the first female U.S. Supreme Court Justice.

Newcomers and visitors often think there's not much history in Arizona, but nothing could be farther from the truth. The Grand Canyon, the world's open-air geology textbook, begins with ancient schist strata at the bottom of the canyon that date back 1.7 billion years. From dinosaur tracks to petrified tree trunks, Arizona's prehistoric record is set in stone. Eleven thousand years ago, ancient cultures

ABOVE: *Geronimo and Naiche at Fort Bowie after their final surrender. Courtesy of the Gila County Historical Society.*

ABOVE RIGHT: *Apaches learned the art of basket-making in their youth. Courtesy of the Gila County Historical Society.*

BELOW CENTER: *Apaches are masters of intricate basketry patterns.*

BELOW RIGHT: *Huhugam Ki Museum's modern architecture at the Salt River Pima-Maricopa Indian Community.*

FACING: *The White House cliff dwelling in Canyon de Chelly. Courtesy of Victor Beer Photography.*

hunted Ice Age mammoths through tropical swamps in what we now call Arizona. Several millennia later, while King John signed the Magna Carta and Genghis Khan conquered Asia, ancient farmers built multistoried cliff dwellings and dug hundreds of miles of precisely engineered irrigation canals throughout the Southwest.

Decades before Jamestown and Plymouth Rock, hundreds of Spanish conquistadors traveled thousands of miles from Mexico City to the center of Kansas in their quest for gold, glory, and God. They were followed by missionary priests in the 1600s and then soldiers in the next century, building forts on New Spain's northern frontier.

Next came the mountain men—Jedediah Smith and Kit Carson among them—trapping beaver on Arizona's rivers, learning the mountains and trails from the Native Americans. The Mormon Battalion followed them, heading west to wrest California from Mexico, just before gold was discovered at Sutter's Mill.

Two decades before the Earps fired on Ike and Billy Clanton *near* the O.K. Corral, the farthest-west Civil War battle played out at Picacho Peak. The discovery of big

LEFT: Western music became an Arizona tradition for locals and tourists. Courtesy of the Arizona Historical Society (PC204F38/D).

BELOW LEFT: Canvas radiator bags like this one helped motorists make it across the desert.

BELOW RIGHT: Railroad brochures fostered nineteenth-century tourism.

BELOW: Navajo sheep ranch near Canyon de Chelly.

ABOVE: *Clear skies meant lots of flying time in the Southwest. Courtesy of the Mohave County Historical Society.*

RIGHT: *Resort hotels like the Westward Ho in Phoenix attracted winter visitors in the 1920s and '30s. Courtesy of Dori Griffin.*

nuggets and rich veins in rivers, creeks, and mountains almost everywhere in Arizona attracted California forty-niners still caught in the gold fever's greedy grip. Merchants, gamblers, and soiled doves followed the prospectors. Boomtowns sprang up overnight and just as quickly turned to ghost towns when the minerals played out.

The population boom created tension with Arizona's indigenous peoples, encroachment led to conflict, and then violence led to vengeance. A downward spiral began that brought a fourth of the United States Army to Arizona. Decades later, the struggle ended in exile and confinement, but native beliefs and culture survived through strength and persistence.

The railroad tugged Arizona belatedly into the modern era in the 1880s, and Wild West mythology and "Land of Enchantment" marketing added tourism to mining and ranching as the state's major industries. Ease of travel brought Health Seekers, reclamation dams brought farmers, and, as the century moved into the 1900s, Arizona's "Five Cs" became economic bywords: Copper, Cattle, Cotton, Citrus, and Climate.

The battle for statehood was finally won on Valentine's Day 1912. A few years later, General "Black Jack" Pershing and the Buffalo Soldiers chased General Pancho Villa in Mexico. America fell in love with cowboy stars Tom Mix and Doug Fairbanks in the 1920s, and Arizona cashed in on the dude ranch craze. The Great Depression hit hard, but Arizona got many WPA projects and more than its share of Civilian Conservation Corps (CCC) workers who could keep working in the winter in most parts of the state.

In World War II, Hispanics and Native Americans joined Anglo Arizonans and fought for freedom and

ABOVE: The roadside town of Two Guns fell into ruins when Interstate 40 replaced Route 66.

BELOW: Apache culture meets modern technology at the Coolidge Dam. Courtesy of the Pinal County Historical Society.

ABOVE: *The agave (ah-GAH-vey), commonly known as the century plant.*

BELOW: *Ranching is still picturesque in the Sulphur Springs Valley near Dos Cabezas. Courtesy of Carol Wien.*

FACING: *Oak Creek Canyon, one of Arizona's many scenic attractions. Courtesy of Victor Beer Photography.*

democracy as members of the Navajo and Hopi Code Talkers unit and Bushmasters (158th Infantry Regiment). On the Home Front, Arizona's warm climate and open spaces finally began to pay off as there were plenty of opportunities for citizens to serve their country by working in airplane factories and training bases.

After the war, the state was proud home of Senator Ernest McFarland, father of the G.I. Bill, which quadrupled college enrollments and started a housing boom that has grown quite steadily ever since. A new freeway system and booming economy brought more and more tourists and vacationers to Arizona. The aircraft and electronics industries boosted the economy, and Del Webb developed the first senior community, Sun City.

Arizonans got national attention in the 1960s when Stewart Udall served as John F. Kennedy's Secretary of the Interior and Senator Barry Goldwater, whose grandfather arrived in Arizona just after the California gold rush, won the 1964 Republican Party nomination for U.S. president. César Chávez worked with other leaders to create the United Farm Workers.

Recent decades served science with the giant telescopes and Mars Phoenix Lander technology, computer hardware and software production, and, most recently, genetic engineering, cancer research, and other groundbreaking medical successes.

But through all its progress, Arizona's enduring treasures are still its scenic wonders. The Grand Canyon, Monument Valley, the red rocks of Sedona, and the Painted Desert are only the best of show in a state where more than 80 percent of the land is set aside as national forests, national and state parks, wilderness areas, preserves, and nature conservancies.

Whether you are a native Arizonan, a longtime resident, or a new arrival, we hope this book gives you new appreciation for your state. If you live elsewhere, we hope it encourages you to visit for the first time or reminds you to return.

CHAPTER ONE
★ VOLATILE LANDS AND VALUABLE WATERS

Here you have no rain when all the earth cries for it,
or quick downpours called cloud-bursts for violence.
A land of lost rivers, with little in it to love;
yet a land that once visited must be come back to inevitably.

—Mary Austin, *Land of Little Rain,* 1903

Arizona is one of the most beautiful, fascinating, and yet misunderstood states in the Union. For decades it has been saddled with stereotypes in every form of media, from Western movies to Roadrunner cartoons. Portrayed as sand dunes, buzzards, and bleached cow skulls, more than half the state is not even desert. Even the desert portion is not uninhabitable sand dunes but supports hundreds of species of plants and animals. But this book is not intended to be a natural history; rather, it's about people and how they interact with each other and their environment. History is often defined as the written record of mankind, yet for almost 14,000 years, Arizona's unique geology and geography have influenced human civilization so much that the people and their environment are eternally interdependent. You cannot talk about human history without examining what came before it.

Novelist James Michener started all of his epics with the creation of the earth, that giant spinning ball of molten lava. He talked about oceans and continents forming and shifting over

FACING: Shiprock Mesa (October 1942), Arizona, by Maynard Dixon. Courtesy of Mark Sublette, Medicine Man Gallery, Tucson Arizona. ABOVE: Gothic rock towers near Superior, east of Phoenix.

LEFT: "Organ Pipe" rock formations tower skyward in the Chiricahua National Monument.

RIGHT: Fields of icicles grow on Sky Islands, where several life zones blend together. Courtesy of Victor Beer Photography.

incomprehensible time spans. Like Michener, we need to get an inkling of what happened in order to understand what ancient peoples and modern civilizations have had to overcome.

Eons ago, huge chunks of the earth's crust called tectonic plates rammed into each other, gnashing, grinding, and sliding over and under each other, pushing rock formations thousands of feet in the air, creating hundreds of earthquakes and volcanoes spewing molten lava and hot ash over the landscape, tearing open the earth's crust while large rock formations broke apart into sections, creating faults and uplifts that tilted massive pieces of rock thousands of feet in the air. For millions of years, much of the country was under water. Erosion wore away the mountains, creating shallow inland seas. Rivers deposited different colors of silt, including a whitish limestone made of decomposed seashells. Sedimentary deposits are almost a mile thick in some places, indicat-

ing million-year buildups. When the seas evaporated, compressed sediment and silt turned to shale, sandstone, and limestone.

Then the cycle began again. There were more earthquakes, volcanoes, faults, uplifts, and mountains, followed by erosion, oceans, and sedimentation, repeating over hundreds of millions of years until the present, where Arizona boasts the most beautiful, sometimes bleak, landscapes, from the Grand Canyon to "dragon-backed" purple mountain ranges, red mesas, and plateaus.

Fossils indicate that 800 million years ago, single-celled algae, the first evidence of life in what would become Arizona, floated in a vast shallow sea. The sea receded roughly 700 million years ago, leaving a coastal plain with rolling hills and low barren mountains where multicelled green algae developed. After another hundred million years, the first animals, forerunners of jellyfish and sea worms, evolved in Arizona's inland oceans.

ABOVE LEFT: The Petrified Forest hosts the world's largest array of mineralized plants.

ABOVE RIGHT: Ancient fossils can be found all over the state.

LEFT: Dinosaurs left their tracks near Tuba City.

ABOVE: Polished petrified wood is nature's stained glass.

RIGHT: Painted Desert is composed of layers of prehistoric shale, siltstone, and mudstone.

The Smithsonian Institute displayed Petrified Forest logs for many years.

ABOVE LEFT AND RIGHT: *Replicas of dinosaurs at the Petrified Forest visitors' center.*

BELOW LEFT AND RIGHT: *Giant statues along Interstate 40 mark dinosaur territory.*

FACING: *Saber-toothed cats, ground sloths, and mammoths roamed Arizona 12,000 years ago.*

SABRE-TOOTH CAT

As recently as 12,000 years ago,
sabre-tooth cats lived in the cooler,
wetter climates of our region. This
ancient predator pounced
prey, stabbing and
formidable, sabre

GRAHAM COUNTY
DURING THE ICE AGE

ABOVE: *Mammoth skulls and tortoise-like prehistoric shells found near Thatcher.*

RIGHT: *This prehistoric camel shinbone was unearthed along the Gila River near Thatcher.*

MAMM

This is clust
mammal s
include par
some ribs.
Simon Vall

In some eras, prehistoric Arizona was a rainy place with swamps and huge tropical plants. East of the Grand Canyon on a flat layer of mudstone near Tuba City, you can follow the tracks of Tyrannosaurus Rex, Dilophosaurus, and Coelophysis, petrified in time for up to 200 million years. They left large bird-like footprints in the mud, which hardened and was covered by more mud; then rain eroded the sandstone and the tracks were exposed again.

Around 100,000 years ago, the Ice Age made dramatic environmental changes in Arizona. Glaciers developed on Mount Humphreys and Mount Baldy in the White Mountains, there was much more water, and pinyon and juniper woodlands covered areas that are now desert scrub. Fossil records from southern Arizona dated from the Cenozoic Era around 10,000 BC show that mammoths, giant bison, ground sloths, and saber-tooth tigers roamed the area. The last of the glaciers melted around that time, and by 2,000 BC, the climate and environment became much as they are today.

Snow remains on the San Francisco Peaks north of Flagstaff even in June.

PRESENT-DAY GEOGRAPHY, FLORA, AND FAUNA

Arizona is known for its colorful landscapes, from the majestic red rock sculptures of Monument Valley, Canyon de Chelly, and Sedona, to the varicolored palette of the Painted Desert and Petrified Forest.

But back in 1849, travelers on their way to the California gold rush took the southern route through the Basin and Range country because of the warmer climate and flatter terrain; theirs were the first reports the world had heard about Arizona, and it became known only for its harsh deserts, with no mention of the large forests, meadows, creeks and streams, snow-capped mountains, and high plains grasslands.

Arizona has one of the widest ranges of terrain and habitats in the United States. It runs the gamut from tundra-topped rugged mountains to broad valleys and extensive deserts. It is known for its rugged terrain and scarce water supplies, but it actually has a wide variety of climate zones and elevations.

The state of Arizona is roughly 400 miles long and 300 miles wide, and is the sixth largest of the fifty states. To get an overall mental picture of the terrain, you can think of Arizona's surface as a tabletop that tips from the high plateaus and mesas in the northeast corner at Chinle, in the Navajo Nation, down to the near sea-level deserts of the southwest region at the U.S.–Mexico border near the Gulf of California.

From the San Francisco Peaks near Flagstaff at 12,000 feet to the banks of the Colorado River at Yuma at 141 feet above sea level, life zone environments vary greatly from tundra and pine forests to arid stretches of lava, cactus, and, yes, even a few sand dunes.

The Three Geographical Provinces

Geographers divide Arizona landforms into three "provinces": the Colorado Plateau, the Intermontane (or Central Highlands), and the Basin and Range. In the tilted tabletop example mentioned on page 31, the Plateau covers the higher-elevation northeastern half of the state. The lower half, the southwestern section, is the Basin and Range. A wide ribbon of mountains stretching from the northwest corner to the eastern border, about a third of the way up the state, is the Intermontane province.

ABOVE: Picacho Solito (Rio Arriba, NM 1931), by Maynard Dixon. This formation is similar to Picacho Peak in south-central Arizona. Courtesy of Mark Sublette, Medicine Man Gallery, Tucson, Arizona.

BELOW: The Monument Valley "Mittens" are popular with major advertisers.

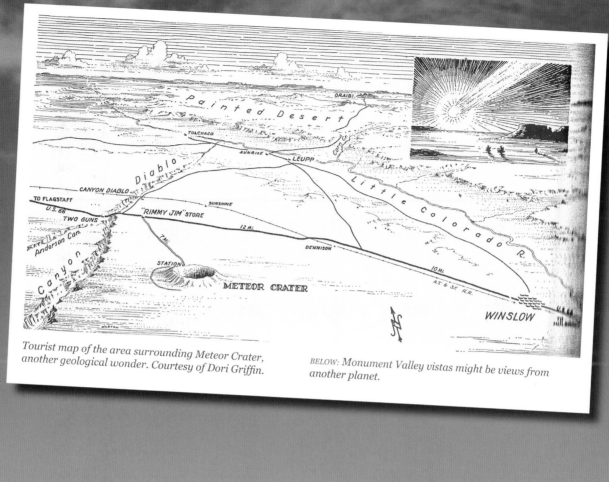

Tourist map of the area surrounding Meteor Crater, another geological wonder. Courtesy of Dori Griffin.

BELOW: *Monument Valley vistas might be views from another planet.*

LEFT: *Stark beauty exists on a grand scale in Monument Valley. Courtesy of Victor Beer Photography.*

ABOVE: *Long mesas mark ancient coastlines in northeastern Arizona. Courtesy of Victor Beer Photography.*

BELOW: *There are still wide vistas on the ranchlands south of Holbrook.*

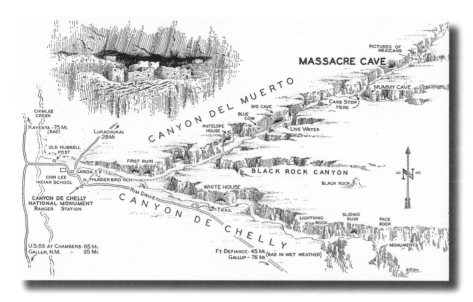

MASSACRE CAVE

PICTURES OF MEXICANS

MUMMY CAVE

CARS STOP HERE

CANYON DEL MUERTO

BIG CAVE

BLUE COW

LIVE WATER

ANTELOPE HOUSE

CHINLEE CREEK

KAYENTA - 75 MI. (BAD)

LUKACHUKAI 28 MI.

OLD HUBBELL POST

FIRST RUIN

GARCIA T.P.

CHIN LEE INDIAN SCHOOL

THUNDER BIRD RCH.

BLACK ROCK CANYON

BLACK ROCK

CANYON DE CHELLY NATIONAL MONUMENT RANGER STATION

RIM DRIVE

WHITE HOUSE

CANYON DE CHELLY

TRAIL

LIGHTNING ROCK

SLIDING RUIN

FACE ROCK

U.S.66 AT CHAMBERS - 85 MI.
GALLUP, N.M. - 95 MI.

FT. DEFIANCE - 45 MI. (BAD IN WET WEATHER)
GALLUP - 76 MI.

MONUMENTS

N

ABOVE: *Three canyons converge to form trident-shaped Canyon de Chelly. Courtesy of Dori Griffin.*

BELOW: *Many find Canyon de Chelly in its own way as beautiful as the Grand Canyon.*

FACING: *Canyon de Chelly is known for its towering red sandstone cliffs. Courtesy of Victor Beer Photography.*

The Colorado Plateau

The plateau is a flat region ranging from 5,000 to 7,000 feet but is dotted with fields of extinct volcanoes. The largest of these are the San Francisco Peaks, which rise almost 6,000 feet above the Colorado Plateau. Arizona's unofficial nickname, the Grand Canyon State, comes from the most outstanding feature of the Colorado Pla-teau. A mile deep, six to ten miles wide, and two hundred miles long, it is one of the most-visited natural wonders on earth. Fifty miles away from the deepest spot in Arizona loom the San Francisco Peaks, the two tallest being Humphreys Peak at 12,633 feet, and Agassiz Peak at 12,356 feet.

The Intermontane or Central Highlands

At the edge of the Colorado Plateau, a large escarpment called the Mogollón Rim (named for eighteenth-century Spanish Capitan General Juan Igna-cio Flores de Mogollón and pro-nounced "moe-go-YONE") separates the Colorado Plateau from the Basin and Range Province. This 150-mile swath of granite cliffs shows how the Colorado Plateau was pushed up by a geological process called uplift, which varies from faulting in that the earth's crust does not tilt, but raises several thousand feet while remaining horizontally perpen-dicular to the original terrain.

ABOVE: *Cholla (CHOY-yah) cactus and saguaros thrive in the wet season. Courtesy of Victor Beer Photography.*

FACING ABOVE LEFT: *Desert blooms create a carpet of wildflowers in the Superstition Mountains. Courtesy of Jack Carlson.*

FACING ABOVE RIGHT: *Arizona's exposed faults are a geology teacher's dream.*

FACING BELOW LEFT: *Saguaros cover the mountain ridges overlooking Roosevelt Lake near Globe.*

FACING BELOW RIGHT: *Rare organ pipe cacti grow amid saguaros at Organ Pipe National Monument. Courtesy of Victor Beer Photography.*

OVERLEAF: *Saguaro forest climbs the walls at Ventana Canyon near Tucson. Courtesy of Victor Beer Photography.*

The Mogollón Rim was the Pinal and Tonto Apache stronghold for centuries, as well as the prehistoric Salado peoples before them. On this southern edge of the Intermontane province, many streams drop down sharply, cutting through the rim to bring mountain snowmelt waters via the Salt, Gila, and Verde Rivers, as well as hundreds of creeks and streams, to the desert floor.

The Basin and Range Province

The Basin and Range Province is flat like the Colorado Plateau, but its vast valleys are interrupted by dozens of "fault block" mountain ranges. These rugged "dragon-backed" chains are usually aligned from northeast to southwest, formed by faulting action tilting large blocks of the earth's crust thousands of feet in the air. They often feature a gentle slope on one side with a much steeper face on the other, and the valleys in between have been filled in with rocks and sand crumbling off the mountains. Arizona's southernmost mountain ranges are an unusual combination of ecosystems that are not often found side by side, creating a phenomenon that natural scientists have named "sky islands."

The Dos Cabezas ("two heads") Mountains, south of Willcox. Courtesy of Carol Wien.

Sky Islands

This poetic name perfectly describes the 70,000-square-mile Basin and Range region of southeastern Arizona, southwestern New Mexico, and northwestern Mexico. About 25 percent of the Sky Islands are found in Arizona mountain ranges, such as the Chiricahuas, Dragoons, Pinaleños, and Tumacácoris.

These mountain ranges got the name Sky Islands because their forested ranges are cut off from other upland areas by "seas" of desert and grassy plains that prohibit wildlife from moving to another mountain range. Unable to travel across miles of hotter, dryer areas, these animals are trapped like castaways on their mountains.

Because of this unique juxtaposition of deserts and alpine mountains, the Sky Islands have some of the world's most diverse ecosystems. They are home to 29 species of bats, 104 mammal species (including rare wolves, ocelots, and jaguars), and more than half the bird species in North America.

The Willcox Playa Wildlife Area, seven miles south of the town of Willcox in the Sulphur Springs Valley in southeastern Arizona, is another world-renowned bird-watching locale. The *playa* (beach) is an ancient closed-basin lakebed that is home to thousands of migratory birds in the winter, especially sandhill cranes, which migrate in numbers up to 40,000.

ARIZONA WATER: A RARE GIFT

Even at higher elevations, most of Arizona is arid or semiarid. From the earliest times, the history of human habitation in what eventually became known as Arizona has been dependent on water supplies. As in other desert regions around the globe, ancient civilizations rose and fell with the water table.

Where the Water Flows

Much of Arizona's rain and snowmelt sinks into underground pockets called aquifers. But of the remainder of water that does not, nearly 90 percent of Arizona's watercourses drain into the Colorado River. Any that is not used by farmers in the Yuma area empties into the Sea of Cortez, also known as the Gulf of California, eighty miles south of Arizona's second oldest town.

Spanish explorers named it the Rio Colorado, or "red river," because of the thick sandstone sludge it contained. Clever pioneers claimed it was "too thick to drink and too thin to plow." The headwaters are in the Rocky Mountains, 16 miles north of Grand Lake in the north-central section of Colorado near the Wyoming border. From there it drops 8,000 feet in 1,450 miles along a southwesterly direction to the Gulf of California. Beginning in the late nineteenth century, a series of massive dams and canals have rerouted the Colorado to serve agricultural and electrical power needs in Arizona, Nevada, California, Utah, Wyoming, Colorado, and New Mexico to such an extent that the water no longer reaches the Gulf consistently.

The Colorado enters Arizona from Utah near the center of the state, turns west almost immediately for about three hundred miles, and then drops directly south to form the state's western boundary. One of the largest rivers west of the Mississippi, the Colorado played an important role in early European history of Arizona,

Riverfront homes along the Colorado River near Parker.

especially with regard to surveys, mining, and military.

The second largest river in Arizona, the Gila, begins in the Black Mountains wilderness more than 100 miles northwest of Silver City, New Mexico. Its 640-mile journey takes it on a meandering east-west path across Arizona, roughly following the 33rd Parallel and separating the top two-thirds of Arizona from the lower third. The Gila River Basin was home to large numbers of prehistoric peoples as well as a great abundance of prehistoric mammoths, camels, saber-tooth tigers, dire wolves, ground sloths, and even glyptodonts (an armadillo-like animal with a shell the size of a large wagon wheel). Fur trappers, surveyors, the U.S. Army, and the forty-niners all followed the Gila River from New Mexico to California.

Its largest tributary, the Salt River, was central to large prehistoric civilizations as well. Ancient peoples dug hundreds of miles of irrigation canals engineered precisely to deliver water on uneven terrain, rivaling the farming communities along the Nile agricultural communities in that cradle of civilization. Five centuries later, prospectors, merchants, and entrepreneurs cleaned out those ancient channels to supply miners at Wickenburg and soldiers at Fort McDowell with produce and fodder for their livestock. A ne'er-do-well Frenchman well-versed in the classics named the new town Phoenix (built on the ruins of another one) after the legendary Egyptian bird that set itself on fire on a nest of cinnamon sticks every five hundred years in order to be reborn.

In southern Arizona along the border, both the San Pedro and Santa Cruz Rivers begin in Arizona, flow south into Mexico, then turn around and flow north into the United States. Like the Tigris and Euphrates, the Santa Cruz and much less so the San Pedro became the cradle of Arizona's Spanish civilization sporadically from 1539 through four centuries of colonization until gold was discovered along the Gila and Colorado Rivers in 1857. The Santa Cruz River Valley provides most of Tucson's water, but much of it is in the form of underground aquifers rather than surface water.

Except for the mountain region, Arizona has always had less water than is needed to support humans. Even in prehistoric times, the Hohokam had to build canals and live near rivers to survive. This lack of water separated Arizona from the rest of the country for centuries. For hundreds of years, pioneers settled first in other places in America where the climate and land were easier to contend with, and then they finally came to Arizona. Even then, they came to mine minerals, build forts, and spread religion, not because it was a good place to ranch or farm.

BELOW: *Mountain men and explorers frequented the marshlands along the Bill Williams River where it enters the Colorado River.*

FACING: *Cathedral Rock, Sedona. These red sandstone formations were deposited 250 million years ago. Courtesy of Victor Beer Photography*

CHAPTER TWO

⭐ ARIZONA INDIANS— PAST AND PRESENT

Some halfway up the limestone wall,
That spot of black is not a stain
Or shadow, but a cavern hole,
Where someone used to climb and crawl
To rest from his besetting fears.

—Robert Frost, "A Cliff Dwelling," 1947

THE EARLIEST ARIZONANS

About 13,000 years before the Spaniards arrived in 1539, prehistoric peoples inhabited almost every area in Arizona. At first they were small roving bands of hunter-gatherers who lived in caves, made stone tools, and clothed themselves in fur. They fed themselves by hunting and gathering seeds, nuts, berries, cactus fruit and buds, and other wild plants. Eventually they developed large sophisticated cities with multilevel apartment houses, hundreds of miles of irrigation canals, fine cotton clothes, and beautiful pottery, jewelry, and baskets. For once, Arizona's arid climate has acted to our advantage by preserving prehistoric artifacts that rotted away in wetter regions.

Archaeologists are still not certain what happened to these ancient cultures, but for some reason they abandoned their homes and arts, and seemed to disappear sometime during the thirteenth or fourteenth centuries. Only a century later, modern tribes replaced the ancient ones, often living in the same locations and restoring canals and buildings. This happened three times where the Salt and Gila Rivers come together. First the Hohokam, then the Pima, and, finally, Anglos tilled the same soil, using irrigation ditches dug centuries earlier.

Today, there are twenty-two recognized Native American tribes in Arizona. Their reservation lands encompass more area, and Arizona contains a larger indigenous population than any other state in the Union. From ancient past to modern statehood, the wide variety of native peoples is the first chapter in the state's history.

Ice Age Big Game Hunters

During the Pleistocene epoch, which began about two million years ago, giant glaciers covered much of the world's northern hemisphere. The ice masses used up water and

Kachina Maker (October 1923), by Maynard Dixon. Courtesy of Mark Sublette Medicine Man Gallery, Tucson, Arizona.

Clovis culture artifacts at Lehner Ranch date from 12,000 BC. Courtesy of the Arizona Historical Society (MS1255f323[f]).

caused ocean water levels to drop, exposing a strip of land between Siberia and Alaska that allowed humans to migrate from the Eastern to the Western Hemisphere across a pathway now known as the Bering Straits.

Sometime around 13,000 BC, the earth's climate began to warm significantly. Over the next four thousand years, the giant glaciers melted and receded northward. The age of glaciers slowly came to an end, and the intrepid Old World traveler populations began to expand and spread out across what would eventually become America.

Ice Age Arizona's well-watered valleys abounded in rich grasses and megafauna (large animals). Discoveries of their chipped stone spear points still lodged in the buried skeletons of the animals they hunted presents "smoking gun" evidence that these Paleo-Indian hunters successfully stalked mammoth, giant bison, horses, camels, antelope, sloth, and even tapir for hundreds, if not thousands, of years.

The Clovis Culture

In 1926, Professor Byron Cummings, director of the University of Arizona Archeology Department, got a call from a schoolteacher in Double Adobe, a small town in southeastern Arizona near Douglas, along the border. The teacher said that people around there had found large elephant-like bones sticking out of the side of an arroyo, or dry creek bed. Unfortunately, Cummings was caught up in a hoax involving lead artifacts that indicated a Roman colony north of Tucson in AD 500, and the Double Adobe prehistoric site did not get the attention it deserved.

Meanwhile, extensive discoveries of the same type and era were found near Clovis, New Mexico, in 1932, and the name of the town has come to represent one of the earliest, most widespread prehistoric peoples in North America.

In 1952, Fred Navarrete and his son Mark discovered mammoth bones near Naco, on the Arizona-Mexico border. Excavations indicated the adult male mammoth died of eight spear point wounds found among the bones. Archaeologists encased the ribs, vertebra, and five spear points in plaster and sent them to the University of Arizona. Other kill sites in the area include Lehner Ranch and Murray Springs.

During the Pleistocene Epoch, the San Pedro Valley was a wooded area with ponds, marshes, and lush grasslands. It supported herds of prehistoric elephants, camels, horses, saber-toothed tigers, ground sloths, and dire wolves. Arizona's San Pedro River Valley can boast probably the largest concentration of Clovis sites in North America, which makes it a prime research location for archeologists from all over the world.

Moderate climate was key to the vast human and animal populations, but climatologists agree that the only thing we can state without a doubt regarding the climate is that it changes. By 8,000 BC, the Southwest began to warm and dry out, eventually reaching modern norms after several thousand years of gradual primeval global warming.

The Archaic Peoples

As the climate warmed and dried even more, the large mammals disappeared. Some researchers say the hunters might have been too good at their job and contributed to their extinction. The Clovis and later Folsom cultures were followed by what archeologists have named Archaic cultures from 7,000 to 2,000 BC. These sparser populations were more nomadic; they sought the cooler mountains in the summer; hunted smaller game such as antelope, turkey, rabbits, and deer; and relied more on

Prehistoric stone axes at Besh Ba Gowah Archaeological Park near Globe.

Besh Ba Gowah Archaeological Park is a treasure trove of artifacts.

collecting plants, nuts, and berries for food than their Ice Age ancestors.

By 1,000 BC or perhaps even a thousand years earlier, southwestern hunter-gatherers began to cultivate corn and squash. Then between AD 200 and 900, people began to live in a scattering of communities year-round but went on long seasonal hunting trips. They had about as much social contact as isolated Anglo homesteads on the Kentucky frontier in the late 1700s.

The Ancient Ones

From about AD 200 to 1450, three major cultures developed in different parts of the Southwest. In Arizona's central highlands, the Mogollón hunted deer and turkey, and gathered piñon nuts, acorns, and berries in the mountains along the Arizona, New Mexico, and Mexican borders. They gardened less than their Hohokam neighbors to the west, who developed a network of hundreds of miles of irrigation canals to adapt to the desert climate of the Basin and Range region of southwestern Arizona.

North and west of these ancient ones, the Ancestral Puebloans lived in the canyons and mesas of the vast Colorado Plateau, stretching from central Arizona to Wyoming. The center of their civilization was in the Four Corners area, the only location in the United States where four states share a common corner. In western Arizona along the Colorado River, the Patayan, who were ancestors of the Yuman-speaking people, lived a more nomadic life, moving from their gardens along the river to desert and mountain camps in different seasons.

Near Flagstaff and south to the Verde River near Sedona, the Sinagua (the people without water) farmed. Near the end of the prehistoric era, the Salado (named for the Salt River that gave rise to the city of Phoenix) irrigated fields in the central and southeastern river valleys. Each had its distinctions, yet many blended together over the centuries, each adopting from the other.

Three major groups of prehistoric people overlap in the Southwest.

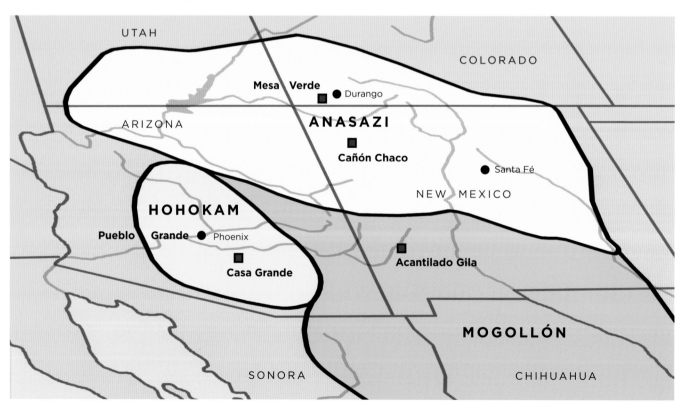

Post holes, circa AD 900, from a Hohokam pithouse excavated in downtown Tucson.

The Mogollón

Around 300 BC, early farmers began to settle into villages close to their farming plots instead of planting, leaving to hunt, and returning later to harvest their crops as their Archaic culture ancestors had. These Mogollón people built pithouses by digging about a foot-deep circle from nine to twenty feet in diameter, erected an upside-down basket framework of sticks over it, and covered that with brush and earth. They began to make pottery around AD 200, a craft that they probably learned from native peoples in Mexico.

The Mogollón culture centered in the forests and upland meadows of southwestern New Mexico and northern Sonora and Chihuahua. Some anthropologists believe they are the ancestors of the modern-day Zuni and other upper Rio Grande River Puebloan peoples. They were named by renowned University of Arizona archaeologist Emil Haury after his first digs in the 1930s in the Mogollón Mountains of New Mexico. The mountains were named for Juan Ignacio Flores de Mogollón, Spanish Governor of New Mexico from 1712 to 1715.

After AD 1000, the Mogollón changed from building pithouses to constructing single-story apartment-like buildings of river rock and adobe. Some complexes had as many as 150 rooms clustered around an open plaza. The Mogollón performed spiritual ceremonies in large rectangular underground rooms called "kivas" or in smaller kivas that could only be entered through a rooftop opening.

The Mimbres, a regional subculture of the Mogollón, were known for their elaborate geometric pottery designs that included fish, birds, and animals, painted with delicate brushes made of a single yucca fiber. Mimbres bowls are often found associated with burials, typically with a hole punched in the bottom to "kill" the pottery and thus prevent further use.

Mogollón tradition underwent a decline beginning around the twelfth century, collapsing throughout the fourteenth century. Some Mogollón may have moved to join the Ancestral Puebloans to the north or Hohokam to the west. The Zuni Pueblo near Reserve, New Mexico, may be partly composed of Mogollón descendants.

The Hohokam

The Hohokam, an Akimel O'odham word for "those who have gone before," lived in the often-bleak and arid desert below the Mogollón Rim along the Salt and Gila Rivers. These waterways flowed intermittently but carried much more water in the centuries before miners, farmers, and city water companies installed dams to capture the water.

The Hohokam homeland boundaries are similar to the natural habitat of the saguaro cactus. Geographically, Hohokam territory covers the Basin and Range region that begins north of Phoenix, includes Tucson and the desert west to the Colorado River, and reaches south into Mexico. However, settlements have been identified as far north as Flagstaff in some periods.

At first they lived like the Mogollón, but later they became master engineers and dug irrigation ditches to divert water from the southern Arizona streams and rivers. Their pithouses were similar to their Archaic ancestors, with four or five houses around a central plaza, about twenty people of the same extended family in each cluster. Eventually they built aboveground mud houses with stone foundations and finally multistory apartment complexes such as those at Pueblo Grande near Phoenix and the famous Casa Grande near Coolidge, Arizona. The latter was established by President Benjamin Harrison in 1892 as the first prehistoric and cultural reserve in the United States.

The Hohokam are known for four outstanding characteristics that differentiate them from other Arizona prehistoric cultures: irrigation canals, ball courts, ceremonial mounds, and acid-etched jewelry. While the first three of these were most likely learned from trade with Mexico, the fourth is unique to their local artisans.

Irrigation Networks

Adapting to the hot, dry climate, the Hohokam became accomplished desert-dwelling farmers. They built an ingenious network of irrigation canals, dams, and con-

trol gates to divert river water to their crops. Covering hundreds of miles throughout the southern Arizona, the complex system rivaled those used in the ancient Near East, Egypt, and China.

The canals ensured steady water supplies and larger harvests, and agricultural expertise allowed the Hohokam to build stable urban centers. Snaketown, at the confluence of the Gila and Salt Rivers just south of Phoenix, was the largest. Population estimates for Snaketown are more than 600 inhabitants in AD 1050.

The Hohokam cultivated cotton, tobacco, maize, beans, and squash. In addition, they harvested a variety of wild plants that grew near the canals. They also grew agave, a cactus plant akin to aloe, on hillside slopes and gathered cactus fruit and buds as well as mesquite beans. Once food was no longer a constant dire concern, full-time artisans developed their skills in making pottery and seashell jewelry inlaid with turquoise.

Their method of acid etching was the first of its kind. First, a shell was coated with resin from creosote bushes or mesquite trees. Patterns were incised and the resin was removed to expose the shell where the finished pattern would be. The shell was then submerged in a weak acetic acid made from fermented saguaro fruit. The vinegar-like liquid ate away the exposed parts of the calcium-based shell anywhere from $1/16$ to $1/8$ of an inch, but it did not affect the areas protected by the coating. Once the resin was scraped away, a raised pattern remained that is still sharp in some artifacts discovered hundreds of years later. The Hohokam also left an abundance of slate rectangles, about three by four inches, with incised decorations around the borders, believed to be used as paint palettes.

Arts and Trade

The Hohokam also developed thriving trade routes into central Mexico to exchange their cotton cloth and jewelry for seashells, parrots, copper bells, and pottery from Mexico, the California coast, and possibly as far north as the Great Plains. The greatest trade period appears to be between AD 800 and 1,000.

Ball Courts and Ceremonial Mounds

Mysteries surround all ancient cultures, and one of the main questions still debated about the Hohokam is their origin. Did they arrive from Mexico around AD 600, bringing their culture with them, or is this a case of "local boy makes good," where the indigenous peoples learned from their neighbors to the south and adapted what they saw on trading trips into central Mexico to their Arizona

The display at Tuzigoot National Monument shows how prehistoric paint pallets were used.

lifestyle. Or, as seems to be the case with many questions, a combination of both answers may be closer to the truth. In any case, the similarities are numerous between Aztec and Mayan cultures and that of the Hohokam, but are not as prevalent with their Arizona contemporaries, the Mogollón and Ancestral Puebloans.

The most impressive and pervasive influence occurs in the numerous ball courts and ceremonial mounds found in hundreds, if not thousands, of sites around Arizona. The walls are mounded up and coated with sunbaked clay, with room for five hundred people to watch around the edge of the field in some cases. A rubber ball was discovered at some sites, similar to the ones used in Mexico ball courts. They also built flat-topped earthen mounds up to 100 feet high, probably for ceremonial dances.

Sometime after AD 1200, the Hohokam stopped making stone vessels, clay figurines, and ball courts. Archaeologists believe that environmental and social disasters caused them to abandon their settlements. Only the ruins of large pueblos, pottery and projectile points, and a huge network of irrigation canals remains.

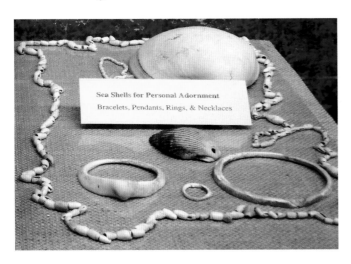

FACING: *Corrugated pottery was one of the first styles created by prehistoric Indians.*

ABOVE: *Replicas of Hohokam seashell jewelry on display at Tubac State Historic Park.*

The Patayan

The Yuma Indians called their ancestors "Patayan," or Old Ones. Culturally similar to the Hohokam, these desert-dwelling Native Americans lived in portions of modern-day Arizona, California, and Baja California between AD 700 and 1550. Evidence of their lives is found particularly along the Colorado River Valley as far north as the Grand Canyon.

They are perhaps the least known of the prehistoric tribes for several reasons: the harsh desert climate prohibited large building projects, they were primarily nomadic, and their sites were easily destroyed by floods and the shifting channels of the turbulent Colorado.

Archaeological studies indicate that these Native Americans may have continued into historic times. It is likely that they met the Spanish conquistadores when they arrived at the Colorado River in 1540. The Patayan practiced floodplain agriculture, hunted with stone tools, and cremated their dead in later periods, as did the Hohokam.

Differing from their other prehistoric cultures, the Patayan built long pithouses with a linear series of rooms, some used for ceremonies or storage.

The Ancestral Puebloans

When most people think of Southwestern prehistoric people, images of cliff dwellings spring to mind, these original high-rises tucked away in the safety of shadowy canyon ledges. The Navajo called them "Anasazi"— Ancient Enemies. These pueblo dwellers were among the first to be studied when the field of American archaeology began in the late nineteenth century. Archeologists and anthropologists have traced their origins, and it seems more appropriate to call them "Ancestral Puebloans," the name preferred by their probable descendents, the Hopi, Zuni, and Pueblo Indians of northern New Mexico and Arizona.

From Francisco Vasquez de Coronado's first encounters with the Pueblo people in 1541, they have been portrayed as a unified homogenous culture, but they are different in many ways. The common points of apartment-like dwellings and farming communities contrast with dramatic differences in language and philosophy.

Thousands of years ago, these archaic foragers roamed the Colorado Plateau's high desert mesas and deep canyons, living in caves and rock shelters. Then between AD 200 and 500, they began to live in pithouse villages and to grow maize, beans, and squash. This early stage of their development is known as "Basketmaker" because they had not yet taken up the art of pottery making.

Between AD 700 and 1100, the Ancestral Puebloan population exploded, probably because of regular rainfall as well as innovations in ceramics, agriculture, food storage, and migrations of peoples from neighboring areas.

During those centuries, they began building the distinctive multiroom apartment complexes associated with southwestern Native Americans and learned to become master agronomists, artisans, astronomers, and architects. Among their many projects, southwestern Colorado's Mesa Verde, the largest cliff dwelling in the United States, contained more than 200 rooms, including two dozen kivas (ceremonial rooms). They linked their vast territory with an elaborate road system and protected it with a series of stone lookout towers.

The Ancestral Puebloans built their elaborate pueblos at New Mexico's Chaco Canyon two hundreds years before Canyon de Chelly, Keet Seel, and Betatakin in Arizona. The latter were built and then abandoned within a mere fifty years between AD 1250 and 1300.

Although we may never know why the Ancestral Puebloans migrated from their large compounds between AD 1100 and 1300, probable causes include global climate change caused by the "Little Ice Age," the 300-year great North American drought, erosion, salinization from extensive irrigation, deforestation, and enemies from as far away as Mexico.

Throughout the twentieth century, leading archaeologists have contended that the Ancestral Puebloans did not mysteriously disappear but simply migrated to areas farther south with more favorable water supplies. They merged into the Hopi and Pueblo cultures that still live in Arizona and New Mexico.

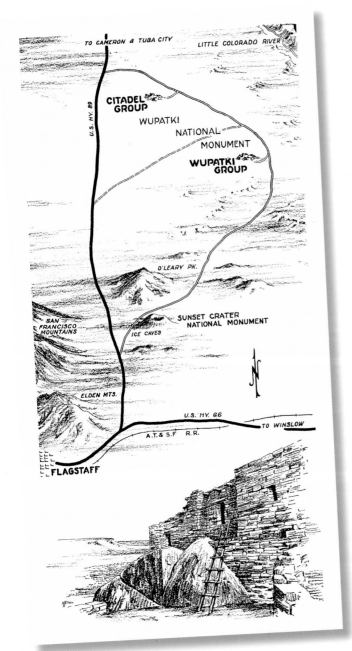

This 1930s map shows the Wupatki ruins north of Flagstaff.

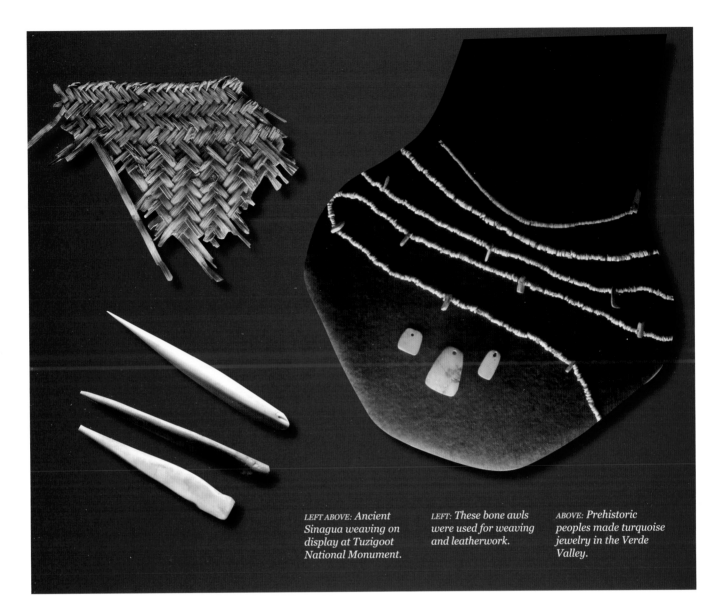

LEFT ABOVE: *Ancient Sinagua weaving on display at Tuzigoot National Monument.*

LEFT: *These bone awls were used for weaving and leatherwork.*

ABOVE: *Prehistoric peoples made turquoise jewelry in the Verde Valley.*

The Sinagua

The Spanish words *sin aqua* mean "without water," referring to the relatively dry country inhabited by these people between AD 500 and 1300. They may have been a migrating band of Patayan peoples from western Arizona who began to live in the forests around Flagstaff and south to the Verde River. The Sinagua irrigated their crops and lived in pithouses, but like the others, they advanced to more sophisticated architecture by the thirteenth century. The Sinagua flourished in the aftermath of a geological cataclysm, benefiting from what we would consider a natural disaster.

Between 1064 and 1067, the volcano erupted that formed Sunset Crater near Flagstaff, raining lava, cinder, and ash over 800 square miles of northern Arizona and causing the southerly migration of the Sinagua. Evidence indicates that the Indians returned in a few years, taking advantage of the agricultural effects of the nurturing minerals in the blanket of ash that covered their homeland.

As their culture developed, the Sinagua expanded their social and trade network to include the four main cultures and perhaps Mesoamericans as well. After

FACING: A Sinagua cliff dwelling at Montezuma Well, near Camp Verde.

ABOVE: Well-preserved Sinagua cave dwelling on the edge of Montezuma Well.

RIGHT: Parrot feathers and copper bells were found at Tuzigoot, near Cottonwood. Courtesy of the Gila County Historical Society.

ABOVE: In addition to cliff dwellings, the Sinagua built freestanding apartment-like structures. Courtesy of the Arizona Historical Society.

RIGHT: Sinagua ruins ranged from Lomaki, north of Flagstaff to Tuzigoot, 100 miles south. Courtesy of Randy Prentice Photography.

FACING: Montezuma Castle was built by the Sinagua people around AD 700.

AD 1100, these influences created a synthesis. The Sinagua adopted Mogollón ceramics, Mayan ball courts, Ancestral Puebloan masonry, and imported parrots and copper bells from Mexico like their southern neighbors the Hohokam.

Similar to the other prehistoric cultures, the Sinagua abandoned their Sunset Crater–area villages in the thirteenth century, probably because of diminishing rainfall. They moved to the south, where they built the five-story Montezuma Castle and most likely moved east and south into New Mexico; they are incorporated into Hopi oral histories as well.

Of all prehistoric cultures, the Sinagua left the best ruins for us to marvel at and enjoy. The archeological sites connected with the Sinagua culture are among the most fascinating national parks and monuments in Arizona: Montezuma Castle, Tuzigoot, Walnut Canyon, Wupatki, and Sunset Crater are all testimonies to the architectural artistry of the Sinagua people.

Tuzigoot inhabitants grew crops along the banks of the Verde River.

The Salado

South of the Sinagua, the Salado (salt) Culture lived in the Tonto Basin between present-day Payson and Globe from about AD 1150 to 1400. Besh-Ba-Gowah, the major excavation along Pinal Creek on the outskirts of Globe, shows evidence of Hohokam pithouses dating back to AD 550 underneath the Salado pueblos. About a mile upstream, Gila Pueblo featured two-story buildings and perhaps three- and four-story ones as well.

The Salado differed from other cultures in their polychrome pottery designs, adobe-walled pueblos interspersed with river rock, and burial of their dead instead of the Hohokam cremation tradition. They irrigated their fields and supplemented their food supply by hunting and gathering plants. Shell artifacts and macaw feathers indicate that they too traded with Californian and Mexican cultures.

ABOVE: The Salado people built the Tonto cliff dwelling around AD 1300.

RIGHT: Reconstructed in the 1930s, Besh Ba Gowah was a large Salado community.

FACING ABOVE: One man's ceiling was another man's floor at Besh Ba Gowah.

FACING BELOW LEFT: Some rooms were living quarters while others stored food and wood.

FACING BELOW RIGHT: These replicas of Salado artifacts re-create daily life in the thirteenth century.

ABOVE: This window offers a glimpse into the past at Besh Ba Gowah.

RIGHT: Low doorways suggest shorter inhabitants 700 years ago.

BELOW LEFT AND RIGHT: Although not as delicate, some Salado patterns are similar to Mimbres designs.

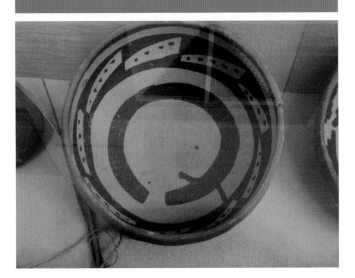

ABOVE: *Well-shaped pots with intricate geometric patterns are similar to Ancestral Puebloan.*

BELOW LEFT: *Intricate Salado bowl patterns suggest Ancestral Pueblo and Mimbres influences.*

BELOW RIGHT: *Although not as delicate, some Salado patterns are similar to Mimbres designs.*

ABOVE LEFT: *Developing later, the Salado incorporated features from other cultures.*

ABOVE RIGHT: *Besh Ba Gowah Archaeological Park exhibits a large collection of artifacts found at the site on the south edge of Globe.*

BELOW: *Shell bracelets and necklaces were also created by the Hohokam farther south and west.*

The Trail from Ancient to Modern

While Arizona's harsh landscape was a deterrent to European settlement, it turned out to be advantageous in several ways. One of the most important of those pertains to the field of archaeology. The combination of dry climate prevents many materials from decaying, and the lack of modern human population often destroys evidence by building on top of dinosaur graveyards and prehistoric cities.

Because of these two factors and countless others, when American scientists began their forays into the archaeology and anthropology at the end of the nineteenth century, Arizona was one of the first and foremost research centers. Though almost all of the prehistoric cultures mysteriously disappeared sometime in the thirteenth or fourteenth centuries, the same situation was true just about everywhere else in the United States. However, there were more clues to be found in Arizona, and many more places to look.

In a way, modern Arizona Indians have benefited from Arizona's remote and difficult landscape and climate. In more hospitable climes and areas suitable for farming, fishing, or even transportation, Native American cultures were eradicated by disease and warfare, relocated by force, or assimilated into Anglo culture decades, and sometimes centuries, before the final days of Indian independence when Geronimo surrendered to General Nelson Miles in 1884.

While the process of Native American genocide and cultural devastation repeated itself belatedly in Arizona as it had across the nation, there are probably more American Indians practicing their traditional ways in Arizona than any other state in the nation.

CONTEMPORARY INDIAN CULTURES

Today, the twenty-two recognized tribes have adapted and blended with each other to the point where it is sometimes hard to say where one tribe leaves off and the other begins. In anthropological terms, a tribe is defined as a social group with a distinctive language, but in the real world, groups create their own distinctions and identities, which change through time. Anthropologist Jack D. Forbes likens the tribal concept to ocean currents: "It is possible to point out generally where a particular current exists, especially at its center or strongest point, but it is not ordinarily possible to neatly separate that current from the surrounding sea." This is an apt metaphor to keep in mind when learning about Arizona Indian tribes.

The scope of this book does not allow descriptions of every Arizona tribe. Since some were larger and more influential, their stories will be told in more detail. Significant events will be put forth in later chapters as they occur chronologically.

However, too many Arizona history books begin with the coming of the Europeans. Who were these modern-era Native Americans, how and where did they live, and what were some of their beliefs and values?

Hopi: The Peaceful People

Very little has changed in the sky city pueblos high up on First, Second, and Third Mesa—not since Coronado's conquistador Captain Pedro de Tovar visited in 1540 and probably not for five hundred years before that. Of all the tribes in Arizona, the Hopi have undoubtedly changed the least. Many maintain some of the same dwelling styles, spiritual ceremonies, and government as they practiced almost two thousand years ago.

The word "Hopi" is short for *Hopituh Shi-nu-mu,* "The Peaceful People." Hopi culture is matrilineal. Children belong to their mother's clan, but many of their

Hopi pueblos are among the oldest communities in the United States. Courtesy of the Arizona Historical Society (PC29f13/Y).

names are suggested by the women of their father's clan, with the final choice up to the parents.

The tribe's teachings relate stories of a great flood and other events dating to ancient times, marking the Hopi as one of the oldest living cultures in documented history. A deeply religious people, they live by the ethics of peace and goodwill.

Each village governs itself independently from the others, but the Hopi Tribal Council makes law for the tribe and sets policy to oversee tribal business as well as national and international relations. They strive for total reverence and respect for all things, and believe that their spiritual ceremonies benefit the whole world.

The Hopi traditional ceremonies coincide with the lunar calendar, and Christian missionaries have had less impact on Hopi spirituality than perhaps any other Native American culture. The Kat'sina (Life Bringer), commonly known to outsiders as Kachinas, are a central part of Hopi spirituality. They can be elements, qualities, concepts, or natural phenomena, and are represented by Kat'sina ceremonial dancers and intricately carved and painted wooden dolls.

The word "Kat'sina" can mean the spiritual beings themselves, the dolls, or the people who dress as kachinas for ceremonial dances, which are understood to embody all aspects of the same belief system. Kat'sinas are also related to historical events and are used to teach children the Hopi way of life.

Over many centuries, Hopis have perfected "dry farming." They create "wind breakers" in the fields to concentrate soil, snow, and moisture, and use special techniques to plant seeds in dry fields. Corn plays a central role in Hopi spiritual beliefs and ceremonies.

Approximately 12,000 Hopis live on a reservation that encompasses about 2,438 square miles of the Colorado Plateau in northeastern Arizona. The Hopi Reservation is surrounded by the much-larger Navajo Reservation.

ABOVE: Fannie Nampeyo carried on in the tradition of her mother, Nampeyo, the matriarch of Hopi pottery.

BELOW: The Hopi are known for creating beautiful pottery.

Apache spirit dancers practice intricate steps and music. Courtesy of the Graham County Historical Society.

Apaches: The Enemy—The People

In contrast to the isolated and relatively unknown Hopi, the name "Apache" is recognized from Finland to the Philippines. They are more feared and revered than any other native people in the world. Their culture is synonymous with courage, stoicism, and guerrilla warfare. Fierce warriors and skillful strategists, they were the last to resist European encroachment.

Like many Native Americans, the Apache are known by another name than what they call themselves. When Francisco Vasquez de Coronado entered Arizona in 1540 in search of the fabled Seven Cities of Cibola, his men asked the Zuni Indians what name their neighbors went by. The Zuni replied that they called those people *Apache,* their word for "enemy." The Apache call themselves *Indeh,* "the People."

Although it is difficult to track seminomadic people, it is generally believed that the Apache moved first into Texas perhaps as early as AD 800 and then moved westward into New Mexico and Arizona several hundred years later as a result of conflicts when Kiowas and Comanches began to move south from the Great Plains into Texas.

Although they speak a common language, the

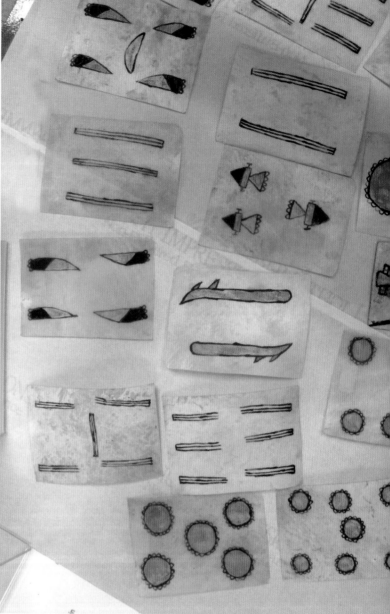

Apache never considered themselves a consolidated tribe with one chief over all, as Europeans are most likely to view all groups. In Europe, after the fall of the Roman Empire, nation states began to form so that by the time they reached the Southwest, explorers and settlers assumed that all peoples had consolidated into larger regional nation-like governments. However, because of their small populations, remote wilderness locations, and seminomadic lifestyles, the largest group of Apache people was the regional band, usually an extended family of no more than two hundred people.

For descriptive purposes, Europeans divided Apaches into several groups: White Mountain, Chiricahua, Pinal, Tonto, Aravaipa, Mescalero, Jicarilla, and Coyotero. These were not always the names they called themselves, however. For instance, those who were called Chiricahua actually recognized themselves as several subgroups: Chi-henne, Chokonen, Nednai, and Bedonkohe. Problems

arose when Europeans made peace treaties with one group but expected all Apaches to comply with the terms.

In earlier times, the Indeh (Apaches) lived near either side of what is now the Arizona–New Mexico border in the mountains and hilly regions where plenty of game and water was available. They probably did not expand to the Santa Cruz River basin in south central Arizona until the eighteenth century, corresponding to the arrival of the Spanish in that area.

FACING LEFT: *Traditional Apache girls wear many layers of skirts. Courtesy of the Gila County Historical Society.*

FACING RIGHT: *The Apaches created European-style playing cards out of rawhide.*

ABOVE LEFT: *This pointed basket would be carried on an Apache back, using a strap to hold it on.*

BELOW LEFT: *Four is a sacred number to several cultures, as incorporated into this Apache basket pattern.*

ABOVE: *Apache couple in traditional garb, weapons, and basketry. Courtesy of the Gila County Historical Society.*

Navajo: The People

The Navajo call themselves *Diné* (or Dineh), "the People," but Spanish conquistadores named them *Apaches de Nabaju,* which means "enemies who farm." The word "nabaju" is believed to derive from a Tewa Indian word meaning "planted fields." Like the Apache, their Athabascan-speaking linguistic cousins, the Navajo probably arrived in the Four Corners area some time after AD 800. Unlike the Apache, however, the Navajo settled near the Pueblo villages inhabited by ancient cliff dwellers long before the Athabascan speakers arrived. Navajo neighbors were descendants of prehistoric farmers, and the Navajo learned farming techniques from them as well as pottery making.

The Diné are the largest Indian tribe in the United States, not only by population but also by reservation land area. The Navajo Nation (*Diné Bikéyah* in Athabascan) is a semiautonomous Native American homeland that stretches 26,000 miles across the vast high desert and red sandstone Colorado Plateau from the east edge of the Grand Canyon to the Four Corners–Rio Grande area of western New Mexico (about the same land area as the state of West Virginia). In 2000, the United States Census recorded 290,000 Dine, with approximately 58 percent of them living within the Navajo Nation's boundaries.

The "Nation" is not just a political designation but is also a larger concept that embraces the relationship with its natural resources, kinship, language, religion, and self-governance. The seat of government is the city

BELOW: *Navajo people are most noted for their weaving, first blankets and now rugs.*

FACING: *Despite struggles climate, terrain, and other cultures, the Navajo prevail. Courtesy of the Arizona Historical Society (PC180B37F362_2304).*

A Navajo woman has her baby strapped into a traditional cradleboard.

of Window Rock, straddling the Arizona–New Mexico border. There are also adjacent Navajo Indian Reservations—Alamo, Ramah, and Tohajiilee—in this area, which often function as subunits of the major reservation, even though they have considerable local autonomy.

The vast stark beauty of the Navajo lands is uniquely southwestern, so much so that the United States created several conservation areas there, including Canyon de Chelly National Monument, Monument Valley Navajo Tribal Park, and Rainbow Bridge National Monument.

Even more than the Apache, the Navajo are the cultural icons of southwestern imagery. Paintings, postcards, and illustrated maps often depict a Navajo woman in her turquoise jewelry and velveteen shirt sitting at her loom

in front of huge red sandstone cliffs, perhaps with a few sheep in the foreground as well. This is not just a stereotype but remains an accurate representation of part of the Navajo culture that continues unchanged.

Like woolen threads on a loom, sheepherding is tightly interwoven into the Navajo way of life. When the Spanish established their first colony near Santa Fe, New Mexico, in 1598, the Diné were quick to see the advantages of adding livestock management to the agricultural lifestyle they had already adopted from the sedentary Pueblo Indians.

But the choice was not just about food, wool production, and weaving. The interplay of values and beliefs related to sheep raising are integral to Navajo society and culture. The daily processes of herding, shearing, and preparing the wool combine with the skills and creativity of weaving to create a profound spiritual tradition and balance between the Navajo and nature.

Centuries later, while in exile from their homeland, the Navajo adapted another skill from their Spanish and Pueblo neighbors: the art of styling jewelry out of silver, turquoise, and other semiprecious gemstones.

The combination of farming, sheepherding, weaving, and jewelry-making are undoubtedly factors contributing to the current size and relative prosperity of the Navajo Nation. However, as Europeans began to enter Arizona, location—especially in proximity to valuable minerals—was a more powerful determiner of their future.

Pimas and Maricopas

The Pimas call themselves *Akimel O'odham,* "The River People." Before the Europeans arrived, their villages stretched for more than 100 miles along the Gila River, thirty miles south of Phoenix. The Pima language is of the Uto-Aztecan family, indicating their relations to indigenous peoples of Utah and Mexico. Many anthropologists and archeologists believe that they are the descendents of the Hohokam, while others contend they are a different group that adapted Hohokam ways. As their population grew, the Pimas restored the hundreds of miles of ancient irrigation canals and grew beans, corn, and squash in the rich silt from the overflowing river.

While the Pimas were probably the first Native Americans to grow cotton in what is now the United States, the species they grew centuries ago is not the now-famous Pima Cotton that graces the labels of better garments. That name was applied to the modern variety in honor of the Pima Indians, who helped develop the cotton on U.S. Department of Agriculture experimental farms in Arizona in the early 1900s.

The Pima Indians thrived along the Gila River until the water was controlled upstream. Courtesy of Dori Griffin.

Pima trade routes for their woven fabric extended as far north as Colorado, west to the Pacific coast, and south into Mexico. In the late 1700s, the Maricopas from the Colorado River asked if they could settle next to the Pima to escape warring tribes in their area. Oral tradition has it the Pimas allowed this with the agreement that the Maricopas would begin farming and not pursue long-range hunting and raiding, which would bring enemies into their homeland.

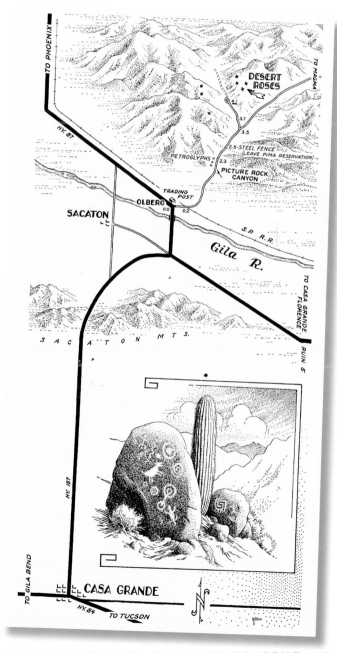

The Pimas lived in a riverside environment with a constant supply of water that could be tapped by irrigation canals and ditches. They lived in their large villages all year round, unlike their seminomadic neighbors. With the coming of Anglo settlers, the U.S. government created reservations using portions of their homeland along the Gila and Salt Rivers.

Tohono O'odham: The Desert People

Also Uto-Aztecan speakers, the Tohono O'odham are closely related to the Pima. In times of need, Pimas invited their southern cousins to help harvest crops and gave them a share. Sometimes the Tohono O'odham were able to return the favor, but the Gila River received more runoff water from the mountain regions to the east than the Santa Cruz did from the south.

The Tohono O'odham are famous for their intricately designed basketry, the most famous being the "man in the maze," which represents I'itoi (Elder Brother) and the path to enlightenment.

Tohono O'odham lived on the mountain foothill bajadas in wintertime near permanent springs, and they farmed in the desert valleys in the summer. Today Arizonans reverse the cycle and stay on the desert floor in the winter and go to the mountains in the summer now that water is more accessible.

The Tohono O'odham live around Tucson and west to Sells and Gila Bend. Many live off the reservation in Tucson and Phoenix, and some still live in northern Mexico as well.

Yaqui: Migrations and Ceremonies

Amid the Pimas and Tohono O'odham live the Yaqui Indians, the Cahitan-speaking descendents of the ancient Toltecs of Mexico. They migrated north in large numbers at the end of the nineteenth century, establishing communities in the Tucson and Phoenix areas. The Yaqui are best known for their elaborate Pascua (Easter) ceremonies, combining ancestral costumes and traditions, such as the deer dancer, with Christian Lenten observations.

Pai People

Like many Arizona tribal names, the heading above is redundant. In the Yuman language, the word *pai* actually means "people," just as O'odham means "people" for tribes of the Uto-Aztecan language group. There are three regional tribes whose names end in "pai": the Hualapai, the Havasupai, and the Yavapai.

The Hualapai, also spelled Walapai, are the "People of the Tall Pine." They are a relatively small tribe, never counted at more than 700 in earlier centuries. Archaeological evidence placed these hunter-gatherers along the Colorado River and the western edge of the Grand Canyon as early as AD 600. With the coming of the Europeans, they took up cattle-ranching and logging. Approximately 1,600 tribal members are currently recorded at the tribal capital in Peach Springs, Arizona.

Owners of undoubtedly the prettiest tribal name, the Havasupai, "People of the Blue Green Waters," take their name from high concentrations of calcium carbonate in the waters of Havasu Creek in the side canyons at the western end of the Grand Canyon. The carbonate forms travertine mineral deposits in the pools below spectacular waterfalls, creating beautiful turquoise- and sky-blue waters.

The third related tribe, the Yavapai, or "Sun People," were mistakenly referred to as Mohave Apache in early U.S. military reports. They are related to the Yuma/Quechan and to other *pai* people, the Hualapai and Havasupai. The Yavapai homelands are located in west-central Arizona from the Mazatzal and Pinal Mountains on the east to the Colorado River on the west. Over many years, the Yavapai and Tonto Apaches of the upper Verde River basin blended together to form a distinct cultural group known as the Yavapai-Apache.

Colorado River Tribes

From earliest prehistoric times, the history of Arizona has been the history of water. It is no accident that in this partially desert state, the majority of Arizona's Indians lived near waterways, even if they do not provide water year-round. The mighty Colorado River, the state's largest water supply, creates Arizona's western boundary, the only side that is not a straight line.

Several Yuman-speaking tribes make their homes along the Colorado River. Closest to the delta, the Cocopah (perhaps a subtle shift from pai to pah) call themselves "People Who Live on the River." They may be the descendents of the ancient Patayan peoples, who practiced floodplain agriculture and hunting and gathering along the Colorado in Arizona, California, and Mexico's Baja, California.

Quechan/Yuma at the Crossing

Just north of the Cocopah, the Yuma, or Quechan, is the largest tribe of the Yuman linguistic stock, to which they have given their name. Unlike the central and eastern tribes, they build their homes with a rectangular pole frame covered with arrow weed, sand, and mud that sloped to the ground in back to keep off the heat. Pre-European Yumas sometimes lived in loose bands averaging 125 during part of the year, but they broke into smaller extended family groups of 25 for most of the year because of the difficulties in obtaining food.

The Yumas were among the first to be encountered by the Spanish Conquistadors, and by the time an American military fort was opened in 1851, they were operating a successful ferry business made profitable by the California gold rush.

Heinrich Balduin Möllhausen painted this picture of three Quechan (Yuma) Indians.

Mohave: The River People

The northernmost of the river tribes, the Mohave were once one of the largest tribes of the Yuma language base. The Chemehuevi lived between them and the Quechans, with the Cocopahs farthest south.

They call themselves *Aha Macave,* "People Who Live Along the River." Some of their villages are on the California side, but the majority live on the Arizona side of the river. In his reports as leader of the steamboat expedition of 1857, Lieutenant Joseph Christmas Ives described the Mohave as "strong, athletic, and well developed."

The Mohave are best known for their artistic tattoos, created with cactus spines as needles and a blue dye made from cactus juice and ground minerals. Many believed that it was not possible to get into Heaven without a ceremonial tattoo.

Unlike most North American river tribes, the Mohave did not make canoes but created rafts out of light wood and reeds. Like their Yuma neighbors to the south, their rectangular dwellings were low with three-foot-high walls supported by posts and roofed with brush covered with mud and sand.

Their major food sources were corn, pumpkins, melons, beans, piñon nuts, and fish. Since they relied on flood tides rather than irrigation, crops often failed during drought years when the river did not overflow its banks.

Fray Francisco Garcés estimated the tribal population to be about 3,000 in 1776, but according to the Arizona school system, that number dwindled to around 1,600 in 1905. Today in Arizona, the Mohaves are part of the combined Colorado Indian Tribes, which number about 3,300 Mohave, Chemehuevi, Hopi, and Navajo people. Another 1,100 live on the Fort Mohave Indian Reservation, which overlaps into California and Nevada.

Other Arizona Tribes

In addition to the tribes described above, there are even more that make up the list of twenty-one federally recognized tribes as well as some that are distinct but not recognized. Among them are the Ak-Chin, Kaibab-Paiute, Pee Posh, and Southern Paiute. We regret omission of any other culturally unique Native American groups in Arizona. The difficult task of listing them all attests to the diversity and scope of Arizona's native peoples.

FIRST EUROPEANS AND HISTORY BEGINS

Although they often overlapped, anthropology left off and written history began when Francisco Vasquez de Coronado and his soldiers, priests, and Indian allies entered southern Arizona from Mexico in the summer of 1540, followed by the larger, more extensive Francisco Vasquez de Coronado expedition in 1540–42. Other than brief encounters with explorers and missionaries, native Arizonans were not affected by Europeans other than the beneficial exchange of tools, crops, livestock, and other goods.

Just as there were many languages and cultures in Arizona before the Europeans, the area would continue to be a multicultural stew, where each ethnic ingredient retains its flavor rather than a melting pot where they all blend together.

The stage is set; the geographical scenery and original cast are in place; now enter the Spaniards.

The Yuma Indians, or Quechan, differed from central or eastern Arizona tribes. Courtesy of the Arizona Historical Society (4737).

CHAPTER THREE
★ SPAIN AND THE REPUBLIC OF MEXICO

They were not familiar with His Majesty, nor did they wish to be his subjects.

—Francisco Vasquez de Coronado, 1541

OLD SPAIN AND THE NEW WORLD

In April AD 711, hundreds of years before the Ancient Ones built cliff dwellings throughout the Southwest, the Moors embarked from Morocco, crossed what is now called the Straits of Gibraltar, and invaded Spain. In less than a decade they occupied all of the Iberian Peninsula.

The Cross and the Sword

Spaniards began a reconquest, or *Reconquista*, of their homelands as early as AD 721, and most of the country was retaken by the twelfth century. However, the Moorish occupation did not end until the last of them were driven out at the Siege of Granada in January 1492. Although Columbus had been petitioning the rulers of Portugal and Spain for funding for his expedition for almost a decade, it was no coincidence that they took action only after the Reconquista was completed.

The Moorish Conquest caused Portugal and Spain to develop differently than other European nation-states. While France, England, and Germany were experiencing the exploration, trade, and cultural developments of the Renaissance, Spain developed a system of military and religious conquest in order to regain their country.

In addition to knights, noblemen, and their serfs from small nation-states, the system relied on mercenaries, whose payments were usually the spoils of war. From the eleventh through the thirteenth centuries, the fight against the Moors became linked with Crusades, with God on their side. After the Reconquista, Spanish rulers used the same combination, often called the "Cross and the Sword," to conquer much larger areas of the New World than their European neighbors.

In Old Tucson *(1907), by Maynard Dixon. Courtesy of Mark Sublette, Medicine Man Gallery, Tucson, Arizona.*

Greed and Fables

Know, that on the right hand of the Indies there is an island called California very close to the side of the Terrestrial Paradise; and it is peopled by black women, without any man among them, for they live in the manner of Amazons.

—Garci Rodríguez de Montalvo,
Amadis de Gaula, 1503

More than a century before Spaniards entered Arizona, the Age of Discovery—led by Prince Henry the Navigator, Vasco de Gama, and Bartholomeo Diaz—inspired dreams of mystery and grandeur. Explorers' reports of strange lands and beasts led people to believe that ancient myths of dragons and treasures might actually exist in far-off lands.

By the sixteenth century, Johannes Gutenberg's moveable-type printing press began to put books into the hands of thousands. It was not a far leap for young adventurers to combine exploration reports and newly published novels to conclude that great treasures awaited them in the New World. When Hernán Cortés sailed up what is now the Sea of Cortez in 1535 and discovered a tall tribe of natives, he named the land "California" after an island of Amazon women ruled by Queen Califia in one of these adventure books.

Those who entered Arizona expected to find large cities overflowing with gold and silver, similar to those found in Peru or Mexico and described in their favorite novels. What they found, however, was entirely the opposite. Any cities that might have been in Arizona had already been vanquished by a silent enemy.

Widowed, not Virgin, Land

With the voyage in 1492, a process called the Columbian Exchange began the widespread transfer of plants, animals, agricultural techniques, and culture between the Old World and the New World—one of the most significant events in human history. Explorers returned to Europe with maize, potatoes, tomatoes, avocados, chili peppers, cocoa, and turkeys, and in turn provided the New World with fruit trees, wheat, horses, sheep, goats, and other products too numerous to mention. In particular, the introduction of the horse changed the lives of Native Americans from the Southwest to the Great Plains, allowing them to increase their hunting range and become seminomadic.

While the new crops and animals created population increases in both hemispheres, European diseases such as the plague, measles, cholera, and even chicken pox were introduced to indigenous peoples with no immunity. Although no accurate data exists for pre-Columbian populations, scholarship of the past several decades estimates declines in the native population of anywhere from 50 to 90 percent between the years 1500 and 1650. Smallpox epidemics are believed responsible for the largest death tolls.

Conquerors and colonists generally believed that they were encountering "virgin land" in the New World, an area sparsely populated and unspoiled. In light of the recent disease findings, historian Francis Jennings coined the phrase "widowed land," a country emptied by epidemics. As the Indians lost their battle with disease, the Spaniards went from a victory in the Old World to several in the New World.

The Conquistadors of New Spain

When Spaniards finally defeated the Moors at Granada, attention turned to new conquests, spreading Christianity and expanding the empire to recover from the devastating costs of the reconquest. King Charles V approached the conquest of the New World with the same strategies his ancestors developed during the centuries-old Reconquista. He granted military contracts to noblemen, who then raised and supplied their own troops with the promise of a portion of the lands and loot gained from their conquest.

The leaders sent to the New World were sons of noblemen called *hidalgos*, a contraction of the phrase *hijos de algo*, or "other sons." Since every first-born nobleman's son inherited all his father's land according to Spanish law, the other sons had to make their own way, becoming priests, soldiers, government officials, or simply courtiers if their family wealth permitted. One of these young adventurous *hidalgos* would be the first to visit the American Southwest, and his stories of legendary wealth brought the first Europeans to Arizona.

Cortés and the Aztec Empire

The rapid success of Conquistador Hernán Cortés in conquering the Aztec Empire in only two years is due in part to the advantages of steel and gunpowder, plus the tactic of allying with conquered peoples to overthrow their tyrants. After reports of riches looted from the fabulous city of Tenochtitlan, explorers expected to find others like

BELOW: Arizona's missions housed many santos *(carved statues of Catholic saints).*

RIGHT: Dedicated Franciscans endured harsh conditions to bring Christianity to Arizona.

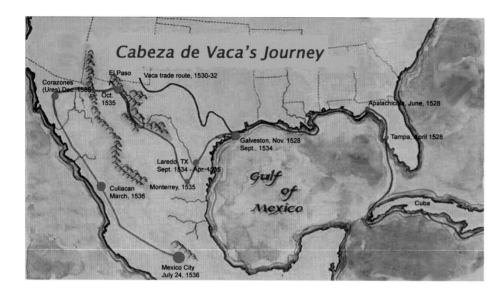

LEFT: *Cabeza de Vaca was the first European to cross North America.*

FACING: *Coronado followed the San Pedro River, and then veered east to the Sulphur Springs Valley. Courtesy of Jerry Jacka Photography.*

it in the unknown lands of the New World. One legend stood out in particular and helped bring the first Europeans to Arizona.

The Seven Cities

For several centuries, Spaniards passed on a story about seven bishops who escaped from the Moorish invasion of AD 711, took their great wealth, and fled to an uncharted island to the west. Believing anything possible after what previous expeditions reported, when explorers reached the Caribbean, they named those islands the Antilles. They found no fabled cities, but the legend was too alluring to be discarded.

FIRST ENCOUNTERS IN THE SOUTHWEST
Conqueror, Slave, Healer

Encouraged by Cortés's success, Pánfilo de Narváez set sail from Cuba in April 1528 with four ships and 400 men, and landed near Sarasota, Florida. To prevent his men from retreating, Narváez sent the ships back to Spain, just as Cortés had done earlier. The major flaw in his strategy doomed the expedition. Where Cortés had hundreds of Indian allies to fight the Aztecs, Narváez met

only fierce natives with powerful longbows who drove them back into the ocean.

The Spaniards then built barges from horsehide and were battered around the Gulf of Mexico from Mobile to New Orleans. All but 40 of the original 400 men were lost in a big storm, and the survivors washed ashore, only to be enslaved by the natives. The Indians told them they would be medicine men, but the ship's treasurer, Cabeza de Vaca, protested they did not have medical training. When the Indians threatened to starve their captives, they soon learned to heal, using a combination of Catholic prayer, sprinkling powders, and blowing on their patients. Vaca then slipped away and became a trader on a route from Galveston to southeast New Mexico.

He returned after two years. By now there were only three Spaniards remaining, two noblemen and a black slave named Estevan. Vaca helped them escape, and their route took them more than 700 miles from Monterrey up near El Paso, west to just south of Nogales, and finally down to Culiacán near the Pacific coast. Their healing brought the castaways many gifts, among them heart-shaped green stones that the Spaniards mistook for emeralds. The survivors said they heard stories about seven rich cities high up on mesas to the north at the Zuni

villages in a place called Cibola. Word spread from pulpits and town squares in New Spain. An expedition was mounted to search for the cities, led by Fray Marcos de Niza and guided by Estevan.

Fray Marcos and Estevan

Miguel Dorantes, one of the survivors of the ill-fated Pánfilo de Narváez expedition, sold his slave Estevan the Moor to the viceroy of New Spain. The viceroy, Antonio de Mendoza, lost little time in investigating Cabeza de Vaca's expedition stories. He commissioned Fray Marcos de Niza, a monk with previous military/missionary experience, to accompany Estevan on the expedition.

For this journey, Estevan collected an escort similar to Vaca's, but he did it without the humility and tolerance shown by his former leader. Flaunting his sacred gourd rattle and copper bells, Estevan demanded turquoises and beautiful women from each village. When he reached the Zuni village of Hawikuh, the elders suspected that he was a spy for would-be conquerors. They resented his attitude and demands, and put him to death.

Francisco Vasquez de Coronado

Decades before Hudson, LaSalle, and Champlain navigated America's eastern seaboard, Spanish conquistadors followed the legend of the Seven Cities of Cibola for thousands of miles across North America in search of gold and jewels. Francisco Vasquez de Coronado, a Spanish hidalgo and governor of the province of Neuva Galicia, and his friend Antonio de Mendoza, the Viceroy of Mexico, invested large sums of their own money in the venture. Coronado's wife, Beatriz, was the daughter of the Treasurer of New Spain, who added another 70,000 pesos to finance the expedition.

The expedition left Compostela, near Puerto Vallarta, in February 1540 with approximately 335 Spaniards, 1,300 natives, four Franciscan monks, and a number of both native and African slaves. They were outfitted with the best supplies money could buy. Coronado wore a gilded suit of armor, and his helmet sported a red plume. His 225 mounted men and 62 foot soldiers wore chain mail, quilted cotton armor, and buckskin jackets; they carried crossbows and several arquebusses, forerunner to the Pilgrim's blunderbusses. While Coronado went north by land along the banks of the San Pedro River into Arizona, he sent Hernando de Alarcón with several ships of supplies up the Colorado River to present-day Yuma. Anywhere along the route, local natives stood for several hours watching the main expedition force of 350 Spaniards, 1,000 Indian allies, and thousands of horses, cattle, and sheep pass by their villages.

Their first battle was the Zuni pueblo of Hawikuh in eastern New Mexico, the six-story "apartment building" that Fray Marcos de Niza believed was one of the Seven Cities of Cibola. The natives knew they were coming and tried to negotiate with them. They also attacked them in a mountain pass before the Spaniards reached their pueblo. Then emissaries from the Old World and the New World met on the plain some distance from Hawikuh. Coronado had a native guide read the famous *Requerimiento,* the Papal declaration stating that the Spaniards had authority from God to rule all of the Americas. It is uncertain whether the Zunis understood much of the translation, but they responded by attacking the Spaniards and retreating to their fortified pueblo, showering arrows, spears, and large rocks down on the invaders, seriously wounding Coronado on the head with a stone.

After fierce attacks in which perhaps 20 Indians were killed and a handful of Spaniards wounded by rocks and arrows, Hawikuh fell to the superior arms of the Europeans. The conquistadors and priests stayed at Hawikuh to recuperate, and Coronado sent Captain Pedro de Tovar to the Hopi mesas; Antonio López de Cárdenas went past

FACING: Carl Oscar Borg depicted Coronado's arrival at the Seven Cities of Cibola.

ABOVE: The conquistador is an integral part of Arizona's Spanish public image.

FACING: Historic artwork at the Tumacácori Mission museum gives an inkling of the church's interior.

them to become one of the first Europeans to see the Grand Canyon.

The Coronado Expedition spent the winter of 1541 near present-day Albuquerque. Overcrowding, famine, and greed strained Euro-Indian relations until another legend sent the Spaniards on their way. Stories of the Gran Quivera, where trees grew silver apples and chiefs ate from golden bowls, led the explorers across the bleak Llano Estacado in Texas and all the way to the center of the United States to the area around Salina, Kansas.

The failure to find great riches or Indian communities willing to convert to Christianity delayed further explorations in North America for almost four decades. The next group of explorers would be looking for Arizona's true mineral wealth, that which was in the ground, not worked into jewelry and other artifacts.

Espejo, Farfan, and Oñate Expeditions

Ostensibly searching for two missionary priests who disappeared in what is now New Mexico the year before, Antonio Espejo led a search party late in 1582 but continued the journey far to the west, responding to stories of minerals told by Mexican Indians whom Coronado left behind. The explorers reached present-day Jerome in central Arizona, where they found turquoise and rich silver deposits.

Several years later, Marcos Farfan de los Godos reported veins of rich ore in what is now central Arizona "so long and wide that one-half the people in New Spain could stake out claims in this land." By 1605, the viceroy reported to King Phillip III that tales of riches were taking on fairy-tale proportions.

Up to this point, the expeditions were small. It was not until January 1598—ten years before the English colony at Jamestown—that Don Juan de Oñate, the last conquistador in the New World, led six hundred colonists, including soldiers, priests, families, Mexican Indians, and African slaves, up the Rio Grande to the village of San Juan near present-day Santa Fe. This 83-wagon caravan, with more than 7,000 animals, stretched for four miles across the landscape on its journey to establish one of the first European colonies in North America, second only to St. Augustine, Florida (founded in 1565).

From his base colony, Oñate also led the longest expedition across Arizona up to that point. In 1605, he retraced Espejo's journey to the Hopi mesas and then traveled down off the Mogollón Rim to Jerome. Oñate continued westward to what is now called the Bill Williams River, following to its confluence with the Colorado. From there, he followed the Colorado south to Yuma. The round trip was approximately 1,400 miles.

THE CROSS REPLACES THE SWORD

Through a change in Spanish royalty with a stronger humanist philosophy, the Pueblo Revolt, and complaints from New World clergy, the cross led the way in the Southwest in the late 1600s, and the Spanish sword was temporarily sheathed.

Missionaries to the Hopi

It was another 20 years before Europeans entered Arizona again. In 1629, four Franciscan missionaries led by Father Francisco de Porras headed west from Santa Fe and established San Bernardino de Awátobi near the Hopi mesas in northeastern Arizona. Missions at Shongópovi and Oraibi were founded soon afterward, with *visitas* at Walpi and Mishóngnovi added later.

The Hopis, with their ancient and elaborate spiritual system, did not take to the new religion, and the missions struggled along until the Pueblo Revolt in 1680, when four missionaries were slain and their churches destroyed. No further attempts were made to convert the Hopis until their homelands became part of the United States two centuries later.

The Pueblo Revolt of 1680

To tell the story of early Arizona, one has to erase state boundaries, and even national borders, and talk about events that affected European settlement of the Southwest on a wider scope. Just as the Coronado expedition sought to spread the Catholic faith by bringing priests along, Oñate's New Mexico colonies did the same. The Spanish sword, the cross, and a process similar to the

Arizona's missions hosted hundreds of beautiful religious statues and paintings.

as well. On the other hand, the new crops, tools, and protection against raiding Navajos and Apaches were welcomed, and the two cultures coexisted in relative peace for four generations.

Drought and famine strained relations in the 1670s, and Spanish soldiers could not defend the Pueblos against raiding enemies as they had in the past. European-introduced diseases increased, and the natives, in their starving condition, turned to their old beliefs for relief. The missionaries responded by putting 47 medicine men in prison. Three were hanged and a fourth committed suicide before his death sentence could be carried out.

In retaliation, Pueblo leaders marched to Santa Fe and forced the governor to release the medicine men. One of the prisoners, an intelligent and charismatic native of San Juan Pueblo named Pope (pronounced POH-pay), gathered 20,000 Indians and led a revolt against the Spaniards beginning on the morning of August 10, 1680. Reports listed 380 colonists killed. With only 150 soldiers to defend them, the remaining 2,000 Spanish

repartimiento system, called the *encomienda*, disrupted the Pueblo Indians' traditional religion and government systems.

Many were forced to labor for the colonists and in the silver mines far south in Chihuahua, Mexico. They were punished for practicing their spiritual ceremonies

colonists retreated under harassment to El Paso, on the current U.S.–Mexico border.

The Pueblo Indians were able to repel the European invasion of their homelands, and the Europeans did not return until Diego de Vargas mounted an American *Reconquista* in 1692.

Padre Eusebio Kino

Another sixty years lapsed between the Franciscan failures at the Hopi mesas and Spain's next advance into Arizona. History is often influenced by extraordinary men of purpose, drive, and perseverance. Just as California had Brother Junípero Serra, Arizona had its "patron saint" of Catholic missionaries, Father Kino. Arizona has erected at least four statues to honor Father Kino: one in Phoenix, two in Tucson, and one in Statuary Hall in the Capitol Building in Washington, D.C.

Eusebio Francisco Chini (Kino) was born August 10, 1645, in the village of Segno in the Val di Non, less than 100 miles south of Innsbruck, Austria. A genius at mathematics, astronomy, and cartography, one of Kino's contemporaries said he was more German than Italian in his thinking.

Kino excelled in school but was struck by a life-threatening illness in his late teens, when he vowed to St. Francis Xavier that he would become a missionary to Asia, like his famous cousin Martino Martini, if God would save his life.

After teaching at several universities in Austria, Kino studied for 12 years to become a Jesuit priest. Although he had hoped to serve in China, where mathematics was revered, the luck of the draw sent him to Baja, Mexico, where his mapping skills were put to good use.

Father Eusebio Kino stands in the National Statuary Hall and in front of the Arizona History Museum, Tucson.

Expeditions in the Pimería Alta

Arriving in Mexico in 1681, the 36-year-old missionary changed his name to Kino, probably because Chino was a sometimes-derogatory Spanish word for "Chinese." Appointed as the royal cosmographer for the California expedition of 1682, Kino drew the first accurate maps of the Sea of Cortez and Baja, California. Later, he created the first detailed maps of northern Sonora, Mexico, and southern Arizona. His 1706 map of the area was drawn so well that it was used for more than a century.

In spite of his willingness to endure hardships, Kino's work in California was short-lived. The Baja Peninsula was so desolate that Spanish officials scrapped the mission there and sent Father Kino to Magdalena, Mexico, where Hispanic and Native American Catholics still make a pilgrimage every year.

In 1691, Father Eusebio Francisco Kino began the

ABOVE: *Completed in 1796, Mission San Xavier del Bac is very photogenic. Courtesy of Dori Griffin.*

BELOW: *San Xavier Mission has been the subject of countless postcards. Courtesy of Dori Griffin.*

FACING: *This recent photograph of San Xavier shows the restoration successes of the 1990s*

first of nine expeditions into Arizona, an area the Spaniards called the Pimería Alta, land of the Upper Pimas. He followed the Santa Cruz River north from Mexico 20 miles above the current border, and visited the area where the ruins of Tumacácori Mission are preserved as a national park today. On his next mission a year later, he visited the village of Bac, just south of Tucson, where the San Xavier Mission still serves the descendents of those he converted three centuries ago.

He counted 900 natives at Bac and 800 at Schookson. Roughly translated, Schookson means "black at the base where it comes up," referring to the volcanic hills to the west; Spaniards translated it to Tucson. The Indians were living in clusters of houses stretched out six leagues (approximately 17 miles) along the banks of the Santa Cruz River, barely in sight of each other. He said the whole area was covered with abundant ditch-irrigated fields. It was the largest native population he had encountered thus far, one of the reasons that the metropolis of Tucson arose from a prehistoric Indian village. Between 1694 and 1701, Father Kino and his companion Captain Juan Mateo Manje covered almost 8,000 miles on horseback from northern Mexico to the Colorado River delta.

The Spanish Mission System

In the seventeenth century, the Spanish mission network consisted of a central *cabacera*, or headquarters, surrounded by missions several days away in several directions from the hub, and farthest out, a series of *visitas*, or places a priest visited regularly. Once a congregation developed, the visita merited a permanent priest, and, like a Methodist circuit rider of the next century, he

BELOW: President Theodore Roosevelt designated Tumácacori Mission as a National Monument in 1908, and it was redesignated as a National Historical Park in 1966.

FACING: Holding hands at San Xavier Mission, a natural state for kids everywhere. Courtesy of Dori Griffin.

manent mission there in 1700, naming it San Xavier del Bac, after his patron saint. In 1701, he set up permanent missions at Tumacácori, farther south on the Santa Cruz River, and at Guevavi, near present-day Nogales, Arizona.

Not only did Kino concentrate on conversion, but he saw to every area's economic and civil development as well. With the 24 missions and countless visitas, he established in his 26-year career, Kino also created 19 ranches to bring cattle, sheep, and goats to the natives. He trained Indians to become cowboys long before any others in the Southwest, and drove 1,500 head of cattle from Mexico to San Xavier del Bac. His horsemanship was noteworthy, and it was said that the "Padre on Horseback" could ride more than 50 miles a day.

Kino brought many new foodstuffs to supplement the meager desert diet, including fruit trees, vegetables, and cold-resistant wheat that provided food during the lean winter months. In addition, he trained the Pimas and Tohono O'odham in carpentry and ironwork.

began traveling to start new visitas on the frontier.

The combination of sound economic planning and a broad tolerance for Indian customs was a major reason for Kino's success in his campaign of peaceful conquest. Where the sword brought failure, now the cross met with success—mostly in northern Mexico, but with modest and lasting beginnings in Arizona as well.

Kino first visited the Tohono O'odham village of Bac in 1691 and set up a visita. According to Spanish records, Father Kino established a per-

FACING ABOVE: The acoustics inside the Tumácacori Mission are phenomenal.

FACING BELOW: The Kino Memorial Association created this plaque north of the Tucson City Hall in 1936.

RIGHT: Behind the main church, a small chapel sits in the center of the cemetery.

BELOW: The granary supplied storage for a thriving agricultural community.

After the Jesuit Expulsion in 1767, Franciscan missionaries took charge.

Padre Kino's Legacy

Father Kino was the first to explore and map the Pimería Alta while establishing more than 20 missions. He was known to be compassionate, understanding, a scholar, a great horseman, and knowledgeable about agriculture and other practical subjects. He earned the respect of the native people, his colleagues, and his superiors.

The Padre on Horseback continued to spread Catholicism in the Pimería Alta, the land of the Upper Pimas, for more than two decades, working with the Akimel O'odham (Pimas), Tohono O'odham, Sobas, Cocomaricopas, and Yumas. He treated them with respect and reverence, and was often acknowledged as generous, kind,

and hard working. In the last years of his service, he estimated that he and his fellow missionaries converted more than 30,000 souls in Sonora and southern Arizona.

Father Kino continued his work until 1711, when he died at age 65. Through lack of funding and far-flung distances, the first missions in Arizona lasted a few years at most. A resurgence of mission building took place in the 1730s. Politics intervened, and the king ordered the expulsion of all Jesuits from the New World in 1767. The mission system was abandoned in some parts of the New World, but Franciscan friars took up where Kino left off and constructed the current missions at San Xavier and Tumacácori.

Return of the Sword

In Arizona, the most effective of the grey-robed Franciscans was Fray Francisco Garcés. Known as the children's priest because of his youthful exuberance and connection with young people, Garcés would have made a great youth leader today. He took charge of the failing mission at San Xavier in 1764, and in 1771, he built the San Agustín Mission at the base of what we now call "A" Mountain, then called Schookson, the village from which Tucson gets its name. It was his suggestion to the Spanish mission inspector that caused the relocation of the presidio, or fort, from Tubac to Tucson in 1776. Sadly, he did not live to see the town that his efforts created. Garcés was martyred trying to establish a mission at Yuma in 1781. He died in service at age forty-three.

Visiting San Xavier is like traveling back to the eighteenth century.

The mission system was destined for difficulty, and the cross alone could not prevail. Spanish missionaries brought horses and cows to the Southwest, and the more sedentary agricultural Pimas and Tohono O'odham obtained them by accepting the religion that came with them. Since Apache culture and traditions favored courage and aggression, they found it much more practical to simply take the livestock, guns, knives, and metal tools.

But more than all the rest, the Apaches' strong belief in revenge for wrongs to their people, especially family members, was the key factor in the clash of cultures they carried on against the Europeans for several centuries and at least one century before with other Arizona native people. Their persistent revenge perpetuated the same

motivations in their enemies, with all sides forever calling for more raids to avenge those killed in the last raid. The downward spiral of attacking and avenging continued until the Apache culture was completely subdued.

But when the Spaniards first entered the Pimería Alta, the avengers' dance with death was just beginning for them. The sword was still needed, and Spaniards took a page from the Roman conquests to forge their frontier strategy.

LANCERS FOR THE KING— THE PRESIDIOS

What could ancient Tripoli, medieval city-states, and Jamestown possibly have in common with southern Ari-zona? From at least AD 74, the Roman Empire defended its frontier colonies with a series of far-flung walled villages. They were called *praesidium*, which eventually evolved into the Spanish word *presidio*. European feudal states adapted the praesidium system with walled cities such as Avila and Girona in Spain and Carcassonne in France.

Although these frontier outposts served as forts, they were much more than that. Presidios included soldiers' families, artisans, servants, and priests—all the roles of a typical village. The army payroll attracted merchants and others, including gamblers and bootleggers as well.

The presidio was also an example of human intrusion into an ecosystem. People did not move there because the climate, water, and food supply were better than where they lived before, but for military, political, and economic

BELOW: A ramada provides shade in the reconstructed Presidio San Agustín del Tucson.

FACING: The Spanish flag flies over the reconstructed presidio at Tucson.

Reglamento of 1729

reasons instead. Tucson is unique in that it is probably the only city in the United States whose citizens lived within a walled city for almost 80 years.

By the time Hernán Cortés landed at Vera Cruz, the need for walled cities diminished in Spain. But the frontier of New Spain presented old problems that brought to mind traditional solutions.

When silver was discovered near Zacatecas, miners rushed to the unprotected lands north of Mexico City. The fierce Chichimec Indians made this a dangerous venture. Faced with the same difficulties as the Romans, the Spanish military began building small presidios as early as 1570. When Kino, his fellow missionaries, and their handful of soldier escorts explored Arizona in the 1690s, no compounds were necessary. However, as the Spanish presence grew in the 1730s, more colonists arrived. After two decades of growth, violent events caused a major shift in the settlement of the Pimería Alta.

After the Pueblo Revolt in New Mexico, Spanish authorities strengthened their forces to safeguard against future uprisings and defend against their European rivals. However, distance from central authority fostered fraud, sloth, and corruption. Frontier soldiers were paid in overpriced supplies instead of silver coin, and service charges reaching 18 percent took a bite out of their pay. As a result, they were often without horses, arms, or ammunition, and in debt.

The viceroy showed concern for their plight but was more concerned about large sums lost to payroll fraud. When soldiers died or deserted, corrupt captains kept them on the payroll and pocketed their pay. Colonel Pedro de Rivera inspected all the presidios and compiled the first set of general presidio regulations, published as the Reglamento of 1729. But the Colonel was more concerned with saving money than protecting the frontier, and major political events in the next 50 years greatly affected the situation in Arizona.

Pima Revolt of 1751

The Spanish policy of combining military and religious motives served them well during the Reconquista, but it gave rise to conflicts from the start in the New World. Priests constantly complained about civilian abuses of the Indians, from the first encounters in the Caribbean, through the Coronado Expedition, through to Kino's time.

In the case of the Pima Revolt, it was not as much the two institutions fighting over treatment of the Indians as it was neophytes being torn between two masters. During his explorations in the 1690s, Kino and his soldier escorts were instructed to appoint civil leaders in each area they reached, creating Indian "captain-governors" by handing out canes of office bedecked with ribbons. These native captains were to serve as civil leaders, negotiating peace with other Pima and Tohono O'odham villages, and serving as war leaders while serving as auxiliaries with the Spanish army.

Starting in 1748, several incidents occurred where Indians defied the priest to go on raiding expeditions against the Apaches, and they were beaten for their insubordination. Over the next three years, extreme punishment by several priests led charismatic Captain-General Luis Oacpicagigua (nicknamed "Luis of Saric") to coordinate other Pima leaders in a several-hundred-mile area of southern Arizona and northern Sonora, Mexico.

In early November 1751, Luis convinced the missionaries at Saric (near present-day Nogales) that they should seek shelter in a house because Apaches were attacking. When they did, Luis had his armed men surround the house and then set fire to it, killing 22, including 9 children.

Other Pimas and O'odham attacked other missions at the same time, killing several punishing priests and more than 80 Spanish men, women, and children as well. Some of the priests had whipped their charges and restrained them in the stocks.

Spanish soldiers quelled the rebellion with a pitched battle at Arivaca on January 4, 1752, when less than 100 Spaniards defeated a force of about 2,000 Indians. Luis of Saric retreated into the hills but surrendered on March 18. In response to the Pima Revolt, the first Spanish presidio was constructed at Tubac in the summer of 1752. Other outbreaks occurred in following months, and Luis died in a Spanish prison in 1755.

Tubac Presidio

Founded in 1752 as a reaction to the Pima Revolt, Tubac was the first Spanish presidio in Arizona and was situated on the Santa Cruz River. It afforded not only water but firewood and feed for livestock. The fort was constructed about three and a half miles north of the mission at Tumacácori, perhaps because the missionary priests did not want the soldiers corrupting their Native American neophytes.

Usually manned by less than 50 men, the *compania volante* (flying company) of soldiers at Tubac conducted successful expeditions against the Apaches and Seri Indians over the next 14 years. The presidio also served as the base for Lt. Colonel Juan Bautista de Anza's expedition to lead about 200 colonists overland and to found a presidio and mission on the San Francisco Bay in 1776. Tourists may now follow historic markers along the 1,210-mile Juan Bautista de Anza National Historic Trail, traveling from Tubac to Tucson and up through California to what is now San Francisco.

Reglamento of 1772

When the Treaty of Paris ended the Seven Years' War in 1763, France ceded the last of its colonial holdings along the Mississippi to Spain. At the same time, Spain's claims of empire in the New World were also threatened by British and Russian fur trading in the Northwest as far north as Alaska.

The expansion of the mission system, new mining ventures, and increased Indian raids brought military policy to the forefront once again, and Spain launched a second reevaluation of the frontier. In 1766, King Charles III commanded the Marqués de Rubí to conduct a 23-month, 7,500-mile inspection tour of the existing 23 presidios. Rubí called for a single chain of 15 presidios spaced 100 miles apart. He recommended some presidios and relocated others to form a unified line of defense. Rubí's recommendations were published as the Reglamento of 1772, and Lt. Colonel Don Hugo O'Conor, an intrepid Irishman, was appointed commandant inspector to enforce the realignment of the forts.

O'Conor was born in Dublin in 1734. The son of a local man of influence, he and other young men of his stature fled British rule to become mercenaries, or Wild Geese. O'Conor joined the Spanish army at 17, and fought for Spain in Cuba and Texas. He was known as "El Capitan Colorado." O'Conor entered Sonora in May 1775 and was back in Chihuahua in September after a whirlwind tour of the Pimería Alta. In less than four months, he relocated three presidios and created a fourth.

Tucson Presidio

When O'Conor reached the Pimería Alta, he found certain aspects of the Rubí plan impractical. According to the Reglamento, the Tubac Presidio was to be moved to Arivaca, 30 miles west in the Altar Valley. But local missionaries and soldiers said Tucson would be a better location, citing illness at Arivaca and several other reasons that Tucson was the better choice.

Both locations had the requisites of water, pastures, and wood, but the large numbers of Native Americans and rich fields and orchards at the established missions at San Xavier del Bac and San Agustín de Tucson were valid arguments given by local authorities for their choice.

Spanish Colonial–era reenactor Tom Prezelski stands beside an ancient cottonwood tree on the San Pedro River.

ABOVE: *Hector Sosa and wife Micky; he is a direct descendent of an eighteenth-century Tucson presidio soldier.*

BELOW: *The Soldado de Cuero, or leather soldier, wore a tunic made of several layers of deer hide.*

The mission San Agustín de Tucson was built in 1771, not by a Jesuit missionary but by a Franciscan friar, Fray Francisco Garcés. Fearing that they had become too powerful, King Charles III called for the expulsion of all Jesuits from the Spanish Empire in 1767. The following year, Father Garcés arrived to serve as missionary at San Xavier del Bac.

Situated on the banks of the Santa Cruz River, Tucson was also a better choice to become a way station on the road to California. In 1775, Juan Bautista de Anza lead approximately 240 men, women, and children from New Spain north to Arizona and up the coast of California to found the first Spanish colony at San Francisco.

ABOVE: *Tucson's birthday ceremony includes Spanish, Mexican, Confederate, Tohono O'odham, and American flags.*

BELOW: *Cannons were ineffective against the Apaches' hit-and-run tactics.*

Don Hugo O'Conor wrote a letter of certification on August 20, 1775, officially stating that the presidio was to be moved to Tucson. Although this date has been adopted as Tucson's European birthday, Spanish records indicate that the soldiers did not make their move until the fall of 1776.

It was not easy to build a presidio so far from European civilization. The Spaniards got very little accomplished under their first commander and lived in tents until June 12, 1777, when a much stronger commandant, Captain Pedro Allande y Saavedra, took charge. Proud and demanding, Captain Allande was known by his superiors to be both valiant and violent. The strict captain drilled his men

constantly and supposedly said he wanted soldiers who would rather sleep with their muskets than their wives.

Under his command, earthen ramparts topped with a log palisade were constructed. The stockade was small, perhaps 100 yards square, but it protected the soldiers and other residents while the larger adobe wall was completed.

The final walled city was made of sun-baked adobe bricks, 18 inches x 1 foot x 3 inches, just the right mixture of clay mud, sand, and straw. The walls were 10 to 12 feet high and 3 feet wide at the base. In all, the presidio covered 300 square yards, or about 12 city blocks today.

Archeologists have found the foundations of one large square tower on the northeast corner of the for-

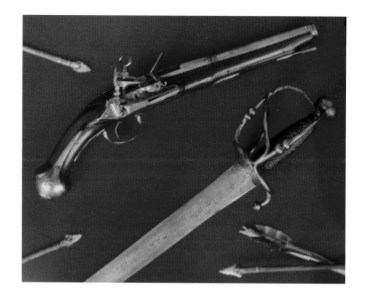

LEFT: *This 1920s tourist book featured mission architecture and a copper cover. Courtesy of Dori Griffin.*

ABOVE: *Spanish steel and gunpowder overpowered Apache arrows and spears.*

mer presidio, and evidence indicates there was a second one on the southwest corner. According to the memoirs of Carmen Lucero, Hillario Gallego, and Mariana Diaz, there was a connected chain of little one-room houses all around the inside of the presidio wall where soldiers could walk guard duty on the roofs and keep watch over the top of the wall.

Only a few of the houses had window openings, and even those did not have glass. The windows had saguaro rib bars to keep raccoons, cats, and other creatures from getting in. The doors were made of brush, sticks, and rawhide. The presidio was completed in December 1783, probably with money contributed by the officers.

Terrenate Presidio

In addition to moving the Tubac Presidio to Tucson, Captain O'Conor recommended that two more presidios be constructed east of Tucson within several days' ride of each other. On August 22, 1775, O'Conor chose a high bluff on the west bank of the San Pedro River (near present-day Tombstone) to relocate the presidio near the vil-

lage of Santa Cruz, near the current international border. The troops moved in early the next year.

The little-known Terrenate Presidio was doomed from the start. Far from reinforcements, the Spaniards were soon cut off from their supply line by the Apaches, who also stole their horses. Those Spaniards who were not killed by frequent raids were wiped out by cholera, malaria, dysentery, and starvation.

Although the inhabitants at Terrenate constantly asked to be moved back to their old location, their pleas fell on deaf ears because they served as a buffer between Mexican villages and Apaches. They were finally allowed to return to their original location in 1782. Ruins of this presidio are preserved and interpreted by the Bureau of Land Management.

San Bernardino Presidio

San Bernardino Presidio was built on the site of a Spanish land grant whose owners gave up their ranch and returned to New Spain (Mexico) in the 1730s because of increased Apache raids. The San Bernardino Presidio suffered a fate similar to Terrenate—too far from Mexico and right in the middle of Apache seasonal migration routes. San Bernardino residents were allowed to abandon their presidio in 1778. The San Bernardino Presidio is now well known as John Slaughter's Ranch, near the border town of Douglas.

Ruins of the Terrenate Presidio are visible seven miles west of Tombstone.

PESOS FOR THE REVOLUTION

In August of 1780, when the Tucson Presidio wall was less than half finished, Charles III fought "the insulting tyranny of the English nation" by calling for support of the American Revolution—a donation of two pesos by every Spaniard and one peso by every Indian to keep Spanish patrol boats on the Mississippi River. The viceroy's instructions were clear that no one would be forced to give the money, and many gave more than the request. Tucson's contribution was admirable. From the decree in 1780 through 1786, Tucson gave 459 pesos. In all, Sonora donated 22,420 pesos, and New Spain donated almost a million pesos. At that time, three pesos would buy an excellent riding horse, which meant one peso might be worth anywhere from $10 to $20,

and thus Tucson's total aide amounted to anywhere from $50,000 to $75,000.

The Viceroy's Peace Plan

Borrowing from the innovations of French traders, Viceroy of New Spain Bernardo de Gálvez designed a dramatic new Indian policy known as the Instrucciones de 1786. The first part of the three-pronged strategy was to wage unrelenting warfare to force the Apaches to surrender. The second prong encouraged Indians to settle near each of the presidios in sites called *establecimientos de paz* (peace establishments). The third prong was to provide the Indians with beef, bad guns, and strong liquor. The idea was to make the Indians dependent on

FACING: Mexican cultural traditions are still a large part of southern Arizona's heritage. Courtesy of the Arizona Historical Society (73821).

ABOVE: Joaquin Murrieta (1903), by Maynard Dixon. Murrieta was a California icon, but this image is reminiscent of Arizona's Mexican era. Courtesy of Mark Sublette, Medicine Man Gallery, Tucson, Arizona.

the Spaniards for gun repair and alcohol. Gálvez believed that a bad peace was better than a good war.

The peace plan worked well for almost three decades. By 1793, there were eight peace camps called *establecimientos de paz* set up near presidios at Janos, Fronteras, and Tucson. Several thousand Apaches settled in the camps and received weekly rations of corn, meat, tobacco, and brown sugar.

Apache raids decreased significantly. A new era of prosperity and peace allowed European settlement to grow and succeed throughout the Pimería Alta. Moving away from missionary dominance, the presidio at Tubac was restored with Indian troops, the Compañía de Pimas, and the area flourished. In a short time, the small band of Apaches became friendly with the Spaniards, Pimas, and Tohono O'odham, and came to be known as the Manso (tame) Apaches, or Apaches de Paz. These Apaches formed an Indian auxiliary and rode with the Spanish soldiers against the remaining raiding Apaches; they were rewarded well for their valor.

Some Silver Linings . . .

Reduced Apache raids allowed growth in several areas for the next 30 years, but major political and economic changes brought an end to if not a golden era, than at least one with a silver lining of growth, relative peace, and prosperity. For instance, some previous writers described the peace period as a golden age where huge ranches and extensive mining operations abounded. Their readers imagined Spanish land barons living in splendor similar to California's legendary Zorro, and lost mines of great wealth almost as far north as Phoenix are still sought after by modern treasure hunters.

More research into the Spanish and Mexican records show that ranching definitely increased, but landowners often exaggerated their holdings in order to obtain larger grants and the use of surrounding lands. Mining was limited to those areas near Tucson and Tubac, where the Indians were friendly and labor, supplies, and water were available.

During the Gálvez Peace, Spaniards and a number of

FACING: *San Xavier, "The White Dove of the Desert," gleams in the bright Arizona sunshine.*

ABOVE: *The Casa de Cordova courtyard in Tucson was perhaps built before the Gadsden Purchase.*

Apaches developed a somewhat symbiotic relationship. This pacification by dependency may have succeeded much longer if the Mexican War for Independence had not intervened.

THE NEW REPUBLIC OF MEXICO

Although far from the action, Arizona's first European settlers were greatly affected by the Mexican struggle for independence. Spain's attention to its New World colonies was severely diverted by the Seven Years War, the American Revolution, and the French Revolution, which were all costly. As a result, the colonists' needs were not met, and they felt neglected and without a voice in their government.

The War for Independence

From the beginning, Mexico was run by the *gachupines*, an upper-class caste born in Spain, even though purebred European Spaniards born in the New World, the *criollos* (creoles), outnumbered them nine to one. Like the rest of Europe, Spanish politics and society was highly stratified and restrictive. Mexico's independence was quite similar to their American cousins, as the upper class born in both countries joined with merchants, artisans, laborers, and Native Americans to form independent nations. In Mexico, however, the *mestizos*, those of mixed European

ABOVE: *Mexican Arizonans practiced Old World culture, grace, and charm.*

ABOVE RIGHT: *Undaunted by strains of the frontier, ranchers dressed with style.*

and Indian blood, made up an even larger portion of the disenfranchised population.

Father Miguel Hidalgo, a member of a liberal intellectual literary club in Querétaro in what is now central Mexico, helped enlist the native Indian, mestizo, and masses of lower-class citizens in the struggle. On September 16, 1810, Hidalgo delivered his revolutionary cry for social and economic reform, the Grito de Dolores, to his parishioners.

This triggered a mob of untrained Indians and mestizos, who overwhelmed the royal army at Guanajuato. They marched on to Mexico City, defeating royalist troops at the outskirts. However, the victories where short-lived, and the rebel forces were soundly defeated by the Royalist armies. Hidalgo and his officers were

executed the following March.

Four years later, isolated guerrilla bands renewed the fighting. But by 1820, the independence movement was again about to collapse. In December, after an initial clash with rebel forces in Oaxaca, Colonel Agustín de Iturbide, a royalist criollo officer, switched sides and joined his army with that of the rebels to win Mexico's independence.

On February 24, 1821, Iturbide drew up the Plan of Iguala. His formerly royalist army was joined by rebel forces from all over Mexico, and on August 24, 1821, the Spanish government signed the Treaty of Córdoba, recognizing Mexican independence. After three centuries of Spanish rule, the people of Mexico were free to govern themselves.

Arizona under Mexico

While great changes took place in central Mexico, life was pretty much the same in Arizona. Soldiers at Tubac and Tucson took the oath to support the new government, but the same officers remained in command.

However, for the next three decades, economic and safety conditions slowly got worse. After independence, strong leaders called *caudillos* warred with each other for control of different areas of Mexico, and at the same time, uprisings of Yaqui Indians drew troops away from Tucson. The new federal government could not afford the price of peace: the rations supplied to Apaches.

In 1832, hundreds of Apaches defected from peace camps, including a few from Tucson. But by 1870, about 100 still lived on the land given to them by the Spaniards. Some moved back to their homelands in eastern Arizona, but many of their descendents may still live around the San Xavier Mission or in west Tucson, intermarrying with other local cultures. Although we may never know who the descendents of the Manso Apaches are, even less is known about a smaller group known as the *Apaches pinto*, the mystery natives with blue eyes.

With troops off fighting civil wars and the Yaquis, the local governments resorted to a war of extermination in northern Mexico and southern Arizona, raising funds to

Ranching artifacts at the Tubac Presidio Museum hearken back to large Mexican land grant days.

offer bounties on Apache scalps. They hired bloodthirsty, sometimes psychopathic, American scalp hunters such as James Kirker and James Glanton to eradicate Apaches, but stopped when the hunters tried to pass off Mexican scalps as Apache. One significant incident involved John Johnson and a small cannon. Finding himself outnumbered by Apaches, Johnson began to trade with them. When trading was done, he lit the fuse of a hidden swivel gun, killing 20 Indians. There are several versions of this story, but most historians agree that the incident fanned the flames of revenge that would last another 50 years, especially for Chiricahua leaders Cochise and Mangas Coloradas.

The major change in style of governance had to do with Mexico's approach to settlement on the frontier. Spain relied on religious and military institutions, which had become too powerful and costly. Mexico now turned to independent ranchers, usually upper-class citizens, to populate Arizona. Spain issued only a few land grants, but Mexico granted thousands of acres to independent families and in some cases sold earlier abandoned Spanish land grants in an effort to colonize Arizona.

As an example, in May 1822, Lieutenant Ignacio Perez purchased the San Bernardino Spanish land grant. The ranch included 73,000 acres in what is now the southeast corner of modern Arizona and northeast Sonora, Mexico. Perez then purchased 4,000 head of cattle to stock his ranch from Father Juan Bautista Estelric of the Tumacácori Mission. The landowners saw the Apache situation as more or less under control and had no idea that within 10 years they would all have to flee for their lives.

Another major difference under Mexican rule was the opening of the Santa Fe Trail and other trade opportunities with the United States. Like Britain, Spain operated a closed colonial mercantile system, where raw goods and resources were provided to the mother country, and colonies had to purchase their finished products from that rul-

The Mexican-era Sosa-Carrillo-Frémont House in Tucson, was the only building spared by urban renewal.

of miles west of these routes, increased profits in trading opened up new routes from Guaymas and Hermosillo as well, bringing much-needed goods to the remote villages of Tubac and Tucson. Free trade also opened up Mexican Arizona to another entrepreneur, the fur trapper.

But before the Santa Fe Trail brought Americans to the Southwest, another chain of events was playing itself out in Texas. It began in 1810 when Spanish officials invited American pioneers to settle there and ended the Spanish-Mexican Era in Arizona with the Treaty of Guadalupe Hidalgo in 1848, and finally the Gadsden Purchase in 1854.

LEFT: *The north wall of the Tucson Presidio was situated about one foot inside this entrance to Old Town Artisans.*

BELOW: *The Sonorans' use of vivid colors on Tucson architecture reminded one U.S. soldier of Morocco.*

ing nation. This was not unlike the company store model, where wages, prices, and profits could be tightly controlled.

However, this resulted in no money or products on the distant frontier and prohibitions on trading with closer American frontier neighbors. Once Mexico formed a republic, the trade situation changed. A major trade route opened up that would bring Mexican and American traders together, creating a blended southwestern economic and cultural frontier.

New Trails

Missouri trader William Becknell opened the Santa Fe Trail the same year Mexico won its independence. Long freight wagons filled with manufactured goods made their way across the frontier to Santa Fe, New Mexico, where they exchanged some of their goods for furs and hides with Mexican freighters traversing the Chihuahua Trail, leading from Santa Fe south along the Rio Grande to Chihuahua, Mexico. Mexican traders such as the Aguirre brothers also ran wagons to the eastern end of the Santa Fe Trail at Franklin, Missouri. While Arizona was hundreds

CHAPTER FOUR

★ MANIFEST DESTINY, THE ARGONAUTS, AND CIVIL WAR

[The Grand Canyon] looks like the Gates of Hell. The region . . .
is, of course, altogether valueless. Ours has been the first and
will undoubtedly be the last, party of whites to visit the locality.

—Lieutenant Joseph Christmas Ives,
survey expedition, 1858

THE FUR TRADE

Fur traders, known popularly as mountain men, often began their careers in their early teens, running away from farm life drudgery to answer ads placed by major fur companies. The first Americans reported in Arizona after Mexico took control were four fur trappers who were told by Pima Indians on the Gila River that they must register with Mexican officials in Tucson.

In the 1820s and 1830s, the father-and-son team of Sylvester and James Ohio Pattie, Kit Carson, Jedediah Smith, Bill Williams, Paulino Weaver, Michel Robidoux, Antoine Leroux, and countless others played major roles in discovering the best trails along the Gila River and points north. Mountain men brought along Indian guides and often chose Indian women as their partners. Later, mountain men served as guides for prospectors and military expeditions, sharing their knowledge of trails with them.

One of these scouts was the second of his family to contribute his skills to mapping the West. Born in 1805 to a French trapper and Indian mother, Jean Baptiste Charbonneau served with Paulino Weaver as a scout for the Mormon Battalion in 1846. His mother, Sacagawea, led Lewis and Clark across the nation with her papoose, baby Jean (nicknamed "Pomp"), on her back. Charbonneau was educated in the East, spoke several languages, and lived in the castle of a German prince for several years before returning to the United States to travel the wilderness as a mountain man.

ARIZONA JOINS THE UNITED STATES

Fueled by a belief in Manifest Destiny, the concept that God intended for Americans to control all the territory from the Atlantic to the Pacific Oceans, politicians and

Saguaro Cactus (c. 1925), by Maynard Dixon. Courtesy of Mark Sublette, Medicine Man Gallery, Tucson, Arizona.

soldiers acted on a series of events—Texas independence, the Mexican-American War, and the Gadsden Purchase—that added more land area to the United States than any other chain of event since the Louisiana Purchase. From 1846 to 1854, the nation doubled in size, and Arizona was now part of it.

The Texas Revolution

Similar to Arizona, Spain's northeastern frontier in Texas was sparsely populated, mostly because of violent Comanche and Apache natives. In order to strengthen its hold on the territory, the Spanish government offered American colonists free land if they were Catholic, hard-working, and willing to become Spanish citizens. Moses Austin and his son Stephen received one of the first and largest contracts to set up a colony. When Mexico won its independence a year later, it continued to grant land to Americans under the same terms.

Trouble developed over political upheaval in Mexican government, stricter federal laws, and land grant disputes between Anglos and Mexicans. After several years of skirmishes, total war broke out in October 1832. After several battles, including Anglo-Texan disasters at the Alamo and Goliad, General Antonio López de Santa Anna was defeated at the Battle of San Jacinto on April 21, 1836. The Republic of Texas was created in 1836.

The Mexican-American War

Mexico refused to acknowledge the new Republic of Texas in 1836, but it was prevented from taking military action against them because the United States, Great Britain, and France gave the new nation diplomatic recognition.

For the next nine years, Texans and American Southerners pushed to get the new Lone Star Republic annexed to the United States. Northerners were opposed to adding another slave state to the Union, and they believed annexation could lead to war.

The Mexican-American War added more than a million square miles to the United States.

When Virginian John Tyler became U.S. president in 1841, he and Southern congressmen encouraged the Texans to create a treaty requesting annexation, which was rejected by the U.S. Senate. The project was tabled and became the major topic of debate in the 1844 presidential election.

Democrat James K. Polk won the presidency on a pro-annexation platform, but Tyler acted quickly in his last days in office and initiated annexation proceedings in Congress before Polk took office. Texas officially became a state on December 29, 1845.

When President Polk took office in March 1845, he sent General Zachary Taylor to the banks of the Rio Grande near present-day Brownsville, Texas, in June of the same year. Since its independence, Texas claimed the Rio Grande as its southern border, while Mexico claimed the Nueces River, farther to the north and east. As the situation worsened, both sides sent troops to the area. After several months of facing each other across the river, Mexican troops attacked U.S. Captain Seth Thornton's cavalry patrol on April 24, 1846. President Polk asked Congress for a declaration of war, which was issued on May 13.

While Generals Zachary Taylor, John Wool, and Winfield Scott led American troops—including recent West Point graduates Robert E. Lee and Jefferson Davis—into successful but horrendously bloody battles in Mexico, General Stephen Watts Kearny (pronounced KAHR-nee) was ordered to lead an "Army of the West" to capture New Mexico for the United States, an area which still included Arizona.

Kearny left Fort Leavenworth, Kansas, in late spring with 1,700 regulars and volunteers. They reached Santa Fe by June 1846, where Governor Miguel Armijo surrendered without a shot being fired. General Kearny sent the majority of his troops south to join the fighting in Mexico and to lead a smaller cadre west to California.

On September 26, General Kearny and 150 dragoons started their march to the Pacific. Ten days later, the army met Kit Carson coming from California with dispatches for Washington. Carson told Kearny that Commodore Stockton and Captain Frémont had captured California, and that no news of the invasion of New Mexico had yet reached California. General Kearny ordered Carson to turn around and guide his army along the Gila River to California.

The Army of the West followed the Rio Grande south from Santa Fe to the copper mines at present-day Silver City, then headed directly west over mountainous territory by following the river. The supply train consisted of pack mules and mountain howitzer cannon, which had to be lowered and raised through canyons by rope. From the copper mines, General Kearny wrote to Colonel Philip St. George Cooke and ordered his Mormon Battalion to blaze a wagon road across Arizona to California.

The Mormon Battalion

At the same time, another group began exploring Arizona for completely different motives. Since the sixteenth century, Europeans established themselves in America through both military and religious approaches. Now new arrivals represented the United States belief in freedom of religion. After escaping violent religious persecution in Ohio, Missouri, and Illinois, the followers of The Church of Jesus Christ of Latter-day Saints (the Mormons) sought freedom in the western wilderness.

After Congress declared war on Mexico, President James K. Polk sent Captain James Allen to Council Bluffs, Iowa, to enlist 500 Mormons to help secure California for the Union. They left Fort Leavenworth, Kansas, in late August, following the Santa Fe Trail. Many suffered from malaria, dysentery, starvation, and exposure. At three different times, detachments totaling more than 150 ailing or older men, women, and children were sent to winter in Pueblo, Colorado.

Colonel Cooke took command of the Mormon Battalion at Santa Fe, New Mexico, on October 9, 1846. The

6-foot 4-inch tough-as-nails career officer was dismayed at the sight of his new army. He said that the mules were feeble, clothing inadequate, and the company "was embarrassed by too many women."

The army followed the Rio Grande River toward Mexico, turning west just south of present-day Las Cruces. Cooke took the Battalion through a steep mountain pass, where soldiers had to lower the wagons down the cliffs with ropes. Men hacked or trampled down obstacles to make a road wide enough for the wagons.

When they reached the former presidio of San Bernardino near present-day Douglas, Arizona, on December 3, it was the first building they had seen in 31 days. Raiding Apaches had driven out the Mexican ranchers in the early 1830s, but they left thousands of heads of cattle behind. By this time, the Indians had killed off most of the cows and calves, which left hundreds of wild long-horn bulls roaming the countryside. The Mormon soldiers killed several while stopping over a few days at San Bernardino and dried the beef for their journey.

For the next few days, the road was stony and tough going. Much of it was uphill through mesquite thickets, and they plodded through rain, sleet, and snow while thorns tore at their skin. Most of the Mormons kept diaries, which, in addition to military reports and officers' journals, give a detailed account of the trip.

As a result, we know that on December 11, the battalion marched alongside the San Pedro River about seven miles northwest of present-day Tombstone. The grass was tall because of the nearby river, and before they knew it, the troops had surprised a group of wild bulls. The bulls panicked, and instead of running away as they had been doing for the past week, they charged the group. One bull gored a mule in the stomach, spewing blood everywhere.

Another trampled a soldier while another man received a deep horn cut in his thigh. According to the diaries, Colonel Cooke was almost struck head on by a large black bull, but a Mormon soldier shot the bull square in the head at close range, and the animal slid to within a few feet of the colonel. Three or four men were badly wounded, but no humans were killed during the Battle of the Bulls, the only skirmish of the Mexican-American War to take place in Arizona.

The Mormon Battalion continued its march on through Tucson and reached San Diego on January 29, 1847. Colonel Cooke commended them for their courage and determination for a trek that lasted more than seven months and 2,000 miles. One of the longest military marches in history, the Mormon Battalion opened the way for thousands of forty-niners heading for the California gold rush. Parts of the road they blazed were used by the Butterfield Overland Stage and the Southern Pacific Railroad. Modern highways still follow the Mormon road in some places.

Pima Indians and the Oasis at a Cultural Crossroads

From Father Kino's first encounter with the Pimas in the 1690s, explorers, trappers, and soldiers benefited from the Pima Indians' plentiful crops and hospitality. These Gileños (people of the Gila River) preferred farming to fighting (with the exception of the brief Pima Revolt), and their successes against Apaches guaranteed safe havens anywhere within two days ride of the Pima villages.

For the first 170 years, only handfuls of Europeans reached the villages. However, on November 11, 1846, General Stephen Kearny's 120-man "Army of the West" reached the Gila River villages en route to California. Hearing that Kearny wanted to trade for provisions, the Pimas rushed to meet them, briskly walking the nine miles from the villages to the approaching troops in three hours, arriving out of breath, loaded down with corn, beans, honey, and watermelons. Although they traded some, this orderly expedition required little assistance.

The situation was much different when Colonel Cooke's 340-man Mormon Battalion arrived at the villages a month later in desperate need. Ill-equipped and exhausted, they suffered during the grueling 90-mile stretch of desert between Tucson and the villages. Sergeant Henry Bigler reported that their canteens were empty and the weather as hot as June. Soldiers dropped by the wayside, begging for water. The battalion marched with very little rest, traveling at night to avoid the heat. Bedraggled, the next scene the Mormon Battalion encountered must have seemed like a mirage. Miles before they reached the villages, Pima and Maricopa women and children came out to meet them. A soldier wrote in his diary, "These Indians appear glad to see us, many of them running and taking us by the hand."

Arizona and the Rush for Gold

Carpenter James Marshall's gold flake discovery at Sutter's Fort on January 24, 1848, gripped the imagination of almost everyone on earth. A decade later, the word "California" was being spoken with many accents all over the world. Before the gold rush, the gold stock of the world was about 1.5 billion dollars. But in one decade, with the production

THE CAPTURE OF THE OATMAN GIRLS

Many gold seekers came to Arizona ignorant and unprepared, and met their fate as a result. In 1851, Royce Oatman and his family became the most famous of these immigrant tragedies. In late February near Gila Bend, the Oatman family struggled to push their wagon up a steep riverbank. Around sunset, about a dozen Yavapai Indians attacked the family, clubbing Royce, his wife Mary Ann, and four of his seven children to death. They hit 14-year-old Lorenzo Oatman on the head and threw him over a cliff.

The Yavapai dragged Olive Oatman, age 13, and her sister Mary Ann, age 8, back to their village. The girls suffered cold, starvation, and slave labor for a year, and then were purchased by the Mohave Indians and taken to the banks of the Colorado near present-day Needles, California.

The Mohaves were much nicer to the girls and gave them their own seeds and a piece of land so they could grow their own food. The Mohaves were famous for their elaborate tattoos and marked the girls' chins with rows of dots and triangles, an action that would make Olive famous but embarrassed the rest of her life. Already ailing from her ordeal with the Yavapai, Mary Ann Oatman died of starvation, perhaps two years after they came to live with the Mohave.

Meanwhile, young Lorenzo, who was left for dead, managed to crawl away and was rescued by Pima Indians. Eventually Lorenzo got a job in California, where he tried for five years to get someone to help rescue his sisters.

By this time, rumors had spread that the girls were at the Mohave villages. Finally, in February of 1856, the U.S. Army authorized a Yuma Indian named

Olive Oatman and her sister Mary Ann were captured by Indians in 1851.

Francisco to ransom Olive Oatman for a white horse.

Brother and sister reunited at Fort Yuma and eventually moved to Oregon to stay with family. There they met a missionary named Royal Stratton, who interviewed them and wrote a book, *The Captivity of the Oatman Girls*. Interested in raising funds to convert the Indians, Stratton had a much harsher view of Olive's captives than the story she told him. Eventually, the book sold more than 27,000 copies. Stratton took Lorenzo and Olive on the lecture circuit to sell the books, and Olive became one of the first national superstars. By the 1870s, America was full of little girls who had been named for her.

After several years on the circuit, Olive married a businessman named John Fairchild and settled into a big house in Sherman, Texas. Although plagued with migraine headaches and other nervous conditions, Olive became involved with many church activities and charities. She lived a long life, always insisting that the Mohave Indians were kind to her and her sister.

from California and similar strikes in Australia, the world's gold supply almost doubled.

Word of great riches always travels fast, and by August, the *New York Herald* said the strike was having a profound effect on hundreds of people. In his annual message to Congress in December, President James K. Polk confirmed the magnitude of the gold discoveries. Reporters said that "yellow fever" had struck the East, and young men of all classes stampeded to seek their fortune.

In addition to providing capital for railroads and giving birth to joint stock enterprises that paved the way for big business, the gold rush planted the idea in everyone's consciousness that mining meant wealth. From then on, mining was seen as a way to change one's social and economic status drastically overnight, just like hitting the lottery is today.

Once individual opportunities ceased to "pan out," Arizona received the backwash of the California rush. Still struck with gold fever in the 1850s, backers from Ohio and New York reopened the Spanish mines at Tubac, Arivaca, and Patagonia. Miners found gold along the Colorado River and then in the Prescott area. As a result of the American preoccupation with mining, it became the principal part of Arizona's economy for more than a century.

Mr. Bartlett's Survey

The vast quantities of land acquired from Mexico, followed almost immediately by the rush for gold in California, prompted a series of military expeditions across Arizona, some to set the new boundary lines and others to survey for the best possible wagon roads and railroad routes across the state. Like Lieutenant William H. Emory with the Army of the West, most expeditions included a geologist, a naturalist, a botanist, and an artist, or a combination thereof in the same man.

A most unlikely candidate to lead an expedition into the western wilderness, John Russell Bartlett was appointed United States Boundary Commissioner in 1850, charged with surveying the U.S.-Mexican border. He was born in Rhode Island but acquired political connections as a book dealer in New York City. He seemed more interested in writing his a book about his adventures and spent much of his two-year trip touring Mexico.

The Boundary Commission was canceled because of gross errors on the Disturnell Map of 1847, which located the eastern end of the border more than 100 miles west and 30 miles north of El Paso, the town stipulated in the Treaty of Guadalupe Hidalgo. Bartlett and Mexico's minister General Pedro García Conde agreed on a compromise, but the American surveyors refused to sign it because the United States would have lost hundreds of square miles of land. The border issue was resolved several years later with the Gadsden Purchase Treaty.

The Railroad Surveys

Since the Santa Fe Trail had been taking pioneers at least halfway across the continent for more than 20 years, it seemed reasonable that the route directly west of that venerable New Mexico town would be the best place to start.

In 1851, Captain Lorenzo Sitgreaves of the U.S. Army Topographical Engineers and 50 men began the first major road survey from Zuni, New Mexico, to the Colorado River, roughly following the 35th parallel. He reached the river 160 miles above Fort Yuma and followed the east bank south to the fort.

The years following the California gold rush brought increasing attention from mining corporations, railroad investors, and potential pioneers who prompted Congress, led by Senator Thomas Hart Benton of Missouri, to take action. In 1853, Congress appropriated $150,000 for six railroad surveys across the continent.

Lieutenant Amiel Weeks Whipple led the first expedition, assisted by topographical engineer Lieutenant Joseph Christmas Ives, in 1853–54. Escorted by a

Arizona's first decade as a U.S. territory was mostly mining shacks and rough wagon roads.

company of Seventh Infantry soldiers and supplied with more accurate survey instruments, they roughly followed the Sitgreaves route but went on to California instead of down the Colorado River.

Lieutenant Ives and the Steamboat

Although Whipple and Sitgreaves had no trouble from the Mohave Indians, later conflicts made it necessary to create an outpost on the upper Colorado's northern crossing. The difficulty in transporting supplies across the desert prompted the U.S. government to send an expedition to research the possibility of supplying troops by boat, up the river from Fort Yuma.

Lieutenant Joseph Christmas Ives of the U.S. Corps of Topographical Engineers was assigned to the task, and a handful of soldiers and scientists arrived at Fort Yuma in January 1858. There they assembled the USS *Explorer,* a small paddle-wheeled steamboat shipped up the Gulf of California in pieces. The little iron-hulled

steamer was only 54 feet long and could float in 18 inches of water. Theirs was not the first steamboat in Arizona. The *Uncle Sam* was launched in 1852, and the *General Jessup* in 1854. Ironically, the first mechanized vehicles in Arizona traveled by water.

However, the *Explorer* went farther north than the others. It steamed up the river to the rapids at Black Canyon, near present-day Las Vegas, Nevada, and could go no farther. From there, the men proceeded overland, becoming the first Anglos to enter the floor of the Grand Canyon.

The expedition was successful, and the steamboat route was put into operation at once. According to the military reports, Indians along the river did not know what to make of the steamboat at first. They are quoted as saying, "The devil is coming, blowing fire and smoke out of his nose and kicking water back with his feet." As was the case since first European encounters, they were quick to adapt and soon developed a lucrative business supplying wood for the steamers.

The Latter-day Saints Look for Eden

At the same time the steamboat navigated Arizona's northwest coast, the Latter-day Saints, known as Mormons, began to explore northern Arizona. In the autumn of 1857, Mormon leader Brigham Young directed missionary Jacob Hamblin to lead an expedition into southern Utah and northwestern Arizona to convert the Paiutes and Hopis. Hamblin forded the Colorado River where the Spanish friars Domínguez and Escalante crossed it in 1777 (known as The Crossing of the Fathers) and discovered another crossing point that would later be known as Lee's Ferry.

The Beale Expedition and Its Experiment with Camels

Traveling up the Colorado in 1857, the *Explorer* became party to one of the strangest juxtapositions in Arizona history. There on the banks of the Colorado River in the middle of the desert, they encountered a herd of Arabian camels led by a Greco-Syrian camel driver nicknamed "Hi Jolly" by American soldiers.

As early as the 1830s, Lieutenant George Crosman and Major Henry C. Wayne, noticed the camels' ability to carry huge loads in the desert with very little water or food. They shared the concept with influential colleagues, including Jefferson Davis, the U.S. senator from Mississippi. When Davis became Secretary of War under newly elected President Franklin Pierce in 1853, he used his influence to obtain Congressional approval on March 3, 1855, for a $30,000 appropriation to purchase camels and hire drivers to test the practicality of using camels as transport in the West.

In June of 1857, part of this "Camel Expedition" was assigned to Lieutenant Edward Fitzgerald Beale to use in his wagon road survey west from Fort Defiance, Arizona, across the 35th parallel to the Colorado River. The party consisted of 25 dromedaries (one-humped camels),

44 soldiers, two camel drivers, and numerous horses and mules. The camels did not meet Beale's expectations at first, but after a few days, they hardened to the duty, often leading the way over terrain where mules and horses balked.

They eventually proved their worth when the surveyors got lost and water grew scarce. The camels persevered and found a river 20 miles from camp. They led the expedition to it, and then looked on indifferently as men, mules, and horses desperately gulped the water. The camels won over the skeptics among the party and pushed on to the Colorado River. The drive continued to Fort Tejon, California, and then Fort Drum near Los Angeles, where the camels transported army supplies and dispatches across the desert.

In spite of the successful trip, the camel experiment was a failure. Army regulars did not like the smell, spitting, gait, temper, and high maintenance of the camels when not in use. But soldiers follow orders, so it was not their reactions that caused the rejection. Charismatic Secretary of War Jefferson Davis was replaced by the less powerful John B. Floyd when President James Buchanan took office in 1857.

But Floyd also believed strongly in the camels and urged Congress to appropriate funds for the purchase of 1,000 more. Once again, personalities and politics affected the tide of history. Floyd's commander in the West, Major General David E. Twiggs, "was outraged when he discovered a herd of camels under his command" and harangued Floyd with a barrage of complaint letters until Floyd gave in and abandoned the experiment. The Quartermaster Department funded camels through 1860, which were then auctioned off. Camel driver Hi Jolly purchased several and used them for prospecting along the Colorado River for several decades after the Army proclaimed them unfit for duty in Arizona.

A diorama tells the story of Lieutenant Edward Beale's Camel Expedition of 1857.

James Gadsden's Purchase

Once the road surveys were finished, officials in Washington realized that the mountain men, the Mormon Battalion, and thousands of forty-niners had already found the best route across Arizona to California; it was known as the Gila Trail, and it is similar to Interstate 10 from Las Cruces, New Mexico, to Casa Grande, Arizona, and then west on Interstate 8 to Yuma.

The Gadsden Purchase Treaty, known in Mexico as the Tratado de Mesilla, was enacted June 30, 1854. It forever reshaped the political, cultural, and economic landscape of Mexico and the United States.

In 1848, the Treaty of Guadalupe Hidalgo ceded lands north of the Gila River to the United States. Then on June 30, 1854, the United States annexed "southern Arizona" with the stroke of a pen. For some, the Gadsden Purchase represented a celebration of diverse cultures coexisting on good terms with dreams of a prosperous future; for others, it impacted their lives and homelands drastically.

President Franklin Pierce sent James Gadsden to Mexico to negotiate a new treaty between the United States and Mexico in the summer of 1853 because surveys indicated that the land south of the Gila River was the best route for a transcontinental railroad. The purchase would also settle boundary disputes in the Mesilla Valley (near present day Las Cruces, New Mexico) encountered through the Bartlett-Conde negations caused by the inaccurate Disturnell Map.

President Antonio López de Santa Anna signed the treaty because he needed money to protect his government from impending revolution, but he agreed to sell only enough land for the United States to build the transcontinental railroad. Mexican officials denied the sale of any seaport lands on the Gulf of California. Negotiators signed the Tratado de Mesilla on December 30, 1853.

However, abolitionists disliked the threat of adding more slave states to the Union, and Senators split into three overlapping factions: 1) those favorable to a southern transcontinental railroad route, 2) expansionists who wanted to pay less and get more land, including a harbor on the gulf, and 3) abolitionists who were against additional slave territories.

During the debates, Senator Thomas Jefferson Rusk of Texas suggested a compromise on what became the final border. The Senate finally approved the treaty and paid Mexico $10 million for the strip of land south of the Gila River. Mexican diplomats were outraged with the new treaty but recognized that they were powerless to oppose their stronger neighbor to the north.

ARIZONA STRIKES IT RICH

The self-styled "Father of Arizona," Charles Debrille Poston, can best be described as "bigger than life"—a flamboyant, charismatic adventurer and storyteller with a knack for embellishment. A native of Kentucky, Poston went west to seek his fortune during the California gold rush. He obtained a post as chief clerk in the San Francisco surveyor's office in 1851. When the political tide turned in 1853, Poston was out of a job. Collaborating with a number of displaced French noblemen who frequented the gambling halls of San Francisco, Poston became part of a mining syndicate to explore the mineral wealth of southern Arizona. The syndicate also recruited German mining engineer Herman Ehrenberg for the expedition.

After surviving a shipwreck off the coast of Mexico near Guaymas, the prospectors traveled to the fabled site of Arizona but found nothing there. They arrived at Fort Yuma in July 1854, just as the Gadsden Purchase was being signed into law. Poston and Ehrenberg had no trouble convincing Major Samuel Heintzelman of the value of their ore samples, and they began arrangements to raise capital in the East for a full-scale mining venture.

Poston embarked on a fund-raising tour of New York, Philadelphia, and points east. In 1856, the men formed the Sonora Exploring and Mining Company in Cincinnati, Ohio.

Heintzelman and Poston were concerned with two problems: attracting more investors and protecting their operations and employees. Those required protection from the Apaches, and a separate Arizona territorial government could bring that to pass.

They formed the Sonora Mining and Exploration Company in 1856 with the backing of the Wrightson brothers, railroad newspapermen from Cincinnati, and Samuel Colt of Hartford, Connecticut, whose guns "won the West."

They started with mines in the Santa Ritas that had been previously worked by the Spaniards and Mexicans, as evidenced by ruins of *arrastras* (grinding stones) and smelters. The mining company attracted former Mexican soldiers, who returned with their families to work the fields they had abandoned.

Colorado River Strikes

Meanwhile, 120 miles across the desert near Yuma, another mining boom began, but this time it was gold. In September 1858, Jacob Snively, former secretary of the Republic of Texas, found flakes and nuggets of placer gold (commonly pronounced "plasser," a Spanish term for "sandbanks") near the Gila River about 20 miles east of its junction with the Colorado River at Yuma.

A year later, there were more than a thousand prospectors and gamblers at the site, now the boomtown of Gila City. As the easy pickings no longer panned out and big mining companies began to take over the California gold fields, independent gold seekers began to look around for other get-rich-quick opportunities. At the same time, northern California vigilante groups drove outlaws to the lawless frontier to assume a new identity. "What Was Your Name in the States?" a song from *How the West Was Won*, says it best:

> What was your name in the States, my friend,
> Was it Murphy, MacDonald, or Gates?
> Did you hold up a bank as a juvenile prank,
> And pack up the money in crates, my friend,
> Oh, What was your name in the States?

Journalist J. Ross Browne wrote, "There is everything in Gila City but a church and a jail, which were accounted barbarisms by the mass of the population." But just as it sprang up overnight, once the easy gold was gone, the population dwindled. Although he was prone to gross exaggeration to entertain his readers, Browne said that by the time he and Charles Poston visited in 1864, "the promising Metropolis of Arizona consisted of three chimneys and a coyote."

In the winter of 1861, on the tail of the Gila City boom, Paulino Weaver, one of the mountain men who trapped furs in Arizona in the 1830s, discovered gold about 50 miles north of Yuma, When he took a goose quill full of gold flakes into town to have it assayed, word spread fast and a second rush began. A year later, 1,500 Anglo-Californians quickly outnumbered the Mexican families who were first on the scene, and the town of La Paz sprang up overnight. Philip Drachman and Big Mike Goldwater started their fortunes there as merchants by selling much-needed Levis, shovels, and pans. In the next two years, miners took millions in gold out of the area, and there was talk of making La Paz the capital of the territory. But the gold ran out, and the town sank back into the dust almost as quickly as it had risen.

A Big Bug and a Vulture Create a Mining State

Weaver continued to prospect farther north up the Bill Williams River west of what is now Prescott and found what he named Rich Hill in 1863. They said gold was so plentiful that they could pop nuggets out of the ground with a knife, and that one acre yielded nearly half a million dollars in gold! Weaver and former Civil War soldier Jack Swilling found $100,000 in nuggets at Antelope Hill nearby and said one was as big as a hickory nut.

In 1863, Henry Wickenburg found a ledge of rich gold ore in the same area and called it the Vulture Mine. Records indicated that $2.5 million in gold was taken out in the first six years it operated, not accounting for up to 40 percent theft by mine laborers.

Meanwhile, veteran mountain man Joseph Reddeford Walker organized a gold-seeker party. Union soldiers of the First California Volunteers got permission to join the search. The company struck gold along the Hassayampa River, Lynx Creek, and Big Bug Creek near present-day Prescott. An area covering quite a few square miles became known as the Weaver/Walker mining district, and Arizona became known as a territory rich in mining prospects.

From those strikes on, Arizona became a mining state. While Charles Poston, Samuel Heintzelman, Sylvester Mowry, and hundreds of petitioners had been trying to get Congress to split Arizona away from New Mexico since 1856, it took these major gold strikes to make it happen. However, instead of creating a new territory south of the Gila River, President Abraham Lincoln was advised to draw a north/south boundary in fear that Confederates and Mexican Americans would have too much influence over a combined southern territory. Accordingly, General James Carleton chose Fort Whipple as the first territorial capital and moved it to the mining town of Prescott a few months later.

When Arizona's territorial legislature first convened in 1864, almost half of its members were involved in mining. The state seal contains an image of a prospector as well as the state motto *Ditat Deus,* "God enriches," referring to one of the richest mineral areas in the nation.

MULTICULTURAL MARRIAGES

The settlement pattern in Spanish colonial North America differed in many ways from the rest of the continental United States. Like the rest of the United States, the Southwest was settled much like Kentucky, Ohio, and Tennessee by single men—hunters, trappers and traders—who paved the way for family settlements. In colonial New Spain, however, the pattern was closer to that of New England or Virginia settlements. In the northeast, religious pilgrims sought to practice and spread their beliefs as families, and whole neighborhoods moved in all at once. In the middle colonies, forts were built and groups emigrated from the mother country to establish an economic colony and political rights for England.

In New Mexico, Texas, California, and Arizona, the same two goals brought whole families to the frontier. Missionaries brought families to populate the area and to help convert the Indians to Catholicism, while land grants were offered to families willing to settle the fron-

Former Confederate soldier Jack Swilling founded the town of Phoenix. Courtesy of the Phoenix Public Library.

tier. Soldiers of the lower classes were not discouraged from intermarrying and raising families within the presidio walls.

After Mexico took over and could not pay to keep the Apache peace, Tucson's population, which had been growing steadily to 1,000, dwindled to around 400 by the time the Gadsden Purchase was signed.

When U.S. soldiers officially took possession of Tucson in 1856, the residents were on the edge of despair. According to their memoirs, most locals welcomed the Americans. In her memoirs, Carmen Lucero said:

I have often heard my mother say that the coming of the Americans when the U.S. took over this country was a godsend to Tucson, for the Indians had killed off many of the Mexicans and the poor were being ground down by the rich. The day the troops took possession there was lots of excitement. They raised the flag on the wall and the people welcomed them with a fiesta and they were all on good terms. We felt alive after the U.S. took possession and times were more profitable.

Typical of the American frontier tradition, the first non-Hispanics arrived without wives or relatives, and many married into the area's elite Hispanic families. The famous Kit Carson and pioneer merchant Charles Bent, the first Anglo governor of New Mexico, both married daughters of the wealthy Jaramillo family in Santa Fe.

Arizona differed from the rest, however, because of Apache conflicts. While California, Texas, and New Mexican families were intermarrying as early as the 1820s, the phenomenon did not happen in Tucson for several more decades. The gold rush had more to do with multicultural marriages in Arizona than any other factor. In the Southwest of the 1850s, Anglo men outnumbered Anglo women 12 to 1. When the rush finally played out, men began to look elsewhere for gold, drifting eastward back to Nevada, Arizona, and New Mexico. The majority of Americans who settled in Tucson were merchants who had made their bankroll selling supplies to the miners in the California gold fields and now invested it in stores, farms, livestock, and mining.

But the word "Anglo" doesn't really fit these bachelor prospectors. From California and all points of the globe came emigrant Frenchmen, Germans, Swiss, Irish, Serbian, Jews, and every combination imaginable. History calls them Anglos, or Americans, because they came from the United States to Arizona, but the accents, clothing, and customs gave the territory a cosmopolitan atmosphere.

The number of multicultural marriages in the Southwest, perhaps as many as 85 percent, indicates the open attitude Hispanics held toward other cultures. Unlike rigid New England society, Anglo males had a great deal of opportunity to interact with young ladies of all social strata through frequent fandangos and fiestas. "By invitation only" was rarely heard; "come one, come all" was the order of the day. In addition, the distance away from their dominant culture allowed for a breakdown of cultural taboos among Yankee men. Along the same line, cohabitation among the lower classes was not as unacceptable as it would be in New England and was therefore commonplace in Tucson and in other locations.

Another important aspect of Hispanic culture with respect to marriage was that the mothers, aunts, or grandmothers, in conjunction with the local priest, decided whom their daughters married. While the Yankee man did the courting, whether for romance

ABOVE: *Dangerous and expensive to maintain, freight wagon trains were the only means of supply and mineral export until the arrival of the railroad. Courtesy of the San Pedro Art and Historical Society.*

RIGHT: *Maricopa Wells was an important stage stop along the Gila Trail. Courtesy of the Arizona Military Museum.*

FACING: *Dueñas (chaperones) kept a close watch on the Americans at fandangos.*

Old Patio (September 1931), New Mexico, by Maynard Dixon. This is identical to many patios found in Tucson and Yuma. Courtesy of Mark Sublette, Medicine Man Gallery, Tucson, Arizona.

or social connections, his was not the final word. For all their machismo, memoirs indicate over and over again that the older women of the bride's family (grandmother, mothers, aunts, and even older sisters) made most of the decisions. They let the man feel he was in charge, but women made the final decisions.

One example of cultural blending is Welsh emigrant Samuel Hughes, who came to Tucson in 1858 after a successful hotel and restaurant career in the gold fields of northern California. Doctors told him to seek a warmer climate for his lung troubles, thus he became one of Tucson's first health seekers. Hughes invested in a butcher shop, a hardware store, farmland, ranching, and supplying the military. He claimed to have "a spoon in every soup."

In his diary, Hughes wrote about the exotic beauties he had seen going for water the morning he arrived, their faces mysteriously covered except for one eye, "cunning as foxes." That evening, the town threw a fandango for Hughes and his fellow prospectors, and he said the gathering seemed like one big family. Little did he know how close he came to the truth. What he sensed unknowingly was a web of intertwined kinship networks. Almost everyone was related to everyone else in Tucson at that time, by blood, by marriage, or as godparents.

In 1863, Hughes married Atanacia Santa Cruz, whose well-established family had a great deal of farmland along the Santa Cruz River. Her sister Petra was already married to Hiram Stevens, Hughes' partner.

In addition to Hughes and Stevens, the most cosmopolitan family in early Tucson was that of Federico Ronstadt. Of German-Mexican parentage, Ronstadt moved to Tucson in the 1880s to live with his mother's cousin, making use of the family network. He married Sara Levin, whose father, Alexander Levin, was a Jewish brewmeister and her mother, Xenonia Molina, came from a well-established Mexican family. Sara died young, and Federico then married his second cousin, Guadalupe Dalton. Guadalupe's grandfather, Henry Dalton, was half English and half Mexican and had married his Mexican wife, California, in the 1840s. Her sister Hortensia married Federico's brother, Jose Maria, thus cementing family ties while bringing together four distinct cultural legacies.

In the 1880s, the end of the Apache wars and coming of the railroad made it safer and easier for Anglo brides to settle in Arizona, but the tradition continues, and it is not uncommon to meet someone named Brown or Jacobs whose ancestors served at Tucson's Spanish presidio in 1776.

Apache Pass played an important role in the clash of cultures.

SOLDIERS IN FORCE

In the years following the Gadsden Purchase, a handful of farmers and ranchers began to move into the rich rolling grasslands around Patagonia and Sonoita Creek, providing beef and grains for the surrounding mines and the new Fort Buchanan, established in 1856 near the current international border between the San Pedro and Santa Cruz Rivers, not far from the ruins of the Spanish presidio at Terrenate.

The Bascom Affair

Apaches raided John Ward's ranch on January 27, 1861, taking off with two dozen head of cattle and Ward's stepson, Felix Telles. When word reached the fort, 25-year-old 2nd Lieutenant George N. Bascom received orders to lead a search party and use force to capture Cochise, who was believed to have been in charge of the capture. Bascom invited the Chiricahua Apache chief to meet him near the Butterfield Stage station at Apache Pass, about 20 miles southeast of present-day Willcox.

Cochise and Bascom met in a tent on February 4.

Rock foundations of the Butterfield Stage station at Apache Pass.

The invitation had been amiable, so Cochise brought his wife, two children, younger half-brother Coyuntaro, and two nephews along with him. According to some reports, John Ward acted as interpreter and vehemently demanded the return of his stepson.

Although soldiers had surrounded the tent, Cochise seized his knife, probably cut through the ties that held the canvas tent door closed, and escaped. Generations later, Apaches would retell this story as "Cut Tent."

The next day, Cochise and the Chiricahuas ambushed and set fire to a wagon train, tortured and killed several Mexicans, and captured three Americans.

Cochise then attacked the nearby stage station at Apache Pass on February 8 and captured stage driver James F. Wallace. Even though they outnumbered the soldiers two to one, the Apaches chose not to risk the loss of attacking armed men safely behind stone walls and fled for Mexico instead. Bascom feared their return and called for reinforcements from Fort Buchanan. Seventy dragoons arrived on February 14 under the command of Lieutenant Isaiah N. Moore. They scouted the area and found no Apaches, but they did find the bodies of Wallace and the three American hostages. In yet another spiral of the decades-old cycle of revenge, Moore and most of the officers and soldiers outvoted Bascom and ordered the hanging of Cochise's brother, two nephews, and three captured Coyoteros.

Cochise's wife and children were released. One of them, Naiche, would grow up to be the last chief of the Chiricahuas in Arizona. Another Apache whose name has become internationally famous assisted Cochise in his retaliation. He was known by his people, the Chokonen Apache, as Goyahkla, but the Mexicans named him Geronimo.

As usual, inexperience, misunderstandings, and mistrust exacerbated the conflict of cultures between Anglos and Apaches. But even experienced officers did not always understand the autonomy of Apache bands and tended to see them as a cohesive larger tribe. While earlier writers may claim Bascom's and Moore's actions caused Cochise to call for all-out war with Americans, raids and deaths did increase over the next 10 years, and violence between several bands of Apaches and Europeans had been going on for more than a century. Other events contributed to the situation as well.

In April 1861, the same month Fort Sumter was attacked and the Civil War began, the Butterfield Stage terminated its service through Arizona. Settlers in southern Arizona began to move to Tubac or Tucson for safety against increased Apache raids, but most of them left Arizona completely when the U.S. Army abandoned and burned all of its forts the following July and moved the troops east.

The Battle of Picacho

On April 15, 1862, Union and Confederate troops exchanged gunfire at Picacho Peak, a geographic landmark on Interstate 10, 40 miles north of Tucson. Known as the Battle of Picacho, it was hardly more than a skirmish. It is significant, however, because it has been called the farthest western battle of the Civil War. And it is, if you don't count some shots fired at Stanwix Station (40 miles west of Gila Bend) a few weeks earlier.

There were only 24 men involved at Picacho, 14 Union troops from the California Column led by Lieutenant James Barrett, and 10 Rebel troops led by Sergeant Henry Holmes. Captain Sherod Hunter's Confederate Dragoons (about 120 men) had captured Tucson in late February, moved north to the Gila River, and were heading west to California.

By April, Captain Hunter knew that Union troops were heading up the Gila River east from California, so he sent a scouting party to the base of Picacho. In return, Union Captain William Calloway sent two groups of soldiers, one led by Lieutenant Barrett, to surround the pass at Picacho. Calloway hoped to capture some Confederates without a fight to learn more about their forces in Tucson.

However, the impulsive Lieutenant Barrett charged ahead without waiting for the other troops to get into place. Military reports said that Barrett and his men could have surprised the Confederates easily, but instead Barrett led his men into thick brush on horseback, single file, even though his scout had warned him twice to dismount. The Confederates shot first and four Yankees fell from their saddles. A fierce battle raged for about an hour and a half, and then the Confederates scattered and headed for Tucson.

Barrett was shot in the neck with the first round of gunfire and quickly bled to death. Two other Union soldiers died as a result of the battle and three were injured. Three Rebels were captured, two were wounded, but none were killed. The Confederates left Tucson soon after the Battle at Picacho, and the California Column arrived, 1,800 strong, in May 1862.

The battle was not all that important, but Civil War policies, politics, and economics had their impact on Arizona history. It began when Federal troops abandoned and burned all military forts in Arizona. The troops were needed in the East, and they did not want to leave anything behind to benefit the Confederates.

With no soldiers in the area, Indians and bandits ran rampant. More than 60 percent of the settlers left Arizona for safer areas, and the stage line stopped running. When Captain Hunter demanded that all Tucson men take a loyalty oath to the Confederacy, several left town instead. Several men had their fortunes confiscated and were not prominent in Tucson after the war. The same thing happened in reverse when the Union troops arrived several months later. Confederate sympathizers had their assets seized and new entrepreneurs came to power.

Civil War politics also decided which way the new territory of Arizona would be split off from New Mexico Territory. The majority of the petitions for separate territory status recommended dividing the two territories with a north/south division, combining the southern thirds of what are now the states of New Mexico and Arizona to form "Arizona Territory." However, concern over the number of Confederate sympathizers in the southern parts of both places led President Lincoln to create the present east/west split on February 23, 1863, and the first territorial capitol was founded near Prescott for fear of Confederates in Tucson. So the impact of the Civil War was felt deeply in Arizona, even though the Battle of Picacho may have only been meaningful to those who fought there.

While we have seen the effects of the Civil War at Picacho Peak and on the propertied men of Tucson, two other actions engaged the blue and the gray, but not against each other. On May 5, 1862, less than two weeks before Sherod Hunter's dragoons withdrew from Arizona entirely, three Confederate soldiers and a Mexican boy named Richardo were ambushed by Apaches near the Dragoon Springs stage station. Not far from Cochise's stronghold, it could have been part of his vengeance, but should not be considered a Civil War action. As historian L. Boyd Finch put it in *Confederate Pathway to the Pacific*, the Apaches did not care whether the Americans wore "blue, gray, plaid, or buckskin." Even today though, visitors are reminded of the short-lived Confederate occupation, not so trivial to the handful of Union and Confederate soldiers who died that spring. Just a few yards from the stone ruins of the stage station, four small rebel flags fly over the rock-piled graves, replaced every year by the local Tucson Sons of the Confederacy.

The Battle of Apache Pass

The ambush at Dragoon Springs probably did not last long, but the Battle of Apache Pass, less than a month later, was the only pitched battle fought against the Apaches in Arizona.

On July 16, a company of infantry led by Captain Thomas Roberts, a detachment of cavalry, and two mountain howitzers, met several hundred Apaches, probably the largest number since the May Day attack on Tucson in 1782. The Union Army volunteers of the California Column entered the draw near the Butterfield Stage station that had been the scene of the Bascom Affair a year earlier. After a 40-mile march, they almost reached fresh water at Apache Springs when, according to Roberts, "we found the Indians posted high above us, where they kept a rattling fire upon us."

The soldiers retreated to the protection of the stage station, where they were pinned down by fire from more than 200 combined Chiricahua led by Cochise and a group of Mimbreño Apaches led by Mangas Coloradas. The soldiers were accompanied by a "jackass battery" of two 12-pounder howitzer cannons. This was one of the first uses of cannon against the Apache, who quickly recovered from their initial shock and retreated to rock breastworks 300 to 400 feet above the springs. After a four-hour battle, the Union soldiers finally stormed the ridge, and at the same time it appears that someone realized that if they broke off or buried the tailpieces of the cannon, they could attain the angle needed not only to reach the Apaches' rock fortresses, but by aiming above them, they could create shrapnel by splintering the hard rocks behind their positions. Three American soldiers were killed, and several were severely wounded. Estimates of Apache casualties ranged from three to 60, but finally settled around 10.

Captain John Cremony claimed that he learned from a prominent Apache who was present that "we would have done well enough if you had not fired wagons at us." According to David Roberts in *Once They Moved Like the Wind,* almost a century later the son of one of the chiefs said, "After they turned the cannon loose on us at Apache Pass, my people were certain that they were doomed."

The First Arizona Volunteers

While cannons roared in southwestern Arizona, gold was being discovered in the Weaver and Walker diggings near Prescott. Miners flocking to the area found themselves much closer to Apache homelands than was prudent. By the spring of 1863, the Apaches had attacked and murdered several small parties of prospectors and miners.

At the request of irate Prescott citizens, John N.

Sergeant Antonio Azul, Pima leader in the First Arizona Volunteers. Courtesy of the Phoenix Public Library.

Goodwin, Arizona's first territorial governor, received federal permission to create a volunteer militia, the First Arizona Volunteers. Regular army officers mustered in 94 Maricopa recruits, designated as Company B, Arizona Volunteer Infantry. By May 16, 1866, there were 103 men in the company. At the Pima villages, Chief Antonio Azul was made a sergeant, and 89 Pimas were recruited to fill out Company C. Five more Pimas were added later at Sacaton.

The Indian soldiers received a blue army tunic, trimmed in red for the Maricopas and blue for the Pimas, one pair of blue pants, and one yard of flannel for a headdress. The volunteer companies left Maricopa Wells with Colonel Clarence E. Bennett's California Volunteers on September 4, 1865, to establish a fort seven miles north of the confluence of the Verde and Salt Rivers. Both companies helped construct Fort McDowell to protect farms along the rivers from Apaches. To the east, Tonto and Pinal Apaches inhabited Tonto Basin, bordered by the Mogollón Rim to the north, the Mazatzal Mountains to the east, and the Sierra Ancha Mountains to the west.

After many successful forays, on March 27, Captain John D. Walker led the largest expedition of Arizona Volunteers on record; an estimated 260 Tohono O'odham and Pima Indian allies as well as 40 Maricopas left the Pima villages. In a fight four days later, 25 Apaches were killed and 16 taken prisoner. Three Pimas were wounded, one of whom eventually died. First Arizona Volunteer actions contributed to the surrender of several Apache groups.

At Fort McDowell on September 11, 1866, because of the legalities of retaining them, Maricopa Company B was discharged from service. The records indicated that Maricopas McGill (probably Miguel), Yose, Goshe Zep, and Duke were killed in battle. The same day, Pima Company C was mustered out by Captain John D. Walker, 1st Lieutenant William Hancock, and now 2nd Lieutenant Antonio Azul. Hownik Mawkum, Juan Lewis, and Au Papat were Pimas listed as killed in battle. All the men were allotted $50 pay and allowed to keep their firearms and equipment. Many volunteers who believed they would get no pay found that all at once they had more money than they had ever had at any time in their lives. In the fall of 1866, the Third Arizona Territorial Legislature passed a memorial commemorating the outstanding service of the First Arizona Volunteers.

The Navajo Long Walk

Although they are most remembered today, the Apaches were not the only culture that clashed with the Europeans. Yumas, Yavapai, Mohave, Pimas, Hualapai, and others had their struggles, but most were subdued before mining brought boomtowns and newspapers to tell the story.

The largest tragedy took place in northeastern Arizona in 1864 and has come to be known as the Navajo "Long Walk." Because treaties had been made with some groups but not adhered to by others, the U.S. Army sent Kit Carson into Arizona to round up 8,000 Navajo and march them in the dead of winter to the Bosque Redondo, a reservation 450 miles away in eastern New Mexico.

Many died along the way of cold and starvation, and as many as 2,000 more died of disease and more starvation in the next four years.

In the winter of 1864–65, the Navajos at the Bosque Redondo were reduced to terrible straits through the destruction of their crops by cutworms. To add to their distress, these people, who make the most serviceable blankets in the world and usually have plenty of them, were destitute of both blankets and clothing by the ravages of their enemies. They had to live in holes to shelter themselves from relentless dust storms.

In 1867, the crops failed from bad management and hail storms; as reported, the Comanches attacked and robbed the Navajos several times, and many of their horses died from eating poisonous weeds.

Finally, General William T. Sherman and Colonel Samuel F. Tappan, Peace Commissioners, reached New Mexico in May 1868. They evaluated the situation and then permitted the Navajo to return to their homeland in Arizona.

In the 1840s and '50s, Arizona became part of the United States. Explorers and surveyors mapped the future state, while the California gold rush brought hundreds of prospectors to the state, blending many cultures and creating Anglos north of the Gila River. The Civil War had a brief impact, but expanding encroachment accentuated the clash of cultures. Once the world learned of Arizona's vast mineral wealth, frontier populations and their Wild West institutions inevitably followed.

HOW THE GRAND CANYON BECAME GRAND

A little more than 10 years after Ives proclaimed that no one would ever again visit the Grand Canyon, a one-armed Civil War veteran and geology professor proved him wrong. In 1869, Major John Wesley Powell, using mostly private funds, became one of the first men on record to brave the wild rapids of the Colorado River through the Grand Canyon. Powell and nine other men started on the Green River in Colorado and followed it until it merged with the Grand River (the upper part of what is now known as the Colorado), and rowed, towed, and carried four sturdy boats through the depths of the Grand Canyon. After a second trip in 1873, Powell combined his notes into a series of magazine articles for *Scribner's Monthly*. Illustrated with Thomas Moran's engravings drawn from Jack Hillers' photographs, the articles, published later in book form, brought national attention to the canyon's majestic beauty.

THE CAÑONS OF THE COLORADO. 399

NOONDAY REST IN MARBLE CAÑON.

Major John Wesley Powell led the first Colorado River expedition through the Grand Canyon, 1869.

But it would be at least another decade before tourists felt save enough to arrive—the Wild West decade of Geronimo, Tombstone, and Wyatt Earp.

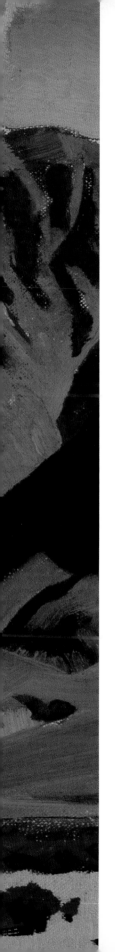

CHAPTER FIVE

★ CONFLICTS OF CULTURE AND LEGENDS OF THE WILD WEST

Now the very rocks had gotten soft. They couldn't put their foot anywhere without leaving an impression by which we could follow, that they could get no sleep at nights, for should a coyote or fox start a rock rolling during the night they would get up and dig out, thinking the soldiers were catching up with them.

—Delshay, Apache leader, 1873

THE APACHE DECADE

Although there were more than 20 American Indian tribes in Arizona, the Apaches affected the course of its history more than all the others combined, from their first encounters with seventeenth-century Spanish soldiers to Geronimo's final surrender in 1886. Their lifestyles, traditions, and skills in warfare delayed American settlement for several decades compared to the rest of the Southwest, while at the same time bringing more than a quarter of the U.S. Army to the territory.

In the 1850s, however, things were different. When several boundary survey crews followed the Gila River across southeastern Arizona, Apaches supplied them with deer and other game. According to his autobiography, Geronimo met with the boundary surveyors in 1851, and expressed his hope that the Apaches would be able to get along better with the Americans than they had with the Mexicans.

Up to that point, raiding was a less important factor of the Apachean culture. Raiding increased when the Spaniards and then Mexicans brought metal tools and livestock to the area, but when they abandoned Arizona in the 1830s primarily because of the raids, it waned again. Apaches then increased their raids into Mexico, whose European population grew faster than Arizona's because they were closer to the mines in Sonora and Chihuahua.

The Apaches' seminomadic way of life involved more hunting and gathering than farming. When large numbers of prospectors arrived in the 1860s, the Indians traded their game and corn for livestock and manufactured goods. But then whites started hunting, and game got scarce.

Morning After Snow *(1929), by Maynard Dixon. Courtesy of Mark Sublette, Medicine Man Gallery, Tucson, Arizona.*

Even before the Europeans, vengeance was central to the Apache way of life; it perpetuated the conflict of cultures. Unlike modern individual outlaw rampages, this was a sacred duty for the whole group. Courage and bravery were revered among the Apache. They didn't have to kill the actual person who harmed their friend or relative, but rather the same kind of people. They believed it was a way to restore balance to the universe. In some cases, it might take more than one avenger, many deaths, and many years to right a grievance, whether the lives taken were Mexican, Anglo, or even other Apaches.

The revenge cycle was not just on the Apache side of the equation either. As Confederate commander of Texas and New Mexico in the early 1860s, Colonel John Robert Baylor wanted to wipe out all Apaches. His orders were to lure them in with whiskey and other goods, then kill all the adults and sell the children into slavery. At the same time, Union General James Carleton was obsessed with his hatred of the Apaches. He ordered the Navajo Long Walk and agreed with commanding General Philip Sheridan's famous phrase, "the only good Indian is a dead Indian."

In southern Arizona and New Mexico, the 1861 Bascom Affair was only partly to blame for increased violence by Cochise and other Apaches. The withdrawal of troops during the Civil War added to the situation, but the main cause

BELOW: Once an Apache conflict hub, Fort Lowell is now a Tucson city park.

RIGHT: Geronimo was detained at Fort Bowie after his final surrender in 1886.

of the rising death toll was the larger number of Americans moving into Arizona to mine, ranch, or farm.

To protect the immigrants, the U.S. Army reoccupied several camps and forts it had abandoned in 1861 and established more than a dozen new ones after the Civil War, including Forts Apache, Thomas, Huachuca, Whipple, Verde, and McDowell.

In addition to military maneuvers, another battle raged against Arizona Indians, this time on paper. As with much of Arizona's history, mining played a part. More than any other event, the California gold rush spurred a boost in interest of news of the West. At the same time that Eastern papers reported western mining news, boomtowns started their own local papers. While eastern media bemoaned their fate by echoing eighteenth-century poet Alexander Pope's line "Lo, the Poor Indian," Arizona journalists and pioneers, living in a real or imagined state of terror, tended to exaggerate Apache atrocities and called for their annihilation.

Just like the soldiers, newly arrived pioneers had no sense of the centuries-old Apache conflicts. They did understand revenge, however, and many new citizens of the territory joined the cycle themselves, avenging deaths of their loved ones. Nor did national leaders understand the pioneers' fears and attitudes. Just as New Mexico pioneers completely opposed central Mexico's policies in the 1840s, Arizonans strongly disagreed with the national view of the Apache conflicts from the 1860s on.

The Camp Grant Massacre

By 1870, Tucson citizens were so upset with the increasing deaths from Apache raids that they petitioned the government for help. After receiving a noncommittal response from General George Stoneman, Tucsonans held several meetings to seek solutions. No decision was reached, but a local group eventually took matters into its own hands. They focused on one location where they especially opposed government inaction.

Early in 1871, Lieutenant Royal Emerson Whitman took command of Camp Grant in southeastern Arizona. Whitman felt compassion for the Apaches, and he gave four Aravaipa Apache women permission to camp near Camp Grant. Soon, more than a hundred gathered there, and Whitman gave them a contract to supply hay for the fort. This was not an official reservation; Tucsonans were convinced that these Apaches used Camp Grant as a base to raid remote settlements, attack whites on the road, and then return to their camp undetected.

Outraged, a self-appointed "committee of public safety" made up of about six Anglos, 20-some Mexican Americans, and almost 100 Tohono O'odham, attacked the Aravaipa camp at dawn on April 30, killing more than 130 Apaches with clubs and guns. According to later reports, all but about eight of the victims were women and children. President Ulysses S. Grant demanded that a jury trial be held for what would eventually be known as the "Camp Grant Massacre," but local feelings were so strong that the jury returned a verdict of not guilty in less than 20 minutes. This was probably the first instance where members of one tribe were brought up on criminal charges for attacking another tribe.

Federal Indian Policies and the Apaches

Back in Washington, D.C., newly elected President Ulysses S. Grant developed a national plan to deal with Native American issues. It was dubbed the Peace Policy. In March 1871, just before the Camp Grant Massacre, Grant signed the Indian Appropriation Act, nullifying all previous treaties with American Indians and making them all wards of the United States government. Although there were already some Indian reservations, Grant's plan called for *all* Native Americans to be confined and controlled. He also replaced military-appointed reservation administrators with Quakers, Methodists, and missionaries of other Protestant denominations.

General George Crook was known by the Apaches as Santan Lupan *("Grey Wolf"). Courtesy of the Arizona Historical Society (25624).*

President Grant appointed Quaker missionary Vincent Colyer to set up reservations in Arizona, but settlers and local editors were outraged by his benevolent attitudes. Some called him a romantic fool; most called him worse. Nineteenth-century historian Hubert Howe Bancroft called Colyer a "fanatic pacifist," and the Prescott *Arizona Miner* suggested that they "dump the old devil down a mine shaft and pile rocks on him."

Confining Indians to reservations run by missionaries was an improvement on the genocidal attitudes held by most westerners, but without power to enforce the plan, it was doomed to failure. Just two days after the Fort Apache Reservation was established, Indians left the reservation, attacked Camp Crittenden, and drove

off the horse herd. Almost a century earlier, the Gálvez Peace Plan used a three-prong approach to convince the Apaches that they had no alternative but to surrender and move to the reservations. The Spanish combination of cross and sword was about to be revived.

General Crook Takes Time to Learn

Even before the verdict was delivered for the Camp Grant Massacre, division commander General George Stoneman brought in veteran campaigner Lt. Colonel (soon to be General) George Crook. He arrived in June 1871 but had to put operations on hold while Colyer tried his peaceful means. A 6-foot-tall stocky man of 42 with muttonchop sideburns, Crook spent 13 years fighting Indians, and then established a distinguished Civil War record. He gained a reputation for treating each situation fairly and individually, coming down hard when necessary.

Crook's limitless curiosity about the Indian way of life helped him plan successful military operations on his first tour of duty in Arizona. Unlike his predecessors, he talked with everyone who had experience with Apaches as soon as he arrived. In addition to knowing the enemy, Crook developed other methods that contributed to his success. He understood the Apache use of guerrilla warfare tactics—strike unexpectedly and then disappear—and put his men on horseback so they too could move quickly, unfettered by slow-moving supply wagons.

Crook also used the age-old strategy "the enemy of my enemy is my friend" to play one band of Apaches against another. Most importantly, General Crook recruited newly surrendered Apaches to form a Native American unit of Apache scouts. While this may seem unusual for tribal members to fight against each other, Crook understood what most before him did not: there were no Apaches—that is, not as a unified tribe or nation. Instead, they identified themselves with their regional band—Chihenne, Chokonen, Bedonkohe, etc., and not as Apaches.

Crook was able to explain to the Apaches what Captain John Bourke, Crook's right-hand man, reported in his book *On the Border with Crook*: "These white people were crowding in all over the Western country, and soon it would be impossible for any one to live upon game; it would be driven away or killed off. Far better for every one to make up his mind to plant and to raise horses, cows, and sheep, and make his living that way; his animals would thrive and increase while he slept, and in less than no time the Apache would be wealthier than the Mexican."

Indian Scouts Make the Difference

More than a hundred Indian scouts served in the Apache conflicts from the early 1870s well into the twentieth century. A few Yuma and Mohave Indians were recruited as well, but as more Apaches were subdued, Indians from their own bands, such as the Chiricahua, were used because of their close ties and understanding of individuals and their patterns. German emigrant Al Sieber was the leading civilian officer in charge of the scouts, and White Mountains pioneer Corydon Cooley served

BELOW LEFT: Al Sieber, civilian leader of the Apache scouts, was respected by his enemies. Courtesy of the Gila County Historical Society.

BELOW RIGHT: Captured and raised by Apaches, Felix Telles served in the Apache scouts. Courtesy of the Sulphur Springs Valley Historical Society.

FACING: Apache scouts helped end more than a century of cultural conflicts. Courtesy of the Arizona Historical Society (19762).

83732

as a civilian leader as well. Mexican-born captives Merejildo Grijalva and Felix Telles were raised by Apaches and served as guides and interpreters for General Crook's Apache scouts. Telles was the famous stepson of John Ward, the one Lieutenant Bascom accused Cochise of abducting. Renamed Mickey Free after a popular fictional character of the day, Telles had actually been captured by Aravaipa Apaches in 1861 and later raised by White Mountain Apaches.

RIGHT: Indian Agent John Clum created an Apache police force and court system. Courtesy of the Arizona Historical Society (4691)

BELOW: Apache police helped keep the peace on the San Carlos Reservation. Courtesy of the Gila County Historical Society.

Apaches adapted quickly from their gambling games to American card games. Courtesy of the Gila County Historical Society.

The Winter Campaign

In November 1872, General Crook mounted a winter campaign that did more to change the Indian situation than any other action since the Gálvez Peace Plan. His strategy was thorough and methodical. Captain Bourke said that "the Apaches should be induced to surrender in all cases, but where they preferred to fight they were to get all the fighting they wanted, and in one good dose instead of a number of petty engagements, as they were used to . . . They were to be hunted down until the last one in hostility had been killed or captured. Every effort should be made to avoid killing women and children."

Crook himself said that every Indian "must feel keenly every deprivation, and more that they are without an article of clothing, particle of food, or any necessaries. The bitter winds will cause them to perish upon the tops of the mountains." It was not by accident that Crook began in winter and stayed in the field for almost

five months. Like the Russians against Napoleon, climate was this general's ally.

The White Mountain Apache surrendered first, then the army focused on the Yavapai and Tonto bands of central Arizona. Bourke said the winter campaigners traveled 1,200 miles and killed more than 500 Indians. The campaign was brutal, bordering on genocide. In the Mazatzal Mountains in December 1872, the Skeleton Cave Massacre resulted in the deaths of several women and children. Writing about it, Bourke said he would have blushed if he still had the ability.

The winter campaign broke the Apache spirit. They were finally convinced resistance was futile. General Crook paraphrased the words of Delshay, a fierce Apache leader:

Now the very rocks had gotten soft. They couldn't put their foot anywhere without leaving an

Waiting in line was a daily routine for Apaches at the San Carlos Reservation. Courtesy of the Graham County Historical Society.

impression by which we could follow, that they could get no sleep at nights, for should a coyote or fox start a rock rolling during the night they would get up and dig out, thinking the soldiers were catching up with them.

By April 1873, the U.S. Army believed there were no Apaches still at large in the United States. Crook thought he had solved the Apache problem, and he was transferred to the Great Plains to lead U.S. forces against the Sioux.

The San Carlos Reservation

Before and especially after the winter campaign, several bands of Apaches were sent to live on the San Carlos Reservation. It had been established in 1871 in eastern Arizona, between the White Mountains to the north and the Gila River to the south. Every Indian had to wear a brass tag and line up for a head count every day to make sure no one left the reservation.

General Crook had Apache men punished for fermenting corn beer called *tizwin* (also called *tulapai*) and for beating their wives. Some civilian Indian agents gave them inadequate rations, often bad flour and beef, and stagnant waters on the reservation caused malaria. To make things worse, several Apache bands that were natural enemies were herded together at San Carlos.

In February 1875, another grueling exodus similar to the Navajo Long Walk took place when officials closed the Fort Verde Indian Reservation and forced 1,500 Yavapai and Tonto Apaches to march up the Mogollón Rim and across the White Mountains to the San Carlos Reservation.

The Chiricahuas' Blood Brother

Not all Apaches were sent to San Carlos after Crook's winter campaign, however. The Chiricahua Apaches, led by Cochise, were granted their own separate reservation, thanks to two unusual men. Traditionally, the Chiricahuas lived most of the year in the Dragoon and Chiricahua Mountains of southeastern Arizona, a striking labyrinth of cliffs, crevices, and granite spires. The Gila Trail, the main southern route to California, wound through their homeland. It offered many ideal spots for hiding and ambushing hundreds of American travelers in the decade following the Bascom Affair.

In an act of bravery usually saved for Hollywood screenplays, Butterfield Overland Stage agent Tom Jeffords is said to have ventured alone into Cochise's stronghold sometime

RIGHT: Every Apache at the San Carlos Reservation was required to wear a metal identification tag.

BELOW: Geronimo was held for two months at this San Carlos guardhouse in 1877. Courtesy of the Graham County Historical Society.

between 1867 and 1870. Cochise was impressed by Jeffords' courage, and they became "blood brothers," a term used as a title for a western novel by Oren Arnold, and later made into the movie "Broken Arrow" in 1950, in which Jimmy Stewart played Jeffords and Jeff Chandler played Cochise. The novel and movie are romanticized, of course, but they are "based on a true story" that played a part in reducing hostilities.

By this time Cochise began to see the futility of resistance. Jeffords convinced him to meet with another of President Grant's Peace Policy emissaries, General Oliver Otis Howard, in 1871. Howard, a strongly religious officer who lost an arm in the Civil War, considered himself "Moses to the Negro" and felt a similar calling to preach Christianity to Native Americans. Howard, like Jeffords, was brave enough to meet Cochise in a remote area with only Jeffords and Lieutenant Joseph Sladen for protection. After 10 days of talks, Howard designated a large portion of the Chiricahuas' homeland near Fort Bowie as their official reservation.

The Chiricahuas insisted that Jeffords be their Indian agent, and he gave them more freedom than the other agents, with no number tags or head counts. Tucsonans were outraged; they were sure these Apaches were still raiding. Some Chiricahuas did continue to raid in Mexico, and lack of control got worse when Cochise died of intestinal cancer in 1874. After a trader was killed for refusing to sell more whiskey to some drunken renegades, Department of Interior officials fired Jeffords, closed the reservation, and moved the Chiricahua to San Carlos in 1876. Several hundred, including Geronimo, fled to Mexico instead.

In 1877, San Carlos Indian Agent John Clum invited Geronimo to meet with him at Ojo Caliente, New Mexico. At a prearranged signal, 80 Apache police surrounded Geronimo and his men. Geronimo surrendered three times in later years, but this was the only time he was captured by force. He was locked in the guardhouse at San Carlos, and Clum began discussions with the Pima County sheriff to convict him on at least seven counts of murder.

On several different occasions in the late 1870s and early 1880s, Apache leaders Victorio, Geronimo, and others left San Carlos, at times with as many as 300 followers. They terrorized southern Arizona, New Mexico, and Mexico, killing and torturing Americans and Mexicans, stealing livestock and kidnapping children. They often returned to the reservation in cold weather for food or because the soldiers and scouts tracked them down.

Eventually, all but Geronimo and his small band of followers gave up. In *Once They Rode Like the Wind*, Thomas Reynolds quoted Apache leader Juh's speech to his warriors in 1876: "Their strength in numbers, with their more powerful weapons, will make us indeed *Indeh, the Dead.*"

Now that the majority of Arizona's tribes were confined to reservations, the land was now open for American settlers. As word got out that the territory was relatively safe from Indian raids, farmers and ranchers came by the hundreds, and eventually thousands, to homestead and start a new life.

But Arizona's rough terrain barely provided food for its indigenous peoples, much less the Americans who began to populate the area in the 1850s. Since Father Kino first arrived in the seventeenth century, European pioneers knew they would have to raise their own food, which included cattle, sheep, goats, and pigs.

ARIZONA RANCHING

Among the many misconceptions about Arizona history, most prominent is the idea that the state was primarily cattle ranching territory, teeming with cowboys taking huge herds on long cattle drives to railroad connections and stockyards in the Midwest. For more than a century, dime novels, western movies, and advertisers taught the world that everyone in Arizona wore cowboy hats, boots, leather vests, and spoke with a Texas drawl.

While cattle were important, the story starts much earlier, and other livestock played a part as well. Sixty years before the Jamestown Colony, Francisco de Coronado's army of Spanish conquistadores drove thousands of cattle, sheep, goats, and swine through southeastern

Arizona. In 1700, Father Kino and his Indian cowboys drove herds into Arizona. He knew the Indians were more likely to accept his religion if plenty of good food came with it.

For 70 years after the presidio was established at Tubac, soldiers, settlers, and Indians raised large herds of longhorn cattle and sheep around the missions and forts at Tubac, Tucson, and other southern Arizona locations. The Spanish, and later Mexican, government attracted settlers by providing large land grants for them to raise livestock in southern Arizona.

But the golden age of Hispanic ranching ended in the 1830s when the Mexican government could no longer afford to supply Apache settlements with beef, blankets, and guns, and the Indians increased their raiding again. Ranchers fled to Mexico, leaving their herds to fend for themselves.

After the Civil War, Texas ranchers spread out into Arizona, selling their cattle to the Army posts that sprang up to fight Arizona's Indians. As the number of troops and forts increased in Arizona, the cattle business grew quickly. The boom reached its peak in the 1880s.

Homesteaders took advantage of the Desert Land Act of 1877 and settled small herds on their allotted 640 acres. Other ranchers started out by borrowing large amounts of money from investors "Back East" or in Europe. Many chose to raise cattle, but sheep, swine, and goats were also raised in parts of Arizona where the climate would support them. In addition to large herds of sheep and goats raised by the Navajo Indians since the 1700s, Anglo and Mexican American settlers drove large herds of sheep from New Mexico into Arizona's highlands in the 1870s.

RIGHT ABOVE: Working cowboys usually wore bandannas to keep the dust out of their mouths. Courtesy of the Sulphur Springs Valley Historical Society.

RIGHT: The Hashknife Ranch created a large market for boots, saddles, and tack, hence the ad for this boot company in Holbrook.

FACING: *African Americans found freedom ranching in the West. Courtesy of the Phoenix Public Library.*

RIGHT: *Real Arizona cowboys didn't always dress like the Hollywood movies.*

BELOW: *In the 1870s, men gathered at the La Paloma Cantina in Florence to play pool, have a cool drink, and hear a little music. Courtesy of the Arizona Historical Society.*

ABOVE: *There were very few cattle drives in Arizona. Most drives ended at the nearest railroad siding. Courtesy of the Sulphur Springs Valley Historical Society.*

BELOW: *A cowboy who griped about chuckwagon food might become the next cook.*

FACING: *His saddle and guns were the cowboy's most important possessions.*

RANCHES OF
SULPHUR
SPRING VALLEY
ARIZONA
1913

FT. GRANT
Sierra Bonita Ranch
J.H. Ranch
Circle I Ranch
Railroad
O. T. Ranch
WILLCOX
Riggs Ranch
DOS CABEZAS
202 Ranch
Hope Ranch
Willcox
Playa
COCHISE
14 Ranch
Allaire's Ranch
Halderman Ranch
DRAGOON
Warren Ranch
Star Ranch
McCalls Ranch

Legend
■ Ranches
🌲 Towns

PEARCE
Railroad

Whitehead Ranch
Rucker Ranch
COURTLAND
GLEESON

Southern
Pacific
Arizona
Eastern

243_062

ABOVE: *Ranchers on the Wien Ranch near Willcox invented "cowboy golf." Courtesy of the Arizona Historical Society.*

LEFT: *The Sulphur Springs Valley in southeastern Arizona was ranching country.*

FACING: *The Adamsville Cemetery near Florence memorializes many forgotten founders.*

Forgotten Founders

When former Secretary of the Interior Stewart Udall wrote *The Forgotten Founders: Rethinking the History of the Old West* in 2004, he examined the myths created by Hollywood, novelists, and previous historians about who really settled the frontier. His "forgotten founders" are ordinary folks he calls "wagon settlers," courageous families who came west before the railroads to homestead small farms and ranches. They created what historian George Ellsworth called "small footholds of civilization."

While mining probably had the biggest impact on Arizona's development, the motivations and labor of individuals played an equal role. Udall correctly points out that religion had a great deal to do with settling the West.

From the Catholic missionaries in the seventeenth-century Southwest to Methodists in Oregon and Mormons in Utah and Arizona, as well as countless other Protestant denominations, religious communities created the towns and cities all over the state that remain today.

Udall points out another important misunderstanding about Western history that applies to Arizona during this period as well. While movies and novels would have us believe that the Wild West was populated by gunslingers, stage robbers, gamblers, and dance hall girls, a large portion of Arizona's population were ordinary farmers, just like those in Iowa or Indiana. While it is true that Tombstone "had a man for breakfast" for several years

ABOVE: *This flash flood on Pinal Creek shows too much water was a problem too. Courtesy of the Gila County Historical Society.*

FACING ABOVE: *Farmers contributed as much to the settlement of the territory as ranchers did. Courtesy of the Gila County Historical Society.*

FACING BELOW: *Board cabins were common in Springerville's lumber country.*

ABOVE: Harry S. Truman dedicated Springerville's Madonna of the Trail in 1928.

BELOW: The theater at Levin's Gardens in Tucson featured minstrel shows and operettas. Courtesy of the Arizona Historical Society (25294).

RIGHT: As shown by this early view of Pennington Street in Tucson, adobe was the main construction material before the railroad arrived. Courtesy of the Arizona Historical Society (B109289).

MADONNA OF THE TRAIL

N·S·D·A·R· MEMORIAL
TO THE
PIONEER MOTHERS
OF THE
COVERED WAGON DAYS

The Sisters of Saint Joseph of Carondelet started a Tucson hospital in 1871. Courtesy of the Arizona Historical Society (62509).

running, the per capita violence quotient in New York City would have been equal to that. In addition, most mining booms sprang up and disappeared in a matter of years, leaving the farming communities of the Verde Valley, those around Prescott, and almost all of eastern Arizona to raise upstanding, churchgoing families. To further prove Udall's point, another group of peaceful farming towns became a desert metropolis without the benefit of even one Western movie, novel, or TV series being written about it.

tiersman and missionary to the Indians, and a group of men built a raft and became the first to cross the Colorado River at what would eventually become Lee's Ferry, a crucial stop on the main settlement route between Arizona and Utah, nicknamed the Honeymoon Trail because Mormon couples traveled along that road to be married in the St. George Temple in southwestern Utah.

John D. Lee built homes of stone and wood for two of his wives and families at Lee's Ferry, and built a dam and an irrigation system as well. As tensions between Navajos and Mormons increased, the settlers built a fort, which later became a trading post, then a home, school, and mess hall at various times. When Lee was executed in 1877 for his role in the Mountain Meadows Massacre near St. George, Utah, his wife Emma Bachelor Lee, a hardy pioneer woman, operated the ferry and farmed the area for several years.

In the 1870s, the Mormons arrived in steady numbers to colonize the Little Colorado River Basin and along the Gila and San Pedro Rivers as well. Starting new farming communities was hard going, as towns suffered from crop failures due to heat, frost, drought, and floods—sometimes more than one per year. On top of that, hailstorms, insect plagues, and heavy winds added to their misery. Through community efforts, faith, and determined persistence, the Mormons succeeded, and their communities still thrive today through the efforts of their descendents.

Mesa, now one of the largest towns in Arizona, was founded by the 85 members of the first Mesa Company, who arrived in the Salt River Valley in 1877. They cleared the land and re-dug the ancient Hohokam canals to grow their crops. Lehi, a nearby town, was prone to flooding and had fewer irrigation ditches, so Mesa eventually grew larger, absorbing Lehi in 1970.

Many towns got started on the rich soil alongside the Gila River, the most notable being Safford, Thatcher, Duncan, and Pima. Likewise along the San Pedro, the towns of Saint David and Pomerene were established in

THE MORMON VISION

The Mormon Battalion experience of 1846 was not lost on the growing religious group, and many veterans passed on the word that Arizona would be a good place to expand their movement. In 1864, Jacob Hamblin, fron-

RIGHT: *Family farming near Duncan was not lucrative, but it was usually wholesome. Courtesy of the Graham County Historical Society.*

BELOW: *Farmers along the Gila River bought stock in canal companies to ensure water. Courtesy of the Graham County Historical Society.*

CAPITAL $ 10,000.

No. 915 Solomonville, A.T. Jan'y 31 1906 ½ Shares.

This Certifies that J. J. Quinn is the owner of One Half Shares in the Capital Stock of

THE MONTEZUMA

CANAL COMPANY.

Transferable on the books of the Company by endorsement hereon and surrender of this Certificate.

H. L. Castle
Secretary.

Geo. A. Olney
President.

400 SHARES $25. EACH.

ABOVE: This sandstone fort at Pipe Spring was an early Mormon settlement. Courtesy of the Arizona Historical Society.

BELOW: When they first arrived, Mormons built forts such as Fort Moroni, later called Fort Rickerson, nine miles north of Flagstaff. Courtesy of the Phoenix Public Library.

this era. The Mormon philosophy favored farming over ranching because the former favored community participation, whereas individual ranchers were separated from the community by their multi-acre ranches. Today, there are just as many Mormon ranchers as there are farmers, as well as professionals, politicians, and businessmen in every aspect of Arizona's economy.

SETTLING THE SALT RIVER VALLEY: PHOENIX RISES FROM THE ASHES

While General Crook and his Apache scouts forced large numbers of Native Americans onto reservations, Arizona's future metropolis grew slowly along the banks of the Salt River. Centuries before, the Hohokam people dug thousands of miles of irrigation canals in the same location. By the late 1860s, former Confederate Jack Swilling, Yuma ferryboat owner Louis Jaeger, Lord Darrell Duppa, and several other partners created the Swilling Irrigation and Canal Company. They scraped out the ancient ditches and grew large amounts of food and fodder to supply the miners at Wickenburg and the soldiers at Fort McDowell, 20 miles northeast of town.

As with many cities, the origin of its name is still not clear. The majority thinks it was Darrel Duppa, whose notable English family saw fit to make him a remittance man by paying him a regular allowance to stay far away in order to keep him from further besmirching the family name. Duppa's Cambridge University education led him to make a connection between this new town built on the ruins of a large prehistoric civilization and the mythical Egyptian phoenix, a bird that was reborn every 500 years on a fiery nest. At least 60 years later, archaeologists estimated that the ancient Hohokam cities were abandoned sometime around AD 1400, placing the new Phoenix within decades of the mythical bird's 500-year cycle.

Just as they had in prehistoric times, the well-engineered canals carried rich silt from the Salt River, ensuring abundant crops. But unlike the prospectors who flocked to Gila City and Prescott, Salt River Valley pioneers were not looking to get rich quick. The town founders were predominantly Anglo and were proud of their new location. In his seven-volume history, Arizona state historian Thomas Farish quotes a local newspaper:

> Lately hundreds of ornamental trees have been set out, which, in a few years, will give the town the appearance of a forest city, and will add to its beauty and comfort. When it has become the capital of the Territory, which it will, undoubtedly, at no very distant day, and when the iron horse steams through our country on the Texas Pacific road, Salt River will be the garden of the Pacific slope, and Phoenix the most important inland town. The Indian is now a nuisance, and the Sonoranian [Mexican] a decided annoyance, but both of these are sure to disappear before civilization as snow before the noonday sun.

After heated debate on which farming community would become a town, three commissioners were appointed to survey town sites in 1871 and sell lots. According to Brad Luckingham in *Phoenix: History of a Southwestern Metropolis,* the state's future capital was not a boomtown in the 1870s. Since the mining districts were some distance away, the town did not mushroom overnight like Gila City and Tombstone, but instead grew steadily with the increase of farmlands made available by the development of more irrigation canals. Luckingham quotes a Phoenix reporter of the era, saying, "We are in fact, a very sober, industrious people, and we have been, at least the greater part of us, hard at work putting in our crops and taking care of them."

ABOVE: *In this 1907 photograph, looking north on Central Avenue at Jefferson Street in Phoenix, the first building on the right is the Commercial Hotel.*

BELOW: *Natural beauty at Watson Lake, near Prescott. Courtesy of Randy Prentice Photography*

WHEN SILVER WAS KING

The 1850s and 1860s brought thousands of prospectors and mining entrepreneurs, searching mostly for gold around the Colorado River, Prescott, and Wickenburg. Although Poston, Mowry, and Heintzelman got a good start with silver near Tubac and Patagonia (pages 129–30), the Civil War forced them to abandon their mines, and things never quite picked up again. But in the 1870s, two big strikes, one east of Phoenix and the other in southeastern Arizona near the border, put Arizona on the map and created the Wild West image that still lingers today.

Sullivan's Global Nuggets

Mining in Arizona was always a dangerous prospect, especially in the Pinal Mountains southeast of Phoenix. A series of prospecting and Indian fighting expeditions combined ventured into the hills in the 1860s, and signs of rich minerals were noted, but no one dared stay to work the mines. Then in 1870, General George Stoneman directed his men to build a wagon road up the Mogollón Rim, and a steep section near present-day Superior came to be known as Stoneman Grade.

Returning to camp one day after working on the road, a soldier named John Sullivan found some heavy rocks that bent when he struck them instead of breaking apart. By the time he found out what it was, his army hitch had run out, and he was working on Charles Mason's ranch. Sullivan showed Tempe residents the ore, but no one wanted to risk going into Apache country to get it.

ABOVE: *Farmers and ranchers settled near these red rock cliffs in the Sierra Anchas east of Phoenix. Courtesy of Randy Prentice Photography.*

BELOW: *Sure-footed burros made it possible to mine in rugged terrain near Oatman. Courtesy of the Mohave County Historical Society.*

OVERLEAF: *By 1898, mining made Broad Street in Globe one of Arizona's major thoroughfares. Courtesy of the Gila County Historical Society.*

Other prospectors filed claims in 1871, but fear of Apaches kept them from working the claims until after General Crook removed the threat with his winter campaign. In the summer of 1873, mining began, even though they were attacked by the remaining renegades. Sullivan left the area in the winter of 1874–75, but not before he described the location of his find to Mason, who finally found it and called the rich new mine the Globe Ledge, which eventually came to be known as the Silver King. The name may have come from a nine-inch ball of almost pure silver valued at $12,000. Supposedly, it had black figures on it that looked like continents, and it reminded someone of a globe. Like many Arizona town names, the facts are lost to history as well.

A few hours after the news of the rich claims reached Florence, Arizona, hundreds of men swarmed over the future mining towns of Globe, Superior, and Miami,

hoping to find more. The Silver Queen, Rescue, and Big Johnnie mining claims were filed in the area, and camps sprung up. Globe City, as it was optimistically called back then, became a town in 1876 and began to boom in the 1880s.

More and more Americans began to arrive, including ranchers and miners, who supplied the forts and Indian reservations with beef and other foodstuffs. Globe became a true Wild West town, pretty close to what we love to see in the movies. They had a hanging tree on Broad Street, opium dens, dance hall girls, and "soiled doves" (prostitutes). The town was so rough, even as late as 1907, that when Gila County Clerk George Smalley read a letter from back home relating that his Aunt Sally died, his five-year-old daughter asked, "Who shot her, Daddy?"

Although it grew to be a large copper mining town

BELOW: At the intersection of Broad and Cedar Streets, Globe boasted the Silver Belt building, the F.W. Westmeyer store, and the two-story Pascoe Hotel, c. 1882. Courtesy of the Gila County Historical Society.

RIGHT: Ripley's Believe It or Not *noted the Globe Elks Building, erected on Mesquite Street in 1910, as the world's tallest three-story building. Courtesy of the Gila County Historical Society.*

ABOVE: The real Tombstone was more about mining than it was about theaters and saloons.

RIGHT: Prospector Ed Schieffelin found his "Tombstone" and several other silver claims. Courtesy of the Arizona Historical Society (49714).

up through the 1970s, and mines are still in operation and development today, Globe never received national attention in books and movies for its frontier roots. Farther south near the Mexican border, a soldier's warning and a prospector's eerie retort created another silver boomtown—Tombstone, "a town too tough to die"—that continues to upstage all the rest of Arizona history combined.

The Indestructible Legend of Tombstone

When the soldiers at Fort Huachuca asked prospector Ed Schieffelin where he was going, he told them he was headed out into the hills to find silver; they joked, "All you're gonna find is your tombstone." So when he struck a rich vein, the wry miner called it the Tombstone claim. The silver in the area was so pure and soft that they said when you hit it with a pick it would stick in it and stand up.

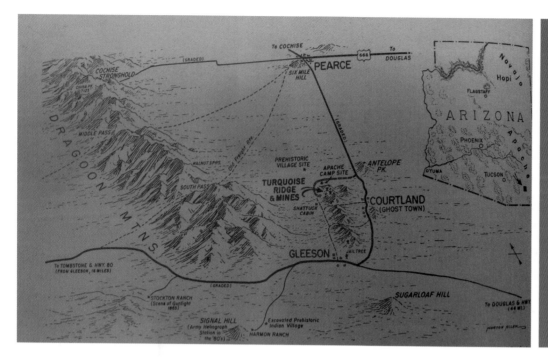

Schieffelin found the silver in 1877, and in less than two years there were thousands of miners, gamblers, dance hall girls, and all the supporting citizens to fill the Arizona boomtown. But not many seem interested in the mining history because something happened there that steals the show.

The Gunfight at the O.K. Corral

No single event in the history of the Wild West is as famous, deeply researched, and contested as the gunfight at the O.K. Corral. Even its name is misleading since it actually took place in a narrow vacant lot next to C. S. Fly's photography studio. As Arizona's Official State Historian Marshall Trimble says, however, "Gunfight at Block 2, Lot 17 is too long to fit on a movie marquee."

It happened on Wednesday, October 26, 1881, around three in the afternoon. About 30 gunshots and 30 seconds later, it was all over, and yet it continues to play out to this day, with new books and movies about Tombstone entertaining eager audiences every year, and daily reenactments in the "town too tough to die" performed before international audiences of fascinated tourists vicariously

participating in the Wild West's biggest legend.

Like any fight, no one cause brought it on. It was a political and economic power struggle, federal versus local rule, Yankee Republicans versus Southern Democrats, property ownership, and a rivalry for the affections of an attractive actress as well. There have been as many interpretations as there are reporters, including a neo-Marxist view, with the Earps on the side of capital and the Clantons representing labor.

But the gunfight at the O.K. Corral was not over when the gunshots quieted and the air cleared of smoke. Violence begat more violence, and another cycle of vengeance began. In a three-week clash between March and April 1882, Morgan Earp was assassinated in a billiard parlor, and Virgil Earp's left arm was permanently crippled by a sniper's bullet. This allegedly led to the Earp faction's murder of Curly Bill Brocius and three others of the Cowboy faction. In a convoluted example of frontier law enforcement, the Earps formed a federal posse to pursue the Cowboys for the death of Morgan, while Cochise County Sheriff Johnny Behan formed a local posse of Cowboys to pursue the Earps!

Wyatt Earp and Doc Holliday caught up with one of their enemies, Frank Stillwell, at the train station in Tucson on March 20 and killed him with a barrage of bullets and buckshot. At that point, the remaining Earps and Holliday left Arizona to avoid arrest, never to return. They had only been in Arizona a few years, but their continued fame far outshines the sacrifices of any man or woman who dedicated their lives to bringing peace, justice, and prosperity to Arizona.

It is significant that this last outburst happened at a train depot, for the locomotive would do more to influence the history and character of Arizona than any other factor since the arrival of the Spaniards, the discovery of rich mineral wealth, or the forced containment of Arizona's Indian tribes on reservations.

THE FAMOUS "BIRD CAGE THEATRE" WHERE LOTTA CRABTREE AND EDDIE FOY APPEARED IN THE EARLY 80'S AND WHERE BUCKSKIN FRANK LESLIE SHOT THE COWBOY'S BOOT HEEL OFF, TOMBSTONE, ARIZONA

FACING: *In 1882,* The New York Times *said that "the Bird Cage Theatre is the wildest, wickedest night spot between Basin Street and the Barbary Coast." Courtesy of the Arizona Historical Society (13-5778).*

ABOVE: *Next to the Grand Canyon, the O.K. Corral is Arizona's most popular tourist attraction.*

BELOW: *This stage ran from Fairbank to Tombstone and was refurbished for the movie* Arizona *in 1939.*

APACHE TRAIL

Southern Pacific Lines

CHAPTER SIX

★ RAILROADS, COPPER, AND STATEHOOD

> I remember when Arizona became a state because my parents had a party. I was supposed to be in bed. But I spent my time in the kitchen with Hin Que, our Chinese cook. Every so often he would raise his champagne glass and say, "Happy Fourth of July, Yndia!"
>
> —Yndia Smalley Moore, born in Tucson in 1902

CHANGES COME BY RAIL

While the shriek of the railroad whistle signaled the closing of the American frontier, in Arizona it meant drastic changes. Charles Poston, self-styled father of Arizona, said the "Chariot of Fire is the messiah of civilization," but Latino and Native American cultures found it a threat to their traditional way of life. Railroads changed the world, especially Arizona, more than any other phenomenon before or since. Change was widespread and rapid, not just in the technological and economic sense, but socially and culturally as well.

Fueled by a large influx of capital from the 1849 gold rush, mines and railroads became the first large joint stock corporations in America. On top of that, the federal government subsidized the transcontinental railroad with inducements of 20 free sections of public land for each mile of track laid.

The Southern Pacific Railroad, moving eastward from Yuma, officially reached Tucson on March 20, 1880. By 1881, the southern route connected the continent from

Facing: Apache Trail *(1926), by Maynard Dixon. Travel poster for the Southern Pacific Lines. Courtesy of Mark Sublette, Medicine Man Gallery, Tucson, Arizona.* ABOVE: *An engine similar to the one that first arrived in Tucson in 1880. Courtesy of the Arizona Historical Society (19475).*

erable markup in prices from point of origin to their destination on the Arizona frontier.

But everything changed the day the railroad arrived in Tucson. Because of the speed and ease with which goods now reached Arizona, prices dropped as much as 75 percent immediately. Storeowners were stuck with inventories they could not profit on, and the leading freighting companies soon went bankrupt. Ironically, Estevan Ochoa, a leading citizen who introduced the railroad bill in the Arizona Territorial Legislature, lost his fortune as well. The silver spike he presented to Southern Pacific President Charles Crocker Jr. might as well have been driven into his heart.

The changes wrought by the coming of the railroad were not only financial but also impacted the social and cultural fabric of Arizona. Its remote location and danger of Indian and bandit attacks brought mostly single men

LEFT: *Mining, ranching, and the railroad made Tucson a cosmopolitan town. Courtesy of the Arizona Historical Society (B112839).*

BELOW: *Smaller engines like this one from the Clifton-Morenci mines were invaluable to copper production.*

coast to coast. Chinese laborers laid the track because they were desperate enough to work in the extreme heat for lower wages than any other ethnic group. As tracks were laid, ramshackle railhead towns sprang up for the Irish, Chinese, and other emigrants working on the track. Following behind came the merchants, gamblers, barkeeps, and dance hall girls to separate them from their money. Similar to mining boomtowns made of canvas and raw lumber, these towns enjoyed a brief moment of glory and then calmed down when track moved on.

Since Spanish rule, Arizona forts and missions remained remote supply stations on the route between more populated colonies in Texas, New Mexico, and California. Tucson was in the freight and mercantile business, led by the Anglo-Mexican firm of Tully and Ochoa. Goods moved by wagon trains of mules or oxen, and the manpower, time, and danger involved created a consid-

The Clemenceau Museum train room in Cottonwood features flat ears loaded with copper ingots. Courtesy of the Verde Historical Society.

to Arizona, and they married the Mexican women already living there. Successful Anglo merchants wed daughters of well-to-do Mexican merchants, creating a multicultural social elite—at least until the railroad came to town.

Mining and Timing

Timing, technology, and mineral wealth combined to turn Arizona economics and society upside down. In the four decades between 1844 and 1884, several inventions created a market for something Arizona had plenty of—copper. The telegraph, telephone, and electric light depended on large quantities of copper wire, which was supplied in large part by Arizona mines. Large machinery was needed to process the ore into heavy copper ingots.

By transporting the equipment to Arizona and exporting the weighty metal ingots to eastern manufacturers, the railroad played an important role in the transformation of Arizona into what historian Thomas Sheridan calls an "extractive colony" for eastern mining corporations.

The new jobs created by the railroad and the mines changed Arizona. Hispanics were rarely promoted to upper echelon jobs and were usually paid less than Anglo co-workers in similar positions. The new corporations employed eastern professionals as lawyers, doctors, engineers, and managers for the railroads and mines. Thus, the richest men in Arizona no longer lived there. Instead, they headed up mining and railroad corporations in New York, Ohio, and Montana.

Railroads bring Cultural and Economic Changes

Once the Native Americans were subdued, the increased safety and ease of transportation provided by the railroad allowed the new professionals to bring their wives and daughters with them. Whole families began to immigrate, and the number of multicultural marriages waned with the influx of marriageable Anglo women.

The railroad changed every aspect of southwestern living as building materials, including complete kit houses from Sears, Roebuck and Company, could be shipped by rail and assembled amid the traditional Sonoran adobe row houses. Everything from American foodstuffs to furniture was now available, and Anglo pioneers hurried to shed Tucson's Spanish trappings and become an all-American "Main Street" town.

Meanwhile, in 1883, the Atlantic and Pacific Railroad, which would eventually become the Atchison, Topeka, and Santa Fe Railway, crossed Arizona from east to west at the 35th parallel, creating the towns of Winslow, Holbrook, Williams, and Kingman, along a forested route that eventually became Route 66 and is now roughly paralleled by Interstate 40. Named after railroad administrators, these towns began with a midwestern flavor, populated overnight by those who built

and served the railroads. A timber industry developed to provide railroad ties, and federal railroad land grants created the Arizona Territory's largest ranch, the Aztec Land and Cattle Company, also known as the Hashknife Outfit for the shape of its brand.

Railroad and Industry

A decade earlier, unbridled railroad speculation and overexpansion caused bank failures, plummeting stocks, and substantial unemployment known as the Panic of 1873. Facing deficits in the tens of millions, the railroads turned to their only remaining asset, the land deeded to them by the federal government.

Major railroads sent agents to Europe to promote their land. In tune with the new scientific age, their brochures claimed that once arid lands were tilled for farming, rainfall in the area increased, creating a "rain follows the plow" phenomenon. Facing difficult times at home, many Europeans emigrated on the dream of this bogus theory.

Although exaggerated as well, a second plan was at least based in fact. In part due to urbanization and poor living conditions, the nineteenth century experienced a decades-long tuberculosis epidemic. Studies found that clean dry air alleviated the symptoms. Railroad agents

Before the railroad, Grand Canyon tourists roughed it by stagecoach and wagon. Courtesy of the Phoenix Public Library.

claimed that no one ever got sick in the American West, and the chambers of commerce in Tucson and Phoenix got on board. Their promotions brought a class of health seekers unlike the western pioneers of earlier decades. A larger number of intellectuals, artists, and America's wealthy found themselves living in Arizona to save their lives, and they contributed to the changing culture.

Tourism by Rail

The most enduring strategy to increase railroad ticket sales was to capitalize on the tourism industry. The Industrial Revolution and rise of factories, Big Business, and urbanization combined to create a middle class of managers, clerks, and other supporting professions. A leisure class emerged, leading to the novel idea of a vacation from work. At first these were only for the upper classes, but as the economy grew, so did the opportunity for more Americans to take time off and travel. Crammed into overcrowded polluted cities, Americans now yearned for the untouched wilderness that just a few decades earlier they saw as something to be conquered or avoided.

Through the booming popular magazine industry and by subsidizing writers and artists, the Santa Fe Railway created an idyllic Southwest filled with enchantment and nostalgia. They transformed the Grand Canyon from an ugly hole in the ground to one of the scenic wonders of the world. Through a chain of railway resorts run by entrepreneur Fred Harvey, travelers could enjoy a stylized southwestern experience without leaving the comfort of their hotel. "Indian Detours"—limousine trips led by well-scripted guides from hotels to ancient pueblos— enhanced the effect. The Harvey Company also created a museum and craft industry, employing Native Americans

Special Train de Luxe — The Eighth Season

Gates' Tours

Mexico, California, Grand Cañon of Arizona

First Tour leaves New York and Boston Feb. 5, 1901. leaves Chicago and St. Louis Feb. 6, 1901.

Second Tour leaves New York and Boston Feb. 19, 1901. leaves Chicago and St. Louis Feb. 20, 1901.

Mexico—Land of enchantment, country of tradition and romance, paradise for tourists, strange and delightful. All places heretofore visited, included. Also, for the first time, beautiful Lake Chapala (5000 ft. alt.) and unique ruins of Xochicalco and Teposteco.

Grand Cañon of Arizona on the SANTA FE ROUTE, most wonderful scenic panorama in the West; 217 miles long, 13 miles wide, more than a mile deep, and painted like a flower.

California—Special arrangements for visiting the noted California resorts. Tickets good to return independently on any train within 9 months.

Train de Luxe—Special train, equipped with compartment cars, drawing-room Pullmans, dining car and observation car. Large observation parlor for ladies and smoking parlor for gentlemen. In service for entire railroad portion of each tour. All expenses included. Number of passengers limited. Send for itinerary describing these ideal winter tours.

CHAS. H. GATES, TOLEDO, OHIO.

W. H. EAVES, AGT., 201 WASHINGTON ST., BOSTON.

LEFT: Tour companies joined with the railroads to promote the Southwest. Courtesy of Dori Griffin.

RIGHT: The Santa Fe Railway hired artists and writers to extol the wonders of the Grand Canyon. Courtesy of Dori Griffin.

BELOW: By the 1890s, Bright Angel Hotel on the South Rim of the Grand Canyon was a popular accommodation as tourism began to accelerate. Courtesy of the Phoenix Public Library.

ARIZONA THE WONDERLAND

GEORGE WHARTON JAMES

ABOVE: *The Harvey Girls brought civilization and sanitation to railroad dining. Courtesy of the Mohave County Historical Society.*

FACING: *The El Tovar Hotel on the South Rim of the Grand Canyon copied the popular Norwegian hunting lodge design. Courtesy of the Phoenix Public Library.*

to create jewelry, baskets, blankets, and pottery of Harvey design. He also employed single women in his cafes, giving these "Harvey Girls" career opportunities and bringing a little respectability to the West.

Of the many changes the railroad brought, the impact on Native Americans was the most dramatic. While earlier miners, farmers, and ranchers depleted game and used up the water, the railroad increased these problems tenfold within only a few years. Restricted to reservations, sometimes on unproductive land, Arizona Indians got work with the railroad or began making rugs, jewelry, or baskets. A schism developed between the trading post "blanket Indian" and those who chose to remain far from the railroad and continue in their traditional lifestyle. These people of ancient isolated farm communities found their past and future on a collision course with a virtual train wreck of modern American values

MEXICAN AMERICANS UNITE

As the railroad brought more and more Anglos and their culture to Arizona, Mexican American residents, especially businessmen, professionals, and ranch owners, formed *mutualistas* (mutual aid societies) to help the less fortunate, advance their interests, influence politics, and defend their rights. The first organization was probably founded in 1875 by community leaders such as Estevan Ochoa, Jesús Pacheco, and Juan Elías. Some members were *descendientes* (descendents) of the first Spanish soldiers to arrive at Tubac in 1752, and others were heir to large Spanish or Mexican land grant ranches.

In 1894, Carlos Velasco, Mariano Samaniego, and about 50 other prominent Hispanics founded the Alianza Hispano-Americana, a fraternal society and mutual insurance organization. By the late 1930s, the Alianza

had become the largest organization of its kind in the United States, with more than 17,000 members throughout the western United States and northern Mexico.

One of its organizers, Carlos Velasco, had been a leader in many *mutualistas*, especially in mining towns across Arizona, and was also the founder of the first Spanish-language newspaper in the territory, *El Frontizero*. Trained as a lawyer, Velasco served as a judge and state legislator in Sonora but fled to Tubac in 1865 because he supported liberal Ignacio Pesqueira, while Emperor Maximilian and the French regime backed his political rival, Manuel Gándara. From the 1870s to his death in 1914, Velasco served his Mexican countrymen of both countries through his editorials and his leadership.

BELOW: This rare photograph shows black soldiers in their quarters at Fort Huachuca. Courtesy of the Arizona Military Museum.

THE APACHE CONFLICTS

Although Arizona pioneers, the federal government, the U.S. Army, and General Crook thought the Apache conflicts were over by the time Crook left for the Great Plains in 1876, the situation was far from settled. The final act would include an unlikely combination of setting one minority against another in the form of African American soldiers in pursuit of Geronimo.

The Buffalo Soldiers

In 1866 and 1867, an act of Congress created four regiments of black soldiers: the 9th and 10th Cavalry and the 24th and 25th Infantry. In light of post–Civil War attitudes, they were stationed only in the West and served

FACING: Known as the Buffalo Soldiers, African American soldiers of the 9th and 10th Cavalry served with pride, as shown in this reenactment at Fort Verde State Park.

ABOVE: *A solid bond developed between the calvarymen and their horses.*

BELOW: *Sometimes Buffalo Soldiers owed their lives to their horses.*

ABOVE: *Many black soldiers made a career out of the military.*

FACING: *Geronimo and Cochise's son Naiche at Fort Bowie after their final surrender. Courtesy of the Gila County Historical Society.*

under white officers, with the exception of Lieutenant Henry O. Flipper, the first black West Point graduate. Native Americans gave them the name Buffalo Soldiers because of their courage, or perhaps their curly hair reminded them of buffalo. Whatever the reason, the term was used with respect and honor.

Stationed in Kansas, the Great Plains, Texas, and New Mexico in the 1870s, the Buffalo Soldiers didn't arrive in Arizona until the 1880s. After extensive breakouts from the Arizona reservations in 1881–82, General Crook was recalled to Arizona. In 1885, as the Indian situation cooled in Texas and New Mexico, the 10th Cavalry was sent to several Arizona forts. The 10th Cavalry took a major role in pursuing Geronimo and his followers through the rugged mountains of southern Arizona and northern Mexico for several years. Thirteen enlisted men and six officers from the four African American regiments earned the Medal of Honor during the Indian Wars. They were cited for coolness, bravery, and good marksmanship in pursuit of the Apaches. After Geronimo's surrender, the Buffalo Soldiers served under General John "Black Jack" Pershing in the Spanish-American War next to Teddy Roosevelt's Rough Riders. They chased Pancho Villa's rebel army just before World War I and saw action in the Battle of Nogales, where U.S. troops fired on Mexican rebels across the international border. The Buffalo Soldiers were stationed in southern Arizona into the 1920s, and many of them remained in the state after their service in the military. But the Buffalo Soldiers' most important, and underappreciated, contribution to Arizona history was their role in the final chapter in the Apache conflicts.

Family over Freedom: Geronimo's Decision

Although most of Arizona's indigenous peoples were put on reservations by 1874, conditions and control issues left a lot to be desired. In June 1881, a medicine man named Nochaydelklinne developed a new spiritual practice known by outsiders as the "ghost dance." Instead of inciting his people to fight Anglos, as many leaders had in the past, his plan to save Apache culture was based on resurrection. Instead of urging his people to resist,

Nochaydelklinne created a special dance that he said would bring back dead Apache warriors to drive out the whites. The medicine man held secret meetings away from the reservation headquarters, exciting the Indians in a way that reminded one officer of revival meetings. Concerned about the situation, Colonel Eugene Asa Carr sent two Apache scouts to a place called Cibecue Creek, about 46 miles west of the White Mountain Apache Reservation headquarters. When the soldiers didn't come back after six days, Colonel Carr took about 80 soldiers, six officers, and two dozen scouts on the march to see what happened. The soldiers reached the medicine man's camp on August 30, 1881.

Agent J. C. Tiffany, already noted for corrupt practices that contributed to the Apache misery of disease and starvation, requested that additional troops be assigned to the reservation because so many Apaches were sneaking off to attend the dances. Nochaydelklinne was arrested and taken to the soldiers' camp, where Indians crowded around them, and someone fired a shot. Several soldiers were killed instantly, and the U.S. Army retaliated by killing Nochaydelklinne.

At this point, the Apache scouts mutinied and began firing on the army troops. The battle lasted until dark. Juh, Geronimo, and Lozen took part. When it was over, six soldiers and one officer lay dead, as well as 18 Apaches, including six scouts. Outnumbered, Colonel Carr led a retreat to Fort Apache. On September 1, the Apaches attacked Fort Apache from two sides. The battle at Cibecue and the attack on Fort Apache were the last pitched battles between soldiers and Indians in Arizona.

Fearing punishment for the incident, Geronimo, Naiche, and Juh fled the reservation on September 30. Nana joined them in Mexico, and they numbered in the hundreds, the largest band of Apaches at large since Cochise's followers 10 years earlier. For the next five years, Geronimo's breakouts from the reservation and raids in Arizona and old Mexico gained him the reputation of the most dangerous Indian who ever lived. According to the newspapers, Geronimo's path was marked by atrocities throughout southern Arizona.

In response, President Chester A. Arthur called for General Crook's return to Fort Apache in September 1882. General Crook understood the Apache situation and claimed that 99 percent of the trouble stemmed from corrupt agents and traders. While his job was to beat the

Camillus S. Fly took this famous photograph of Geronimo and General Crook at Canyon de los Embudos in March 1886. Courtesy of the Arizona Historical Society (78165).

COPYRIGHT
1886 by C. S. FLY
Tombstone Ariz

This photo by C. S. Fly shows Geronimo (right) and part of his band at Canyon de Los Embudos. Courtesy of the Arizona Historical Society (78153).

Apaches into submission, he praised his opponents' acuteness of sense, perfect physical condition, keen knowledge of the territory, and superb abilities of self-protection. "We have before us the tiger of the human species," Crook said. Of their enemy commander, whom they called *Nantan Lupan,* or "Gray Wolf," Nana said, "He was an enemy, yes, but he was an honorable enemy. His promise was good; his understanding of the Apaches was fair."

In March, Chatto and his men crossed the border and raided into the United States, killing several settlers and capturing a six-year-old boy named Charlie McComas. Young Charlie became a rallying point, and Crook used the raid as justification for pursuit. His soldiers and scouts crossed the border into Mexico in May 1883. By this time, some of the Chiricahuas who did not think it wise to leave the reservation had joined the Apache scouts, making it that much easier to know where Geronimo would go.

Lieutenant Charles Gatewood, Captain Emmet Crawford, civilian scout Al Sieber, Mickey Free (the captive boy of the Bascom Affair more than two decades earlier), and Captain John Bourke—all prominent figures in the Apache conflicts—were involved in this campaign to return all Apaches to the reservation. Soldiers attacked a small group of Apaches, killing nine and capturing others. With help from Apache guides, General Crook managed to gain access to the hidden fortress of Geronimo and his co-leader and brother-in-law, Juh (pronounced variously *who, ho,* or *huh*).

The Apaches were alarmed that the troops had tracked them to Juh's stronghold, indicating that they could no longer hide, even in the mountain wilderness. Crook told the Apaches that the Mexican Army was closing in on all sides, which convinced the Apaches to return to the San Carlos Reservation. As several historians have pointed out, Geronimo chose "family over freedom" and eventually surrendered in May 1884.

The situation had not improved on the reservation, however. Apaches were banned from making *tizwin* and jailed for beating their wives—restrictions that they did not feel were part of the surrender terms. At the same time, Geronimo had heard from soldiers and Apaches alike that he was going to be jailed and hanged for his killings. Finally, after a short stay, Geronimo, Nana, Naiche, Chihuahua, Mangas, Lozen, 42 warriors, and 100 Apache women and children left the reservation in the middle of the night. According to reports, they killed 17 whites on their way to the Mexican border and stole 150 horses.

Mass hysteria broke out among Arizona settlers for the next 15 months. The army went into the field in full pursuit, astounding Geronimo at their ability to catch up and stay close on his tail, no matter how far up into the Sierra Madres they went. The Chiricahua Apache scouts had a lot to do with that situation. Finally, on March 24, 1886, Geronimo met with General Crook at Canyon de los Embudos. According to witnesses, Geronimo told Crook: "I give myself up to you. Do with me what you please. I surrender. Once I moved about like the wind. Now I surrender to you and that is all."

But it was not over yet. The night after the negotiations, a whisky dealer made his way to Geronimo's camp and sold the Apaches alcohol. While they were drinking, the bootlegger told them they would all be hanged if they surrendered. The next night, the Apaches got drunk again. Geronimo and several dozen followers sneaked away in the middle of a rainstorm. Later, when General Crook asked them why they drank, Naiche replied, "Because there was a lot of whiskey, and we wanted a drink."

Crook returned to Fort Bowie with a majority of the Apaches but learned that the previous terms allowing the Apaches to return to Arizona after two years confinement elsewhere were rescinded by President Grover Cleveland. Once in government hands, the Chiricahuas would never be allowed to return to their homeland. General Crook resigned in frustration and protest, and General Nelson A. Miles was sent to replace him.

General Miles did not believe in the use of Apache Scouts, even though it had proven successful for Crook. Instead, Miles received 2,000 additional troops, making the total 5,000—approximately one quarter of the total U.S. forces, set to bring in less than fifty Indians. In the next four months, U.S. soldiers traveled more than 3,000 miles across southern Arizona and northern Mexico. They experimented with a mountaintop mirror communication system called a heliograph, but not one Apache was brought in. In addition, there were now at least 3,000 Mexican troops guarding every water hole and ranch along the border.

Finally in mid-July, General Miles sent experienced campaigner Lieutenant Charles Gatewood and his Apache scouts back into the field. A month later, Gatewood sat in Geronimo's camp smoking tobacco with him. Gatewood explained that all the Chiricahuas must surrender and allow themselves to be sent to Florida or every one of them would be tracked down and killed.

On September 4, General Miles met with Geronimo at Skeleton Canyon, in the southeastern corner of Arizona. After the surrender, all the Chiricahuas, including those still on the reservation and even the Apache scouts, were sent east. The women and children were sent to Fort Marion, near St. Augustine, while the men were sent to Fort Pickens, an island off of Pensacola.

From there they were all sent to Mt. Vernon, Alabama, and eventually to Fort Sill, Oklahoma. Geronimo was given some freedom to travel and even rode in President Theodore Roosevelt's inaugural parade, but he died a prisoner at Fort Sill in 1909. More than 100 Chiricahua and Warm Springs Apaches chose to join the Mescalero Apaches on their reservation in New Mexico when the government gave them the option in 1912. The majority chose to stay at Fort Sill, where many descendents still live today.

Indian Boarding Schools

Geronimo's surrender ended two centuries of Native American conflicts in the United States, with exceptions such as Wounded Knee or the Apache Kid. In the meantime, the rest of the nation had moved on to a government-sponsored program of assimilation through education. Although missionaries and charities had taught Indians to read and write on a small scale since colonial times, it was not until 1879 that it was carried out on a national level.

Lieutenant Richard Henry Pratt, an officer in charge of the 10th Cavalry Buffalo Soldiers in the Indian Territory, began teaching English to Indian captives at Fort Marion, near Saint Augustine, Florida. Pratt was convinced that eliminating the cultural traditions and training them in vocations so that they could merge with white society was preferable to the starvation and disease he witnessed on the reservations.

In addition to Quaker and other missionary support, Pratt received federal funds to create the Carlisle Indian Industrial School in 1879. There he cut the students' hair short, made them wear uniforms, and punished them for speaking their native languages. Pratt's famous quote epitomized his philosophy: "You have to kill the Indian to save the man."

Within a few years the Bureau of Indian Affairs had established a number of schools throughout the West. They used Carlisle as their model and were usually led by missionaries.

Indian schools in Phoenix, Tucson, and Holbrook were mandatory for Arizona Indian tribes. Many families hid their children when educational staff came to take them to school. In some cases, students were not allowed to return to their families for several years.

BELOW: Indian schools, like this one in Tucson, were run like military academies, with discipline and uniforms. Courtesy of the Arizona Historical Society (19822).

FACING BELOW: Boys were taught carpentry and blacksmithing, while girls learned to be maids or seamstresses at Tucson Indian School. Courtesy of the Pinal County Historical Society.

Navajo Thomas Torlino before entering Carlisle Indian School in Carlisle, Pennsylvania. Courtesy of the Arizona Historical Society (19831).

Torlino after his arrival at Carlisle. Courtesy of the Arizona Historical Society (19830).

Indian boarding schools, like the Theodore Roosevelt Indian Boarding School at Fort Apache, became mandatory for all Arizona Indians. Courtesy of the Graham County Historical Society.

Reports of physical, mental, and sexual abuse at the school were widespread. Both Native American and Anglo writers have discussed the problems of students returning to the reservation after many years of boarding school, angry, alienated, and not able to fit in with either culture.

The Arizona schools paralleled those outlined in *The Phoenix Indian School: Forced Assimilation in Arizona, 1891–1935*, where Professor Robert A. Trennert states that lack of funds meant students had to sew uniforms, do laundry, cook, and do the menial labor for the schools in addition to their studies. Many ran away from the drudgery, and even those who stayed returned to their reservations when they finished school.

In 1889, Indian Commissioner Thomas J. Morgan wrote that "the Indians must conform to 'the white man's ways,' peaceably if they will, forcibly if they must." Arizona's Indian boarding schools continued to operate into the late 1980s, when they were replaced by high schools built on the reservations.

THE ARIZONA ROUGH RIDERS

Throughout Arizona history, events occurring hundreds and sometimes thousands of miles away had significant influence on the state's future. Tension between the United States and Spain over Cuban independence was a prime example.

The rise of "yellow journalism" in the late nineteenth century, and its emphasis on sensationalism to sell newspapers, prompted the famous quote supposedly stemming from a reply to a telegram from famed western illustrator Frederic Remington. When Remington cabled William Randolph Hearst, publisher of the *New York Morning Journal*, stating: "There is no war. Request to be recalled," Hearst shot back, "Please remain. You furnish the pictures, I'll furnish the war."

Then, after the mysterious explosion of the USS *Maine* in Havana harbor, outraged citizens demanded a declaration of war, and Arizonans of all ages and walks of life—cowboys, miners, railroad men, lawmen, veterans, and even local businessmen rushed to enlist. Congress declared war on Spain on April 24, 1898. Immediately, President William McKinley called for the formation of The First U.S. Volunteer Cavalry Regiment to be enlisted from the western territories of Arizona, New Mexico, Oklahoma, and the Indian Territory (now part of Oklahoma). McKinley called for 1,250 volunteers and appointed his physician, Dr. Leonard Wood, to lead the regiment because of his experience in the Arizona Indian conflicts. Secretary of the Navy Theodore Roosevelt, Wood's close friend, resigned his post to become second in command.

Since leading Arizona citizens Alexander Brodie, Buckey O'Neill, and James McClintock had been recruiting for several months prior to the declaration of war, the task took no time at all. In 10 days, the Arizona volunteers were on a train headed for San Antonio, Texas. The volunteers from the territories were a diverse bunch of men consisting of cowboys, prospectors, Native Americans, and even some of Roosevelt's Ivy League college friends. Most of the men were experienced horsemen, so newspaper reporters soon nicknamed the regiment the "Rough Riders," a popular phrase most likely taken from "Buffalo Bill's Wild West and Congress of Rough Riders of the World."

After six weeks' training at San Antonio, the Rough

Theodore Roosevelt (1st row, 3rd from right), the Rough Riders, and their mountain lion mascot, Josephine, in San Antonio, Texas. Courtesy of the Charles Herner Collection.

BELOW: *Not all the Rough Riders were cowboys, nor were they all young. Courtesy of the Charles Herner Collection.*

FACING ABOVE: *Only 18 years old at the time of his enlistment in the Spanish-American War, Arthur Tuttle was interviewed in 1960. Courtesy of the Charles Herner Collection.*

FACING BELOW: *Territorial volunteers thought they might achieve statehood by fighting in the Spanish-American War, as depicted in this Tucson float. Courtesy of the Arizona Historical Society (13363).*

another assault on the heights and overtook the Spanish positions. Roosevelt called this his "crowded hour." After the capture of San Juan Heights, the city of Santiago surrendered and Spain relinquished Cuba on July 17.

The toll from yellow fever, dysentery, and malaria were much worse than the losses in battle. Historian Virgil Carrington Jones stated that "In the period of about four and a half months they were together, 37 percent of those who got to Cuba were casualties. Better than one out of every three were killed, wounded, or stricken by disease. It was the highest casualty rate of any American unit that took part in the Spanish-American War campaign." Many who managed to return to Arizona suffered from poor health to the end of their lives.

The Rough Riders were then sent to Montauk Point, New York, to recover. In his memoirs, Roosevelt said, "it marked the close of the four months life of a regiment of as gallant fighters as ever wore the United States uniform."

In 1901, when anarchist Leon Czolgosz assassinated President William McKinley and when Vice President Theodore Roosevelt moved into the White House, Arizona was not ignored. Since the arrival of the railroad, however, Arizona was getting a lot more attention, not for Geronimo or Tombstone, but for its major export—copper.

Riders were sent to Tampa, Florida. Hasty preparations and not enough transportation caused more than two-thirds of the troops to be left behind, along with almost all the mules and horses. Since the Arizona troops had arrived first at San Antonio, they had first priority for boarding, thus becoming the majority who saw action in Cuba.

The Rough Riders were landed at Daiquiri, Cuba, on June 22, and saw their first action in the Battle of Las Guasimas on June 24. The heavy jungle made it difficult to fight the better-trained and better-armed Spaniards, but American forces prevailed. Nine Rough Riders were killed and 11 wounded. Captain Buckey O'Neill, well-known Arizona newspaperman, lawman, and mayor of Prescott, was struck in the neck by a Spanish bullet and died at this battle.

On July 1, 1898, Theodore Roosevelt, on horseback, led the Rough Riders, on foot, up Kettle Hill with the support of the regular 9th and 10th Cavalry's Buffalo Soldiers. After reaching the summit, heavy enemy fire forced them to take cover, but the Americans rallied for

THE COPPER ERA

Mining has been important in Arizona ever since the Europeans first arrived, but copper was not always the leading product. Even though Antonio Espejo reported rich deposits in the Jerome area in 1583, a number of events had to occur before copper became one of the traditional five Cs (along with cotton, cattle, climate, and citrus). In 1854, the Arizona Mining and Trading Company worked copper veins in the Ajo area, but it was too costly to ship the ore across the sea to Swansea, Wales, for smelting. When the richest red ore ran out, the company folded.

But Arizona is one of the richest copper regions in North America, and miners kept trying to make it pay. In 1864, Henry Clifton found copper along the Gila River in what is now eastern Arizona, but this Apache homeland was too dangerous to mine. In 1873, James and Robert Metcalf began mining copper in the same area, backed

RIGHT: Bisbee prospector George Warren's likeness is on the Arizona State Seal. Courtesy of the Arizona Historical Society (B8438).

BELOW: Minerals were discovered by prospectors, then corporations like the United Eastern Plant in Oatman began processing and smelter operations. Courtesy of the Mohave County Historical Society.

FACING: Rich in gold deposits, the area around Oatman boomed into the 1920s. Courtesy of the Mohave County Historical Society.

UNITED EASTERN PLANT
OATMAN ARIZ.

by the Lezinsky brothers, Henry and Charles, whose New Mexico–based company hired Mexicans because of their expertise in smelting the ore. They shipped their ore to Kansas City in long trains of freight wagons, fighting Apaches along the way.

Then in the 1880s, local and global developments came together and crowned copper king. First, and perhaps most important, the steam locomotive, telegraph, electric lights, and telephone ushered in the Age of Industry. Before that, copper was used for pots and jewelry, and it had to be high grade. Now, medium-grade copper could not be mined fast enough to meet demands.

RIGHT: The train room at the Clemenceau Museum depicts several operations: giant steam shovels dug ore from open pit mines and loaded it onto railroad cars.

BELOW: Seven different railroad lines were used in the Jerome and Verde Valley areas to haul the oar.

FACING: Even in the automobile age, burros remained the leading form of off-road transportation near Oatman. Courtesy of the Mohave County Historical Society.

By the early 1880s, railroads brought in heavy smelting equipment and shipped out heavy copper ingots with ease. The timing of increased need and better transportation could not have been better for Arizona mining.

On top of all that, the threat of Indian raids was eliminated by the 1880s, mainly because most were on reservations but also because it was harder to attack a train than a long, slow, string of freight wagons.

As silver played out, copper mining boomed in several areas, from Jerome to Globe in the central regions, Clifton and Morenci on the eastern edge, Kingman to the north, all the way to Ajo in Arizona's southwest corner.

Close to the Mexican border in eastern Arizona, Lieutenant J. A. Rucker and government scout Jack Dunn found gold and silver in Mule Gulch, where the boomtown of Bisbee is today. Busy on government business, they grubstaked a prospector named George Warren to do the work necessary and file their claims.

Warren, like many others on the frontier, had a penchant for whiskey and conveniently forgot to include his partners' names on the claims. He became rich for a short time, but lost it all when he bet everything that he could outrun a horse in a 200-yard footrace. Warren was not lost to history, however; a sketch was created from a photograph of him in his prospector's gear, and a highly

BELOW: Roberts Ranch *(July 1900), by Maynard Dixon. Courtesy of Mark Sublette, Medicine Man Gallery, Tucson, Arizona.*

BELOW LEFT: *These pre-1920 automobiles in Gold Road took executives and investors to the rich gold mines. Courtesy of the Mohave County Historical Society.*

BELOW RIGHT: *Oatman epitomizes Arizona's turbulent mineral-producing past. Courtesy of the Mohave County Historical Society.*

RIGHT: *Mining towns like Morenci were a conglomeration of stately buildings, shacks, and tents. Courtesy of the Phoenix Public Library.*

FACING BELOW RIGHT: *Route 66 went through Oatman, but when the gold diminished, it almost became a ghost town. Courtesy of the Mohave County Historical Society.*

ABOVE: *One man's treasure . . . Courtesy of the Mohave County Historical Society.*

FACING ABOVE: *Mexican miners, such as these at Clifton, experienced discrimination in pay and promotions. Courtesy of the Graham County Historical Society.*

FACING BELOW: *Gold promoters and a Native American are pictured in this Oatman juxtaposition. Courtesy of the Mohave County Historical Society.*

stylized version still graces the official Arizona State Seal.

The era of big business coincided with Arizona's copper boom, and refining plant manager "Rawhide Jimmy" Douglas recommended the Bisbee claims to the well-established Phelps-Dodge Company, which became one of the leading mining corporations in the state for many decades. In the private sector, mining magnate William Clark bought out major claims in Jerome, founded the United Verde mine, and became the richest mine owner in the world. Big mines took root in almost every area except the Grand Canyon, becoming a major part of Arizona's economy for the next hundred years.

ABOVE: *Smelter smoke in Clarkdale drifted all across the state in the boom years. Courtesy of the Verde Historical Society.*

BELOW: *Seven smokestacks meant large mineral production in the Globe-Miami mines. Courtesy of the Gila County Historical Society.*

RIGHT: *In the 1920s and '30s, the Clarkdale smelter ran shifts around the clock. Courtesy of the Verde Historical Society.*

LEFT: *Jerome is now an artist haven and tourist attraction. Courtesy of Dori Griffin.*

BELOW: *Many buildings in Jerome lost the battle with gravity and slid down the mountain. Courtesy of Dori Griffin.*

The Copper Collar

No phrase better describes the labor conflicts in Arizona's copper mines than Professor James Byrkit's book title, *Forging the Copper Collar*. At first, skilled hard rock miners were brought in from the mines in Scotland, Ireland, and Wales. Most plentiful and notable, however, were the "Cousin Jacks," the men from Cornwall.

Hard rock mining was grueling dangerous work. Men worked 10-hour days deep underground in dark and dank tunnels, sometimes going home just long enough to warm a bed before being called back during a shift change. Hands and feet were crushed with hammers and other equipment, and men were crippled or killed by falling rocks and explosions. Those who survived the obvious dangers often succumbed to silicosis, or "brown lung," the effect of inhaling too much dust over many years in the shafts. The mining companies offered little

BELOW: All miners, including these from Bisbee, worked under grueling, dangerous conditions. Courtesy of the Mohave County Historical Society.

RIGHT: Standardized signal bells for mine shaft hoists promoted safety.

ARIZONA STATE CODE OF MINE BELL
SIGNALS
1 BELL STOP IMMEDIATELY IF IN MOTION.
1 " HOIST MUCK.
1 " RELEASE CAGE. SKIP OR BUCKET.
2 BELLS LOWER.
3-1 " HOIST MEN. IF BELLS RUNG SLOWLY
3-2 " LOWER MEN. MOVE SLOWLY.
4 " STEAM ON OR OFF.
5 " BLASTING OR READY TO SHOOT.
THIS IS A CAUTION SIGNAL AND IF THE ENGINEER IS PREPARED TO ACCEPT IT HE MUST ACKNOWLEDGE BY RAISING BUCKET OR CAGE A FEW FEET THEN LOWERING IT AGAIN. AFTER ACCEPTING THIS SIGNAL ENGINEER MUST BE PREPARED TO HOIST MEN AWAY FROM BLAST AS SOON AS SIGNAL "1 BELL" IS GIVEN AND MUST ACCEPT NO OTHER SIGNAL IN THE MEANTIME.
6 BELLS AIR ON OR OFF.
7 " DANGER SIGNAL. FOLLOWED
BY STATION SIGNAL CALLS CAGE TO THAT STATION THIS SIGNAL TAKES PRECEDENCE OVER ALL OTHERS EXCEPT AN ACCEPTED BLASTING SIGNAL.

STATION SIGNALS
1-2 BELLS. COLLAR OF SHAFT.
1-3 BELLS. 1ST LEVEL		4-5 BELLS. 13TH LEVEL	
1-4 " 2D "		5-1 " 14TH "
1-5 " 3D "		5-2 " 15TH "
2-1 " 4TH "		5-3 " 16TH "
2-2 " 5TH "		5-4 " 17TH "
2-3 " 6TH "		5-5 " 18TH "
2-4 " 7TH "		6-1 " 19TH "
2-5 " 8TH "		6-2 " 20TH "
4-1 " 9TH "		6-3 " 21ST "
4-2 " 10TH "		6-4 " 22D "
4-3 " 11TH "		6-5 " 23D "
4-4 " 12TH "		7-1 " 24TH "

STATION SIGNAL MUST BE GIVEN BEFORE HOISTING OR LOWERING SIGNAL - THE ENGINEER SHALL NOT MOVE A CAGE SKIP OR BUCKET UNLESS HE UNDERSTANDS THE SIGNAL - ONE COPY OF THIS SIGNAL CODE SHALL BE POSTED ON THE GALLOWS FRAME, ONE AT EACH STATION & ONE BEFORE THE ENGINEER
G.H. BOLL MINE INSPECTOR

106

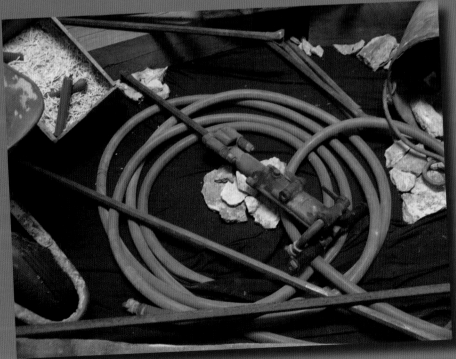

ABOVE: *Miners, like these in Globe, worked together as a team to keep each other safe. Courtesy of the Mohave County Historical Society.*

LEFT: *Once pneumatic drills, like this one shown in the exhibit at the Bullion Plaza Cultural Center and Museum in Miami, replaced hand drills, expert miners from Cornwall and Wales could be replaced by unskilled immigrants.*

FACING ABOVE: *There were many more miners in Globe and in Arizona in the 1880s than there were cowboys. Courtesy of the Gila County Historical Society.*

FACING BELOW: *Miners were a rough bunch who took pride in their work, as did these in Globe. Courtesy of the Gila County Historical Society.*

or no disability programs for the victims of a tough existence. Yet for the most part, miners seemed to be proud of the work they did and gave it up only when they could no longer keep up the pace.

After the invention of the pneumatic drill, less skilled miners could be brought in from countries where the economic or political situation was so bad that immigrating to America was their only hope of improving their lives. Men from Italy, Spain, Serbia, Montenegro, and Bohemia began to arrive, bringing their culture, lifestyle, accents, and clothing with them. In Arizona's mines more than anywhere else, the myth of the Wild West populated by John Wayne types with cowboy hats and Texas drawls could not have been farther from the truth.

Mexicans worked in the mines as well but were usually paid less and were not given skilled jobs that paid better. As labor strikes erupted for better working conditions, better pay, and shorter hours, the age-old divide-and-conquer strategy played Mexican laborers against Anglos to break the strikes.

The strikes began almost as soon as the big companies moved in, first in Tombstone, then in Globe, Bisbee, and Morenci, and just about anywhere there was a significant labor population. The mining boom coincided with the unionization movement all across America, and the Western Federation of Miners often stepped in to support local strikers.

The Bisbee Deportation of 1917

As unions grew and got stronger, mining corporations pushed back. Angry threats led to violence on both sides, and similar to the Apache conflicts, a cycle of fear and vengeance escalated. The unions began with strikes; the mine owners countered with strikebreakers, men who replaced the miners at their jobs. The striking miners

The Bisbee deportation in July 1917 was the largest and most publicized of several. Courtesy of the Arizona Historical Society.

often threatened or attacked the strikebreakers to prevent them from getting to work, at which point the owners brought in law enforcement in the form of company guards, local police, state militia, or federal troops.

The final strategy on the side of management was to round up the miners and force them out of the area so that the strikebreakers could work without fear of violence. These deportations sometimes proved to be an effective method to settle the labor disputes.

Early in the morning on July 12, 1917, nearly 2,000 law enforcement officials and vigilantes rounded up more than 1,200 striking miners connected with the radical Industrial Workers of the World (IWW). They loaded them into cattle cars and shipped them without food or water across the border into New Mexico, where they unloaded them 16 hours later on a remote railroad siding known as Hermanas. There were deportations in other Arizona mining towns before this one, but the numbers of men involved in Bisbee brought national attention. It influenced the labor movement throughout the United States in a time of war, when disruption of production could be labeled as treasonous.

Mining continued to be an important part of Arizona's economy, but the radical period of union building subsided after the war hysteria. The mines as well as the unions continued to grow in the next five decades, fraught with strikes, layoffs, and shutdowns, but nothing as drastic as the deportations ever happened again. Lawmen still had their hands full though, and more than its share of trouble.

THE ARIZONA RANGERS

Since Daniel Boone headed for Kentucky, pioneers found freedom and opportunity on the frontier, but it also attracted outlaws seeking to ply their trade where there was less law to get in their way. As civilization advanced it drove the criminals farther west, but when California finally got organized, their outlaws headed for Arizona as

well. The state with the least population and closest to the border seemed a natural choice for wrongdoers.

But in 1901, Governor Nathan O. Murphy created the Arizona Rangers and seriously reduced the problem. Hashknife Ranch manager Burton C. Mossman was appointed captain and he chose a sergeant and 12 men to fill out the company, including veteran Arizona Rough Riders, lawmen, and qualified citizens. It is said that some of their past records did not read like Sunday school honor rolls. The Rangers reported directly to the governor instead of federal or county authorities, so they were less susceptible to the federal/county/local lawman squabbles that reached their climax in Tombstone after the famous gunfight.

To some, the Rangers were a trained and well-equipped task force that traveled fast and struck without warning. Others saw them as rowdy, power-wielding bullies able to bend the law to make the ends justify the means. It was believed the Rangers may have killed a number of outlaws "trying to escape," thus avoiding the trouble of bringing them in or experiencing failed convictions.

Regardless of public opinion, the Rangers convicted or extradited more than 125 outlaws in their first year, a record that drove many more outlaws across the border. By 1903, the force expanded to 26 men. The Rangers were only in the field for eight years, but were extremely effective in ridding the state of countless outlaws and driving many more south of the border.

The Rangers were a little too effective in some ways. Their ruthless and extralegal reputation led in part to their demise. With the possibility of statehood drawing near, the governor and other leaders could not afford to have the state labeled as a land where lawlessness and frontier justice still prevailed. They did their job in a short time, and were no longer needed as Arizona moved into the twentieth century as businessmen and upstanding citizens, shedding the Wild West image as the population boomed.

STATEHOOD AT LAST

Through a combination of Mormon settlements and other farmers along the Gila and Salt Rivers, Texas cowboys, and foreign miners, Arizona's population exploded in the three decades from the arrival of the railroad to statehood, from 9,600 in the 1870 census to 40,000 in 1880, 88,000 in 1890, and 122,000 in 1900; then it almost double again to make it 204,000 reported in the 1910 census. No state could have grown faster; Arizona was making up for lost time.

In the early 1900s, Arizona politics were overwhelmingly Democratic, with the Mormon settlers and Texas cowboys often bristling under Republican federal appointees as governor and other high offices. The majority chafed at the favoritism shown to the large eastern mining corporations and the railroads.

In an era of Big Business, Arizona's economy focused on copper, cattle, and the railroads that shipped them to eastern markets. Controlled by eastern monopolies and trusts, the miners felt the federal government always came down on the side of business when it came to labor strikes. The rest of Arizona felt the sting because the mining companies and railroads paid little or no taxes, extracting vast mineral wealth and freight profits but returning little to improve the territory.

ABOVE: Governor George W. P. Hunt, a Globe storeowner, helped laborers and mine owners compromise. Courtesy of the Gila County Historical Society.

FACING: The 1901 Arizona Territorial Capitol became the State Capitol on February 14, 1912. Courtesy of the Phoenix Public Library.

After President William McKinley's assassination in 1901, the more progressive Theodore Roosevelt took charge of the White House. His attitude toward trust-busting, anti-monopoly legislation, and pro-labor laws swung the federal pendulum from big business to labor, spotlighting social conscience and support for farmers and the working class. Roosevelt's appointment of former Rough Rider officer Alexander Brodie as territorial governor in 1902 and Joseph H. Kibbey in 1905 disrupted corporation control of the territory and paved the way for a progressive constitution. For the century's first fifteen years, Arizona had one of the most progressive governments of any state or territory. When President William Howard Taft shifted the country back to conservative status, he replaced Governor Kibbey with the more conservative Richard Sloan in 1909.

But miners, farmers, and working-class Arizonans won the Democratic majority for the Arizona legislature in 1908 and felt the time was right to push for statehood. The public sought popular sovereignty, equal suffrage, direct election of senators, public defenders, and a ban on injunctions against strikers. The miners in Bisbee even formed a separate Labor Party, but Globe politician George W. P. Hunt advised the Democrats to adopt planks in the platform favorable to labor lest they split the vote and hand the election to the Republicans.

When permission to create a constitutional convention in preparation for statehood was granted, the election of delegates to that body leaned overwhelmingly toward liberal candidates. They were considered radical for endorsing the eight-hour day, women's suffrage, the right to picket, the recall of judges, work safety laws, and taxation of mining corporation profits.

Arizona's radical rumblings did not go unnoticed in Washington, D.C., however. In 1902, Republican Senator Albert Beveridge from Indiana, chairman of the Senate Committee on Territories, mounted a whirlwind tour of Arizona, bent on proving they were not ready for statehood. Beveridge found the seamy side of Arizona, ignoring orderly mining towns and upstanding farming communities in favor of back alley dregs around Tucson and Phoenix. He also kept a record of how many people did not speak English. Senator Beveridge concluded that "Arizona is a mining camp, and the bill admitting her is gerrymandered so shamefully that if the Republicans were to carry the state by ten thousand, she would still send two Democratic senators to Washington."

As a result of his tour, Beveridge proposed that the territories of New Mexico and Arizona be reunited as they had been prior to 1863 in a process called "jointure."

ABOVE: *The signers of the Arizona State Constitution in front of the Capitol. Courtesy of the Phoenix Public Library.*

FACING: *Crowds like this one in front of the Capitol gathered to celebrate statehood—at last! Courtesy of the Phoenix Public Library.*

Arizona was overwhelmingly against the idea, knowing that the big state would favor the Republicans. Adamant Arizonans claimed they'd rather have no statehood at all rather than jointure. When it came to a vote in 1906, 80 percent of Arizonans voted against it.

Finally, President Taft made a more favorable visit to Arizona in 1909 and admitted that he favored separate states. But Taft did warn Arizonans that writing a radical constitution might jeopardize their chances for statehood. Congress finally passed an enabling act June 16, 1910, allowing Arizona to elect 52 delegates to draw up a state constitution. Arizonans celebrated the event with bonfires, parades, and firing old muskets and cannons.

Taft threatened to block statehood if Arizona came up with a radical constitution like that of Oklahoma, and his main peeve was the recall of judges, since he had held that office in the past. Taft said, "If you want to be certain that I'll veto your constitution, just go ahead and put judicial recall into it."

A Convention Meets in Phoenix

Given the task of creating a convention, political parties organized elections in each county to choose 52 delegates to represent every county in Arizona to draft the document. The Democrats and Republicans presented slates of candidates, with the Labor Party backing the Democrats instead of writing its own slate. The final tally was 41 Democratic delegates to only 11 Republicans. Almost everyone was surprised, but it was thought that the labor unions must have really gotten out the vote.

The group met in the House of Representatives in the State Capitol in Phoenix, and the Democrats chose George W. P. Hunt, successful Globe storekeeper and pro-mine-union politician, as president of the constitutional convention. What followed was 60 days of hard work and hot tempers. As the work came to an end on December 9, 1910, Hunt discovered that someone had stolen his gavel, an item soon to be of historic value. Ever the canny businessman, Hunt simply announced that no one would get paid for their work until the gavel was returned. It was mysteriously returned in no time.

The constitution was then presented to the citizens of Arizona, and they overwhelmingly approved it on February 9, 1911. The constitution produced in mid-December of 1910 was as progressive as the conservatives feared it would be, so much so that only one Republican delegate signed it. In addition to Taft's despised recall, the document also included initiative and referendum clauses that allowed citizens to introduce their own bill or to remove current laws by popular petition.

Even though Territorial Governor Sloan thought the proposed constitution made Arizona's bid for statehood "about as likely as being annexed into the Russian empire," the people loved it, as their overwhelming votes proved in 1911. After Congress reviewed the document, they sent it on to President Taft, who, as expected, sent the bill back to the Arizona constitutional convention members with orders to remove the offending initiative, referendum, and recall clauses.

Arizona's seasoned politicians did just that, knowing full well that once they gained the autonomy of statehood, they could amend the constitution to include them again. In "Ode to Billy Taft," *Florence Blade-Tribune* editor Thomas Weedin jibed:

> . . . as we joyously re-install,
> by the vote of one and all,
> that ever-glorious recall,
> Billy Taft, Billy Taft!

Statehood with all the Bells and Whistles

At long last, after years of frustration, statehood finally arrived. That Wednesday morning, February 14, 1912, felt like Christmas to many. Men, women, and children in every town, ranch, farm, and mining camp waited eagerly to hear that Arizona was finally one of the United States. At 10:30 a.m., President Taft signed the enabling act while motion picture cameras rolled. This was the first time such an event like this had been captured on film. A telegraph operator tapped out some rapid dots and dashes, the message buzzed along copper wires, and, in a matter of minutes, the nation knew Arizona was now a state. All over the state, messenger boys ran everywhere with the news.

Then the celebrations began! It was New Year's and the Fourth of July all rolled into one, no matter where you went. People fired pistols in the air and set off firecrackers. Every factory, mine, and lumber mill blew its steam whistles loud and shrill. Railroad men clanged their bells and tooted their train whistles. Schools and churches rang their bells, too. Arizona was filled with a joyful noise. In Bisbee, miners exploded a stack of 48 sticks of dynamite in one gigantic roar. In Globe, they fired a cannon 48 times to honor the 48th state. When Phoenix tried to carry out a similar 48-gun salute, it rattled the windows and scared the horses so badly that they had to stop after only 38 big booms.

Every community, big, or small, had some kind of festival, and people literally danced in the streets. In Prescott and other towns, fun-loving folks decorated their cars and buggies for a big parade. In lots of towns, bands played while school children and veterans from the Spanish-American War (maybe the Civil War too) marched happily along, rejoicing in Arizona's long-awaited statehood.

And people came from all over the state to fill the streets in front of the Capitol. The first governor of the state, George W. P. Hunt, walked 15 blocks from his hotel to the Capitol in order to carry out his campaign promises of bringing simplicity and economy to the government. By the time he reached the second-floor balcony of the Capitol, the nearly 300-pound man (who didn't mind the nickname "walrus") was sweating, even though the temperature was only in the 60s.

The blare of four trombones, the front rank of the Indian School Band, led off a huge parade. Spectators stood on building ledges and park benches, anyplace they could get a little height for a better view. Fifty young women on horseback from Phoenix Union High School wound up the parade. William Jennings Bryan said, "Isn't that a fitting rear guard, though?"

Bryan, three-time candidate for president of the United States, gave a two-hour speech, the kind known in those days as a stem-winder because you had plenty of time to wind your watch while he was talking.

At 8 p.m. the streets were roped off and people tried to dance to the music of the Indian School Band, but the crowd was too thick. Suddenly the crowd gave out a cheer when they heard 100 voices of the Phoenix Choral Society singing "The Star-Spangled Banner."

Valentine's Day 2012 will mark Arizona's statehood centennial; however, one century is a very short time compared to the perhaps 12,000 years that indigenous people have lived on these same lands. But no matter how you look at it, it is still something to commemorate.

WATERING THE DESERT

Since prehistoric times, communities grew where water was available. When cultures such as the Ancestral Puebloan and Hohokam disappeared from the archaeological record, scientists usually surmise that inadequate water supplies played a major factor in their demise.

Throughout the history of the state, the only thing more important than mining to Arizonans was water.

From the earliest prehistoric times, communities have always been near water. The Hohokam engineered hundreds of miles of canals to flow gradually away from the creek, river, or runoff; later, the Hopi, Navajo, Pima, Tohono O'odham, and many others developed intricate methods for farming with little water, sometimes using the ancient canals.

Water is so important that they named the state's largest city after the canals. Just as the mythical Egyptian phoenix bird reincarnated its life by setting itself on fire in a nest of cinnamon sticks, the town some settlers called "Pumpkinville" (for the abundance of wild gourds that grew in the canals) grew on top of an ancient Hohokam city by inhabitants scraping out the canals and creating an agricultural Eden.

The Spanish, too, knew how to farm with very little water, since southern Spain is temperate Mediterranean geography. Because water was scarce in southern Arizona, the Spanish pioneers developed an elaborate legal system to make sure everyone got their fair share. They formed *communes de agua* (water users associations) and appointed a *juez de agua* (water judge) to settle disputes, as well as a *zanjero* (canal master) to make sure the water was diverted into each private canal system in appropriate amounts.

When the Mormons arrived, they too had a communal system for water use. Their first settlements in far northern Arizona suffered from lack of water resources,

and when water did come, it was in such torrents that it washed out dams and flowed away before it could be put to use in the fields. The Mormons believed that God would reward their hard work and prayer with more water. Just as the railroads claimed that "the water follows the plow,"

The unpredictable Salt River wreaked havoc with the Hayden Ferry at Tempe. Courtesy of the Pinal County Historical Society.

Mormons believed that "water follows the prayer."

Unlike most pioneers, the Mormons settled on the Little Colorado River in northeastern Arizona because no one else would settle in such a remote and desolate location. For the Mormons, this was ideal. Like Salt Lake City, it was far away from nonbelievers and the sins of the cities. The first communities didn't make it because of extreme weather conditions; Mormons then moved to the White Mountains and also founded communities in Phoenix, Tempe, and Mesa in the late 1870s.

Arizona's agricultural industry boomed, thanks to the Theodore Roosevelt Dam. Courtesy of the Phoenix Public Library.

The Laws of Water

Just as the Spanish had laws governing water use, the United States realized that the vast arid lands west of the Mississippi called for new settlement laws. The main proponent of special treatment for western lands was Major John Wesley Powell, Grand Canyon explorer and one of the early administrators of the United States Geological Survey. Powell made a clear case that the current government policy toward government-assisted settlement, the Homestead Act of 1862, would not work in the arid West. The Homestead Act provided 160 acres of public land free to anyone who lived on the land for five years and made improvements on it each year.

Powell and others maintained that a western pioneer did not have enough water to make 160 acres produce enough to make a living. As a result, Congress passed the Desert Land Act of 1877. Designed to aid settlers in arid territories, the new act provided 640 acres to each settler, provided that he irrigate the land. This new act stirred a great deal of interest in irrigation methods, dams, and canals, all of which were not new to Arizona farmers.

Two of Arizona's five C's—cotton and citrus—depend on irrigation. From the beginning, irrigation methods were, for the most part, a community effort. Like the Spaniards before them, Mormon farmers created dams that served the whole community, as did many other farming communities. In many cases, partnerships were formed to create water companies.

The first and foremost in Phoenix was the company formed by Jack Swilling. In 1867, Swilling won the contract to supply hay for the livestock at Fort McDowell, which meant he would need large amounts of water for growing. Swilling raised $10,000, a very large sum for those times, from backers such as Henry Wickenburg, discoverer of the rich Vulture Mine, and Louis Jaeger, who made his fortune with the Colorado River ferry at Yuma. They organized the Swilling Irrigation and Canal Company and excavated more ancient canals than anyone else in the area. Several other joint-stock canal companies sprang up throughout Arizona in the 1870s and '80s.

Farmers purchased shares with cash or by working on the canals. Generally the users' association gave each stockholder enough to raise crops on 160 acres. The purchased shares also paid legal fees for water rights disputes between canal companies, since in lean years companies farthest from the river got little or no water after the older, larger companies had taken what they needed.

The main problem with water in Arizona was that it was either too much or too little, and it was always unpredictable. Rivers flooded after the spring snows thawed in nearby mountains and then dried up when the water was most needed. Farmers knew that dams would ensure a secure water supply, controlling the water and saving it for later use.

These early canal companies were so successful that in 10 years they increased the number of farming acres from 70,000 to 180,000 acres. Although this method worked in many cases, and private or joint-venture dams served their purpose, several of Arizona's rivers were too strong for small dams. In the Mormon communities in northeastern Arizona, dams on the Little Colorado washed out over and over again, and the settlers rebuilt stronger dams each time until the problem was finally solved.

The Salt River in Phoenix was the largest problem in the state, partially because the town's main focus was on agriculture, but also because the river was prone to severe flooding. It wreaked havoc on bridges, crops, and even settlers' homes. In 1889, the Phoenix Chamber of Commerce passed a resolution to create the Salt River Project, an act that single-handedly guaranteed that Phoenix would become the state's largest desert metropolis. At the same time as this resolution, a representative of the United States Senate Subcommittee on Irrigation was looking for a location to implement a brand new innovation in the reclamation of western waters.

A main proponent of federal support for water reclamation was championed by Major John Wesley Powell, who had begun to study the concepts of reclamation in 1888. By networking with like-minded leaders in other territories, Arizonans managed to bring the National Irrigation Congress to Phoenix in 1896. Journalist, lawman, and future Rough Rider Buckey O'Neill championed the cause of national irrigation support, and countless others took up the banner and preached national water reclamation across the country. Congressman Francis G. Newlands from Nevada introduced a bill to use the profits from public land sale money to construct dams. The concept wanted support by western railroads, who wanted to sell the lands the government gave them to build the railroads, and it would only be useful as farmland if there was enough water to keep the crops alive.

The people of Phoenix desperately needed government support for a huge dam, but they had to fight for the project. James McClintock, another Rough Rider and territorial governor, led the survey team that found the perfect spot where the Tonto Creek joined the Salt River east of Phoenix.

Arizona got the help they needed when Theodore Roosevelt became president. The leader of a liberal and progressive branch of the Republican Party, Roosevelt created many government agencies to oversee the nation's business, to make sure that partisan politics did not enter into vital projects. In 1902, the Bureau of Reclamation was formed to implement the use of federal funds to build dams bigger than any private entity could afford to pay for on its own.

Roosevelt Dam Changes Arizona

Next to the huge mineral deposits and the coming of the railroad, nothing affected Arizona's future more than the Theodore Roosevelt Dam. It was the first project to be completed under the Reclamation Act of 1902, also known as the Newlands Act, named after the bill's sponsor, Representative Francis G. Newlands of Nevada. The Reclamation Act set aside money from the sale of public lands in the arid states for the construction of irrigation projects. The dam was 357 feet high and took more than five years to complete. At that time, it was the world's largest masonry dam and, for a time, the largest artifi-

U.S. government the $10 million it cost to build the dam in 1955.

The ability to harness the Salt River Valley water supply led to the rapid expansion of the farm industry in central Arizona. When the Suez Canal was blockaded in World War I, cutting off the Egyptian cotton supply, Arizona became a leading cotton producer, and farm properties increased as much as 800 percent. More and more people came to Maricopa County to farm, and as a result, the 1920 census reported the population of Phoenix to be larger than Tucson for the first time.

ABOVE: *Water and power from the Theodore Roosevelt Dam created the modern state of Arizona. Courtesy of the Gila County Historical Society.*

FACING: *A fascinating sight for any state, massive amounts of water inspire Arizonans. Courtesy of Greg Davis.*

cial reservoir. Originally known as Salt River Dam #1, it was renamed after Theodore Roosevelt in 1959. The dam was also one of the first to generate hydroelectric power. In 1917, Salt River Valley Water Users Association, an independent corporation, took charge of the operation of dam and canals. The association repaid the

With an ample water supply and hydroelectric power, Arizona entered the modern era and left its Wild West past behind. In the decades to come, the state's problems and successes were much more like any other state in the nation, but it still had enough qualities to make Arizona's history one of a kind.

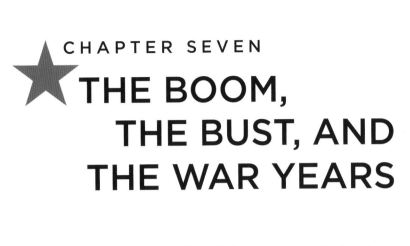

CHAPTER SEVEN

THE BOOM,
THE BUST, AND
THE WAR YEARS

New Deal measures, war installations, and war industries have given the West a far greater and more widely distributed prosperity than it has ever had before.

—Bernard De Voto, *Harper's Magazine,* 1946

From statehood to World War II, Arizona shed its traditional western ways and entered into the modern world of war, peace, and economic fluctuations like any other state in the Union. However, it held on to its unique qualities and revived its past so Easterners could experience the Old West. Arizonans went to war on the border, got rich on cotton, climate, and tourism, survived the Great Depression, and contributed to World War II victory in ways only the Grand Canyon State could manage.

BORDER WARFARE

Spain and Mexico have influenced Arizona in almost every decade since the conquistadors arrived in 1539. The turn of the nineteenth century was no different.

Pershing in Pursuit

Five years after the Mexican Revolution began in 1910, the United States recognized Venustiano Carranza's regime as the official government of Mexico. Pancho Villa felt betrayed by this decision and retaliated by attacking American property and U.S. citizens in northern Mexico. Sometime before dawn on March 9, 1916, Villa led a raid on Columbus, New Mexico, just three miles north of the international border. The Mexican troops killed eight U.S. 13th Cavalry Regiment soldiers, and 10 civilians, and wounded six soldiers and two civilians. More than 70 of Villa's men were killed on the raid or died later from their wounds.

In retaliation, the U.S. Army led what was officially called the Mexican Expedition but came to be known simply as the "Punitive Expedition."

Peace in October (1943), by Maynard Dixon. Courtesy of Mark Sublette, Medicine Man Gallery, Tucson, Arizona.

For several months, General John "Black Jack" Pershing and his troops pursued Villa across Mexico to no avail. As the United States began to prepare for entry into World War I, the Punitive Expedition was abandoned. The 10th Cavalry Buffalo Soldiers took part in Pershing's expedition, and the ruins of Camp Newell, where soldiers were stationed to protect the border near Naco, Arizona, are still visible today.

ABOVE: The Buffalo Soldiers organized into several Arizona military camps before pursuing Pancho Villa's ragtag rebel army in Nogales. Courtesy of the Arizona Historical Society (PC 180 f344 0199).

LEFT: General John Pershing dedicated the University of Arizona's World War I memorial fountain in Tucson. Courtesy of the Arizona Historical Society (19464).

FACING ABOVE LEFT: Although peaceful in this photo, Morley Avenue (on the American side of the border) was the focal point of the Battle of Nogales in 1918. Courtesy of the Phoenix Public Library.

FACING ABOVE RIGHT: An overhead view of the Nogales international border looking west, circa 1918. Courtesy of the Phoenix Public Library.

FACING BELOW: Women received the vote in Arizona in 1912 and rallied for national suffrage in 1916. Courtesy of the Arizona Historical Society (B32100a).

The Battle of Nogales

Warfare continued on the border, most significantly at the Battle of Ambos Nogales, the bloodiest fight involving U.S. troops in the Mexican Revolution. On the afternoon of August 27, 1918, a Mexican civilian did not stop at the U.S. Customs House when returning to Mexico, and shooting began on both sides of the border. The 35th U.S. Infantry and the 10th Cavalry Buffalo Soldiers took part in a four-hour struggle, and around 7:45 p.m., the Mexicans surrendered under a large white flag. Three American soldiers were killed and 29 wounded, while as many as 129 Mexicans were killed or wounded during the battle, including the mayor of Nogales. Although many stories claim involvement by German provocateurs, recent research does not substantiate the stories. Meanwhile, "over there" in France and Germany, Arizona men and boys served their country with courage and honor.

WORLD WAR I
Arizona Goes "Over There" . . .

Just like the Spanish-American War, when President Woodrow Wilson declared war on Germany on April 6, 1917, Arizonans were ready to do their part. Perhaps to quell public fears about his German background, University of Arizona president Rufus Von Kleinschmidt offered the campus as a military training camp, and that year, graduation at the University of Arizona was moved up so that men could enlist in May. More than 320 Arizonans died in the "War to End All Wars," and when it was over, General Pershing dedicated the fountain in front of Old Main to university students, staff, and faculty who gave their lives.

For the first time, Arizona's climate came in handy as veterans flocked to the hospital at Pastime Park in Tucson to recuperate from being gassed in the trenches and from tuberculosis. Ten years later, mercantile storeowner

Albert Steinfeld donated the land to build a beautiful new hospital on the south edge of Tucson. Still operating today, it was and is known as one of the best in the Veterans Affairs system.

The Cotton Boom

Two events combined during World War I to change Arizona's economy significantly, elevating cotton to the lead position of the five C's for several years. British protection of the Suez Canal as well as shipping dangers due to German U-boats led to serious restrictions on the amount of cotton coming out of Egypt. In addition, one of the prime needs for war production was cotton fabric in large quantities for use in tire treads.

Up to this point, citrus was one of the biggest crops in Arizona, but cotton took the lead overnight. For those who planted the "white gold," huge profits caused land values to increase 800 percent during the war, and the company town of Goodyear went into large-scale cotton farming. Land became so expensive that only cotton continued to bring a return. In 1916, only 7,300 acres were planted in cotton, but by 1919, that number increased to 82,000!

Thousands of workers were brought in from Mexico and lived in tent villages near the fields. Although Congress passed a strict Immigration Act of 1917 to increase national security, Arizona was given federal permission to create temporary admission program for farmworkers to help with the huge harvests. This special treatment continued as the Border Patrol was created in 1924. Farmers convinced the Patrol to curtail deportations until after the harvest season.

Approximately 72,000 Mexican workers entered Arizona legally under the new program, and an even larger number arrived without documentation. The larger cotton growers chipped in to send recruiters into Mexico and paid for trucks to bring the farmworkers to Arizona. The recruiters were called *enganchadores*, or hookers, since

Cotton became Arizona's major crop during World War I, shown here in Duncan. Courtesy of the Graham County Historical Society.

they hooked the workers into working in the United States. Getting paid by the number of workers they recruited, these men told the Mexicans they would make so much money that they would need a rake to pile it up, and that transportation back to Mexico would be provided.

As soon as they arrived, the workers saw they had been tricked. The cotton picking camp conditions were unfit even for animals. They lived in tents and drank unsanitary water from irrigation canals, and the camps had no showers, laundry, or electricity—not even outhouses. The workers' wages were immediately impounded for their travel costs, and because they were so far from towns, they had to buy everything from company stores at exorbitant rates, similar to situations described by John Steinbeck in *The Grapes of Wrath*.

Then, almost as fast as they had risen, cotton prices plummeted. Egyptian markets re-opened after the war, and war production surpluses caused an agricultural depression that lasted from the 1920s to the onset of World War II. Without notice, Mexican farmworkers were left stranded. They had no work and no means to get back to Mexico. Finally, church groups and charitable organizations raised the money for trucks to take them back to Mexico.

WHY THEY DID NOT DIE: CLIMATE AND HEALTH IN ARIZONA

In his 1878 book *Picturesque Arizona*, Enoch Conklin quotes Dr. A. M. Loryea: "The heat in Arizona, though high, is endurable in consequence of the dryness." This may be the granddaddy to Arizona's most quoted weather phrase: "but it's a dry heat, so you don't mind it."

And then there are those who never had a choice in the matter. For health seekers more than a century ago, it was live in Arizona or die almost anywhere else. Dr. Loryea dubbed Yuma "Nature's Turkish Bath" and "The

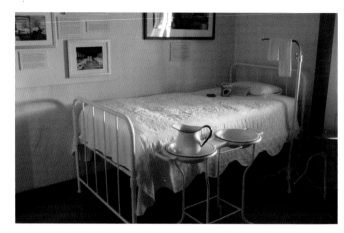

Great Sanitarium of America."

While early doctors prescribed dry air for many ailments from heart disease to asthma, it was an epidemic that brought most health seekers to Arizona—the White Plague. Also known as scrofula, phthisis, or consumption, tuberculosis grew to epidemic proportions at the rise of the Industrial Age, when air pollution and urbanization spread this highly contagious disease. Common beliefs at the time were that clean dry air could effect recovery or at least prolong life.

Best-selling novelist Harold Bell Wright came to Tucson for lung problems in the 1920s and made a major impact on Arizona's recuperative climate by writing "Why I Did Not Die," a 1924 *American Magazine* article describing Arizona's curative climate. Commanding the attention of more than 50 million readers, Wright single-handedly made Arizona the number one destination for health seekers. That same year, the Tucson Sunshine Climate Club, a branch of the Chamber of Commerce, reprinted his article as a brochure and blanketed the country with it.

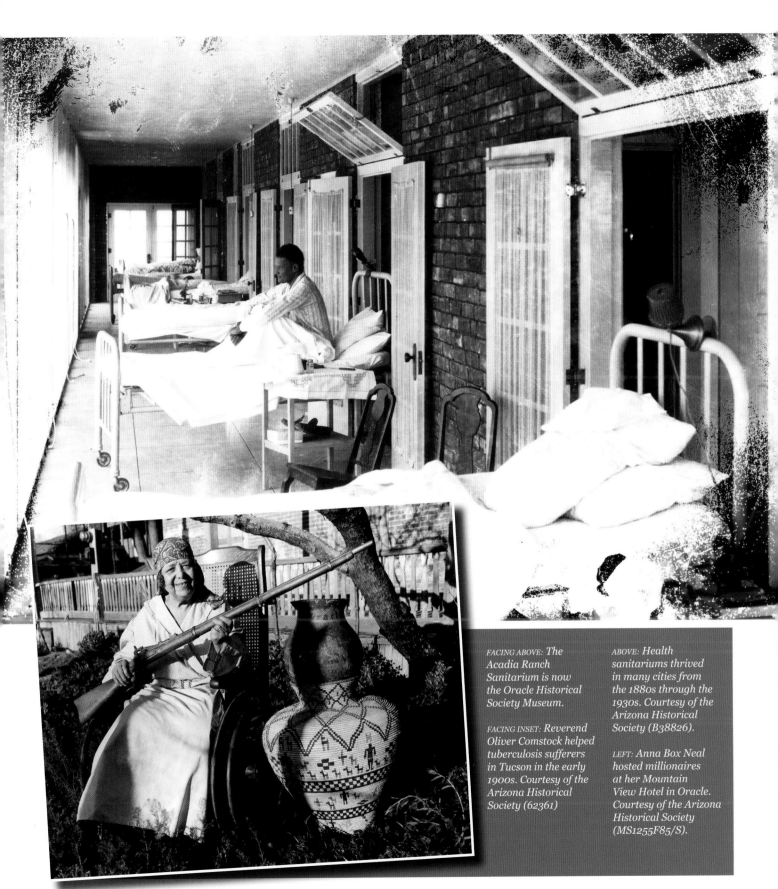

FACING ABOVE: The Acadia Ranch Sanitarium is now the Oracle Historical Society Museum.

FACING INSET: Reverend Oliver Comstock helped tuberculosis sufferers in Tucson in the early 1900s. Courtesy of the Arizona Historical Society (62361)

ABOVE: Health sanitariums thrived in many cities from the 1880s through the 1930s. Courtesy of the Arizona Historical Society (B38826).

LEFT: Anna Box Neal hosted millionaires at her Mountain View Hotel in Oracle. Courtesy of the Arizona Historical Society (MS1255F85/S).

For those who could afford them, large numbers of sanitariums opened in Phoenix, Tucson, Yuma, and many other parts of Arizona in the 1920s and '30s. For those who could not, tent cities cropped up, usually at the edges of town because of the risk of contamination. Church groups and charity organizations helped meet the needs of tuberculosis sufferers. With all these new arrivals, many western states began to think about how many people could possibly live in a desert.

WATER FOR THE WEST

As California began to grow rapidly, the other states adjoining the Colorado River became concerned about demands on their water supplies. A Colorado attorney named Delph Carpenter proposed that the states in question get together and determine each state's water rights. On November 9, 1922, delegates from the seven Colorado River Basin states met to apportion the water. After many objections, the Colorado River Compact divided Colorado River water equally between Upper Basin (Wyoming, Colorado, Utah, and New Mexico) and Lower Basin (California, Arizona, and Nevada).

Unfortunately, the estimates of water available were grossly miscalculated. No state ever got the amount promised, and water scarcity created disputes that continue today. Even though all parties signed the compact on November 24, 1922, Arizona Governor George W. P. Hunt refused to ratify the document. He felt the water should be given directly to each state, not to basin populations, rightly fearing that Arizona could not compete with California's rapid growth. When Congress approved the Hoover Dam project, which gave California more access to the Colorado River, Arizonans objected once more, but they were told that since they had not ratified the Compact, they had no say in the matter.

At the beginning of World War II, Arizona realized it desperately needed their share and belatedly ratified the

Colorado River Compact on February 3, 1944. Arizona legislators were still not satisfied and took their apportionment concerns to the U.S. Supreme Court in 1952. The final decision was favorable to Arizona, giving them almost all the advantages they sought in the original 1922 compact.

The primary answer to desert water shortages came in the form of the Hoover Dam, originally known as Boulder Dam. The huge concrete dam was constructed in Black Canyon, on the border between Arizona and Nevada, between 1931 and 1936, the result of the massive effort of thousands of workers. It was the largest concrete structure ever built at the time, yet it was completed two years ahead of schedule.

The dam generates power for Nevada, Arizona, and California, and controls the flow of water to prevent flooding and droughts. In order to bring Colorado River water to central and southern Arizona, the Central Arizona Project was created by Senator Carl Hayden in 1946. As an indication of how serious and expensive water is for every western state, the project was not begun until 1968 and not completed until 1994. Hayden also understood the importance of tourism to the state economy. He said there were two things people would come to Arizona to see—the Grand Canyon and the Petrified Forest. But they wouldn't come without good roads.

FACING: Completed in 1930, the Coolidge Dam was dedicated by humorist Will Rogers. Courtesy of the Pinal County Historical Society.

BELOW: Through water for agriculture, as shown here in Phoenix, Tucson was eclipsed by Phoenix by 1920. Courtesy of the Phoenix Public Library.

Gallup
Chloride, Ariz.

AMERICANS TAKE TO THE ROAD

As was mentioned earlier, the rise of Big Business as well as huge successes in the mining industry led to new social phenomena not possible before the creation of a leisure class. These two innovations, vacations and tourism, soon became important factors in Arizona's economy. Tourism on a popular scale seems to have begun in the 1860s, when it became fashionable for the well-to-do to take a spiritually uplifting tour of the Holy Land or to do the Grand Tour of Europe, visiting galleries, castles, and cathedrals that one must see in order to

The traveler in Arizona will find excellent highways to serve him on his journey through this delightful land of Sunshine and Scenic Grandeur.

The state is crossed east and west by four transcontinental highways — U. S. 60, 66, 70, and 80 — while the Canada to Mexico highway — U. S. 89 — crosses the state north and south. A network of hard-surfaced highways ties all parts of the state together, and so compact and well planned is the Arizona highway system that modern highways lead to the very door of many of the state's famed Scenic Shrines, and others are of easy access.

Arizona's highways are built and maintained to render the greatest amount of service to the traveler. Adequate signing and striping has been scientifically incorporated into the highway system to insure swift travel with the utmost of safety. The comfort and convenience of the traveler is the first consideration of the Arizona highway department. The traveler into this Empire of the West will find Arizona's highways his constant and good companions.

be considered well-traveled. Mark Twain poked fun at this new fad in *Innocents Abroad*, a lampoon of tourists and other guidebooks, first published in 1869.

Meanwhile, the railroad companies hit hard times because of overexpansion and the Panic of 1873. They turned to tourism to boost ticket sales and later created successful tourist-related businesses that included chains of hotels and restaurants, tour-guided auto excursions called "Indian Detours," and an Indian arts and crafts business, focusing primarily on weavings, jewelry, and pottery. But tourism was still reserved for the upper classes for several more decades.

Auto Camping Brings in Business

Arizona has always been a land of scenic wonders, but ordinary people didn't get to see them until the 1920s. While private car ownership rested at 8,000 in 1900, mass production and the new "buy now, pay later" plan rocketed that number to eight million in 1920! In the early twentieth century, companies began offering their employees vacations for the first time as a means of boosting morale and increasing production. By the 1920s, America's businesses were booming, and even store clerks and fry cooks were playing the

FACING ABOVE: Automobiles and highways made tourism a major industry on Route 66 between Kingman and Oatman. Courtesy of the Mohave County Historical Society.

FACING BELOW: Tourist magazines and maps romanticized the Southwest. Courtesy of Dori Griffin.

LEFT: Early motels called "Auto Courts" varied from rough cabins to full amenities. Courtesy of the Mohave County Historical Society.

BELOW: Cool Springs Auto Court now features a small Route 66 museum.

OVERLEAF: Full-service gas stations along Route 66 catered to tourists' needs. Courtesy of the Mohave County Historical Society.

7 MILES WEST OF OATMAN ARIZONA
HI-WAY 66

stock market. Once people had the time, the money, and the means, all they needed was a road.

The Mother Road Runs through Arizona

On November 11, 1925, the U.S. Highway system established Route 66, novelist John Steinbeck's "Mother Road." Spanning 2,448 miles, the highway began in Chicago, Illinois, and ran through Missouri, Kansas, Oklahoma, Texas, New Mexico, Arizona, and California, ending in Los Angeles.

Route 66 became the most popular road in America, the only one to have both a song and a long-running television show written about it. Its diagonal route from northeast to southwest made it the favorite transcontinental route. The

ABOVE: With improved roads, bus companies began to carry passengers all over the Southwest. Courtesy of the Mohave County Historical Society.

RIGHT: Tucson focused its advertising on its Spanish Colonial past.

FAR RIGHT: An early version of an airport shuttle. Courtesy of the Mohave County Historical Society.

ABOVE INSET: The iconic Route 66 logo made "The Mother Road" famous.

ABOVE: Route 66 saw its heyday in the 1920s but was revived by the 1960s TV show.

FACING ABOVE: Cafes like this one in Kingman thrived on the tourist trade. Courtesy of the Mohave County Historical Society.

FACING BELOW: Businesses like Joe and Aggie's in Holbrook capitalize on Route 66 nostalgia.

road's beginnings coincided with the new auto-camp vacation craze, the best way for middle-class Americans to see the whole country.

Roadside businesses sprang up along the route in every state—auto camps, diners, souvenir stands, and hundreds of roadside museums and menageries to entice tourists to stop and spend their money for pieces of petrified wood, beaded belts, and rubber tomahawks. At the same time, U.S. Route 70, nicknamed the "Broadway of America," snaked across the country in a more southern route, traveling through southern

Arizona. Every town along the route competed for tourist business, but one beat them all. It worked so hard at its Wild West image it is still the Mecca for "fakelore" fans from all over the world. Tourism fostered Helldorado Days, Boot Hill, and "The Town Too Tough to Die," with gunfights daily on the streets of Tombstone.

After it's halcyon travel days in the 1920s, Route 66's tourist focus took a back seat when terrible winds created the Dust Bowl in 1930, ruining crops and displacing thousands of farmers from Missouri, Arkansas, and Oklahoma. Then California growers began advertising in devasted areas, promising farmworker jobs in the Southwest. The Okies and Arkies, as they were called, tied all their belongings onto their cars and headed west. Garnette Franklin was a little girl growing up around her father's gas station in Holbrook, Arizona, on Route 66. She remembered that her father would give the immigrants free

gas just to move them on. Franklin said everything about that movement seemed to be gray—not just the dust and grime from the road but people's moods as well.

The Great Depression gave way to World War II, and gas rationing kept tourists off the road for the duration. But after the war, prosperity brought them back, staying at places like the Wigwam Motel in Holbrook and stopping at countless Route 66 diners along the way. But the route's popularity was again short lived.

Impressed with the autobahn system he saw in Germany during the war, President Dwight D. Eisenhower pressed Congress to pass the Federal-Aid Highway Act of 1956 to improve America's major roads. By 1970, almost all of Route 66 was replaced by four-lane highways; in Arizona, Interstate 40 brought an end to the Mother Road. But the highways didn't just bring auto campers and sightseers to the state. Some of them came to ranches, but not the traditional kind.

ABOVE: *Vacationing is more fun when you send postcards back home. Courtesy of Dori Griffin.*

LEFT: *Tourists also saved postcards as memories of their trip. Courtesy of Dori Griffin.*

ABOVE: *Towns hyped their image to compete with other highway towns. Courtesy of Dori Griffin.*

RIGHT: *Fun-loving tourists enjoyed the comical side of the West. Courtesy of Dori Griffin.*

RANCHES FOR DUDES, AND LITTLE BUCKAROOS, TOO

Dime novels and traveling Wild West shows like Buffalo Bill Cody's started America's love affair with cowboys and Indians, but the movies turned it into a passion. Beginning with the early silent films, low-budget producers and directors favored Westerns because galloping horses and gunfights could portray action and adventure without a sound. As a result, the American public got hooked on cowboys, ranches, and Western stars like Tom Mix and Douglas Fairbanks. Western writers like Harold Bell Wright and Owen Wister added to the mystique, as did artists such as Frederick Remington and Charles Russell.

But of all the Wild West artists, none reached the heart of so many Americans and Europeans as did Zane Gray. This Ohio native wrote more than 90 books romanticizing the Wild West, selling more than 40 million copies to date.

BELOW: Western movies helped dude ranches like the Flying V (now Ventana Canyon Resort) in Tucson become a major Arizona industry. Courtesy of the Arizona Historical Society (BN201601).

RIGHT: Ranch schools like the Southern Arizona School for Boys in Tucson promised a top-flight education in a healthy environment. Courtesy of the Arizona Historical Society (MS1255F522_C).

FACING ABOVE: Aviatrix Katherine Stinson delivered the first airmail to Tucson in 1915. Courtesy of the Arizona Historical Society (B38300).

FACING BELOW: Located in Tucson, this full-size replica of the Spirit of St. Louis is made of cactus! Courtesy of the Arizona Historical Society (BN208922).

ABOVE: Receding Rainstorm *(1924), by Maynard Dixon. Courtesy of Mark Sublette, Medicine Man Gallery, Tucson, Arizona.*

They were so popular that they became motion pictures and television shows. Grey grew up reading dime novels, played minor league baseball, then became a dentist like his father. With his wife Dolly's encouragement, support, and editing, Grey took up writing full time in the early 1900s.

In 1907, Grey attended a lecture given by C. J. "Buffalo" Jones and went with him on a mountain lion hunt on the north rim of the Grand Canyon that changed his life and his writing. Best sellers like *Riders of the Purple Sage* made the name Zane Grey a household word, and his romantic descriptions of Arizona's scenery and characters became reality for his readers. Modern writers continue in the Zane Grey tradition, perpetuating the Wild West myth for generations to come.

Lured by art, literature, and movies, many tourists were not satisfied with fast dashes across the West; they wanted to make Arizona their vacation destination, and that's where dude ranches came in. There were some ranches that accepted eastern guests as early as the 1880s, but the experience wasn't readily available to a larger public until the 1920s. Capitalizing on their western heritage, hundreds of dude ranches opened for business in the 1920s. The Circle Z Ranch near Patagonia, south of Tucson, opened its gates in 1926, as did the Kay El Bar Ranch in Wickenburg, and they are still catering to dudes today, as are quite a

few more recent enterprises. The Great Depression took its toll on most of the early ranches, but with cities and jobs becoming ever more stressful, the appeal of getting away from it all on horseback came back into vogue after World War II.

In the 1920s and '30s, dude ranches branched out to a younger audience in the form of ranch schools. Advertisers convinced parents that letting their children grow up in polluted crime-ridden cities was shameful, and that the caring thing to do

LEFT: Railroads teamed up with dude ranches to bring in customers.

RIGHT: Resort hotels with western motifs also attracted tourists. Courtesy of Dori Griffin.

BELOW: The Hotel Gadsden in Douglas combined opulence with a Southwest motif.

MEXICAN TROUBADORS

WONDERLAND OF ROCKS

CATTLE ON THE RANGE

HOTEL GADSDEN
Douglas, Arizona

1930

was to send their kids to Arizona, where they could grow up big and strong in the Arizona sunshine. While most catered to boys, Hacienda del Sol in the Catalina Mountain foothills north of Tucson was a ranch school for girls. Most schools were near Tucson and Phoenix, but some, like the Little Outfit Ranch School near Patagonia, were farther out.

The Great Depression took its toll on the schools, as it had with the dude ranches, but many of them held on. It wasn't until World War II came along and gas rationing and parents' desire to keep their children close to home in wartime, that business died off. Meanwhile, while well-to-do children from Back East received prep school educations and riding lessons, local kids met with difficulties in the classrooms and on the playgrounds.

Chopping off Mexican Roots

When Clinton E. Rose arrived from Idaho in 1919 to become Tucson School Superintendent, he noted that more than 50 percent of the school children could not speak a word of English. He began a program of beginning English and "Americanization" classes, commonly known as 1C, a system that lasted until 1965. Children were put in the class before entering first grade, theoretically for just one year, but often they were held back for as many as four years, which led to discouragement, demoralization, truancy, and high dropout rates. Just as it was with the Indian boarding schools, children were punished for speaking their native language.

Thomas Sheridan notes in *Los Tucsonenses: The Mexican Community in Tucson, 1854–1941*, that sometimes children were taught in indirect ways to be ashamed of their Mexican heritage and culture. They could not bring Mexican food lunches to school, play Mexican games on the playground, or celebrate Mexican holidays on the school grounds. Community activist Salomón Baldenegro, who grew up in Tucson in the 1950s, put it this way: "Americanization was based on a false belief that we were the foreign population—not true. We were indigenous. The U.S. came to us." An old Mexican *dicho* (or "adage") simplifies his statement: "We didn't cross the border; the border crossed us."

DEPRESSION-ERA ARIZONA

While agriculture foundered and tourism boomed, "America's business was business," according to President Calvin Coolidge, and that meant production. Radios became the latest appliance everyone had to have, and that meant another copper boom. In the 1920s, Arizona became the largest copper producer in the United States. But good fortune did not last long.

Manufacturers overproduced, buyers lost paper fortunes when the stock market crashed in 1929, and copper prices dropped from 16 cents a pound to 5 cents. By 1933 and '34, drought and the market devastated cattle prices so that mining and ranching families had to turn to picking cotton, which was also a failing enterprise.

In 1937, at the height of the Great Depression, another cotton boom prompted Arizona farmers to recruit cotton pickers from the Dust Bowl and the South. Signs were placed along Route 66 and other roads across Arizona to attract migrants who were already on the road advertising the need for farmworkers, and flyers were distributed in towns affected by the Dust Bowl. As a result, 40,000 migrant workers and their families arrived in Arizona by February 1938. The work was over by March, but floods in California kept workers from moving on to fields over there. The Red Cross and state agencies ran out of money to help the workers and their families, but they were stuck in Arizona. When Arizona Governor Rawghlie C. Stanford visited a farm camp near Phoenix, he found disease and starvation. After workers marched on the Maricopa County relief warehouse in protest, the New Deal's Farm Security Administration stepped in and handed out cash to the workers so they could move on.

RECOVERING FROM THE DEPRESSION
Arizona and the New Deal

President Franklin Delano Roosevelt's New Deal programs helped Arizona's economy just as it did most other states, but as usual, the state's unique qualities made for some differences. The Works Project Administration (WPA), Public Works Administration, (PWA), Federal Emergency

FACING: Construction of the Hoover Dam presented challenges that would have been daunting to anyone. Courtesy of the Mohave County Historical Society.

OVERLEAF: Dangerous situations were ever present. Hundreds of Hoover Dam workers died of work-related accidents as well as illness. Courtesy of the Mohave County Historical Society.

Relief Administration (FERA), and countless other "alphabet soup" agencies provided funds to erect buildings, create sidewalks, improve parks and nature areas, and, most of all, give people jobs, just as they did across the nation.

In Phoenix, president of the Valley National Bank supported the 1934 Federal Housing Administration (FHA) by authorizing 200,000 home loans. Working with the banks, contractors like Del Webb started Arizona's housing development industry by building federally subsidized homes and public buildings. But the New Deal was not just for cities, it helped the countryside as well.

The Cactizonians

In April 1933, the federal government created 28 Civilian Conservation Corps (CCC) camps in Arizona, with each camp housing about 200 men. Because of the state's temperate climate and vast undeveloped areas, Arizona hosted CCC men from all over the country, and southern Arizona camps also served as winter camps for workers in Wyoming and Colorado. Many of the men had never been to the Southwest and called themselves "Cactizonians" in the spirit of camaraderie that epitomized the corps, according to historian Peter Booth.

Arizona's state, city, and county relief organizations recruited workers between the ages of 17 and 24 for the project, but World War I veterans and a few older men were enlisted as well. They were not supposed to discriminate, but even though Pima County had a large Hispanic population, only 20 percent of the Tucson recruits were of Mexican heritage. The few African Americans in the camps were given separate barracks and were usually assigned the camp's dirty work.

Arizona's "CCCs" helped preserve the national forests by putting up fences to keep cattle from grazing where they should not be. Like CCC men all over the country, they built dams, recreation areas, and other improvements on government lands. Arizona's Native American men were allowed to enlist in the CCC, and there were

FACING: *Hoover Dam was the largest concrete structure of its kind for many years. Courtesy of the Mohave County Historical Society.*

ABOVE: *Civilian Conservation Corps veterans say the program was a life-building experience. Courtesy of the Colossal Cave Mountain Park.*

no age limits or marital restrictions for them. They often worked from family camps on the reservation.

The most spectacular difference between the CCC in Arizona and anywhere else is the work done at the Grand Canyon. The men constructed a fieldstone wall along the rim of the canyon from the El Tovar Hotel to the Bright Angel Lodge. They also landscaped the Grand Canyon Village area, constructed a community building, and made improvements on the Bright Angel Trail. CCC camps were also established on the North Rim at Desert View and near Phantom Ranch at the bottom of the canyon. Today, more than five million visitors to the Grand

ABOVE: The CCC built a visitor center and walkways at Tucson's Colossal Cave. Courtesy of the Colossal Cave Mountain Park.

LEFT: The Day family acted as overseers at the park. Courtesy of the Colossal Cave Mountain Park.

RIGHT: Irene Vickery, Besh Ba Gowah (ruins excavation director), and unknown persons.

Canyon every year use and appreciate the hard work of the CCC men.

When they learned firsthand that Arizona was not all cactus and sand dunes, many of the young men wound up staying. Even more went directly from their CCC duties to enlistment in the U.S. armed services. After the war, many of those men also came back to Arizona. On the other hand, those who had lived here for many generations did not fare so well during the Great Depression.

The Navajo New Deal

In 1933, the U.S. Bureau of Indian Affairs judged that two-thirds of the Navajo range had been destroyed by overgrazing, and Commissioner John Collier instituted reduction quotas for various types of livestock on specific locations around the Navajo reservation.

At that time, sheep raising and weaving had been the economic mainstay for more than six decades. When they were allowed to return from their Long Walk exile in 1868, each Navajo was given a pair of sheep, which they were able to increase by good husbandry and spiritual reverence for the animals. In addition to selling raw wool, the Navajo wove beautiful blankets and then rugs when the Harvey Company and other trading post owners pointed out American buying patterns.

Their success with the new southwestern tourism market increased the reservation's sheep population from 15,000 in the 1870s to more than a half million

Florence citizens built a tin can NIRA (National Industrial Recovery Act) eagle to boost morale. Courtesy of Pinal County Historical Society.

sheep in the 1920s. Those numbers led to overgrazing, which caused drastic erosion patterns that caused experts to recommend reduction to save the land.

This concept went against Navajo traditions, and since this was their major source of income, they knew it spelled disaster for their economy. Even though they resisted, the federal government slaughtered more than 80 percent of the reservation's livestock.

Unlike some farmers who were paid to plow under their crops or even not plant them, the Navajos were not adequately compensated for their sheep. In addition, the promised government education programs that would have given them alternative jobs did not materialize until after the Great Depression.

On the other hand, emergency soil conservation programs as well as the reduction did save the Navajo lands in the long run. However, the New Deal programs left the Navajos with another taste of bitter distrust to add to their Long Walk experience. In *Navajo Livestock Reduction: A National Disgrace*, historians Ruth Roessel and Broderick H. Johnson offer transcripts from 33 Indians who participated in the reduction program. The testimony shows that most Navajos neither understood nor accepted the fact that their overgrazed homeland would soon become unfit for human habitation if their herds continued to increase.

WORLD WAR II
The USS *Arizona* Memorializes the War

Shortly before 8 a.m. on Sunday, December 7, Japanese aircraft attacked the U.S. Pacific Fleet at Pearl Harbor. One of the bombs hit an ammunition magazine on the USS *Arizona* and caused a cataclysmic explosion that destroyed the forward part of the ship. The blast that sank the *Arizona* took 1,177 lives of the 1,400 crewmen, more than half the casualties of the entire attack.

The wreck became a national shrine on May 30, 1962. The *Arizona* continues to leak about a quart of oil per day in what some call black tears. Surviving *Arizona* veterans claim that it will continue to leak oil until the last of them dies. The bell from the USS *Arizona* now hangs in the University of Arizona Student Union Memorial Center, and its mast and anchor are in the Wesley Bolin Memorial Plaza, just east of the Arizona State Capitol.

The Language of Victory

At the outbreak of the war, Philip Johnston, son of a missionary to the Navajos, approached the U.S. Marine Corps with a plan to use the Navajo language as a military code. One of the few Anglos to speak Navajo fluently, Johnston felt that the language's complex grammar and tonal qualities would make it unintelligible to anyone without years of training.

Military officials liked Johnston's idea, and the first 29 Navajo recruits attended boot camp in May 1942. They created their code at Camp Pendleton, near Oceanside, California, modeled on a system of using agreed-upon words to represent letters of the alphabet. To make it even more difficult, several words could represent the same letter, and communications men interchanged them frequently.

Navajos were not the only tribe in Arizona to serve as Code Talkers, however. Eleven men from the Hopi tribe also developed a code language, which they used to assist U.S. Army Intelligence in New Caledonia, the Philippines, and the Marshall Islands.

At the assault on Iwo Jima, six Code Talkers relayed more than 800 messages with no errors, prompting Major Howard Conner to state, "Were it not for the Navajos, the Marines would never have taken Iwo Jima."

FACING: Navajo and Hopi Code Talkers used their native tongue to help win World War II. Courtesy of the Arizona Military Museum.

LEFT: *The 158th Regimental Combat Team "Bushmasters" flag bore the motto* Cuidado *("take care").*

BELOW: *Many Mexican American and Native American volunteers joined the Arizona National Guard. Courtesy of the Arizona Military Museum.*

FACING ABOVE: *Sunshine and isolation made Arizona a perfect location for air training fields like this one in Kingman. Courtesy of the Mohave County Historical Society.*

FACING BELOW: *The desert terrain along the Colorado River was a good setting for desert tank training.*

Arizona Bushmasters in the Pacific Theater

In addition to the Code Talkers, many Arizonans fought the war in the Pacific as members of the 158th Regimental Combat Team, a unit of the Arizona National Guard known as the "Bushmasters." The unit was comprised mostly of loyal Mexican Americans and Native Americans with a strong sense of duty to fight for their country. General Douglas MacArthur described them as "the greatest fighting combat team ever deployed for battle."

The day the Japanese bombed Pearl Harbor, the officers of the 158th assembled their men to tell them of their secret orders to guard the Panama Canal. There they adopted their nickname, the "Bushmasters," after an extremely venomous pit viper. Their insignia became a snake coiled around a machete, and its motto was the Spanish word *cuidado* ("take care") as a warning against snakes and to their enemies.

After one year in Panama, General Douglas MacArthur summoned them to make good his promise, "I shall return." Following MacArthur's island hopping, they saw heavy combat at Wake Island, Toem-Arara, Noemfoor, and Luzon, where they suffered their heaviest casualties.

Arizona Becomes Important

For most of its history, Arizona was one of those states like Nevada and Utah that no one wanted to come to because it was too far away, too hot, and had too much desert. But once America entered World War II, all these flaws became assets!

The government needed to build factories and military training bases in a hurry. Putting these facilities in the middle of nowhere helped for security reasons, and Arizona's warm weather meant men and women could work all year round without high heating costs. The clear skies and flat ground were perfect for air fields and pilot training, and the deserts along the Colorado River made excellent training grounds. For the first time since the gold and silver booms, people began rushing to the state again.

Military Bases

When war broke out, Arizona towns sent representatives to Washington, D.C., to convince government officials that their town was a perfect place for an army base, air field, or training center. No one was better at this promoting than Carl Hayden, Arizona's longstanding legislator.

An Arizona native, Hayden was sent to the House of Representatives by the voters as soon as Arizona became a state and was elected to the Senate in 1926. By the time

ABOVE: *Kingman residents were good hosts to young airmen far from home. Courtesy of the Mohave County Historical Society.*

FACING: *Kingman kept them flying in World War II. Courtesy of the Mohave County Historical Society.*

the United States declared war in 1941, Hayden's seniority placed him on enough committees and in contact with so many politicians that getting military bases for Arizona was not a problem. The *New York Times* once wrote that Hayden had "assisted so many projects for so many senators that when old Carl wants something for his beloved Arizona, his fellow senators fall all over themselves giving him a hand. They'd probably vote landlocked Arizona a navy if he asked for it."

World War II was the biggest boost to Arizona's economy and the biggest boom in population in the history of the state. The industry that probably benefited the most was construction. Military bases and factories needed lots of buildings. And when the workers came, mostly from the Midwest, to work in the factories, they

needed houses. More people were moving from state to state than had ever done so in the past, and a large number of them moved to Arizona.

The largest military bases were airfields to train pilots and desert training camps. Dozens of airfields in Phoenix, Tucson, Kingman, and Douglas included Luke, Williams, Davis-Monthan, Thunderbird, and Falcon Field. Some of these camps trained Americans, but others included British fliers as well. There were also practice bombing ranges on the vast deserts of western Arizona.

Army bases along the Colorado River near Quartzsite and Yuma prepared soldiers and vehicles for the sand dunes of North Africa. The Arizona desert was a good place to practice, but the Colorado River was also handy for training soldiers in how to build bridges.

Prisoners of War

Another benefit to Arizona's isolation was its perfect location for prisoner-of-war camps, separated from other states by desert, canyons, and mountains. Since the prisoners' only mission once they had been captured was to escape, military authorities made it as hard on them as possible by sticking them way out in Arizona. In all, there were 18 prisoner-of-war facilities housing almost 17,000 prisoners. The camps were located from big cities like Tempe and Yuma to extremely small ones at Bouse, Duncan, and Eloy. Florence was one of the largest, and its 500-acre complex featured barracks, a hospital, bakery, swimming pool, and about a dozen theaters. In 1943–44, it held Italian enlisted men. Later, German POWs were held there.

The prisoners were put to work in all sorts of jobs, from cutting timber to digging canals, but the majority harvested citrus, melons, and cotton, which was in demand once again for war production. Most Ger-

GERMAN TUNNEL ESCAPE

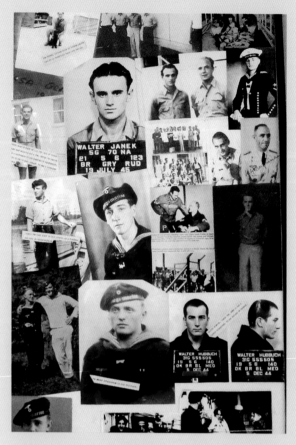

German U-Boat crews held at Papago Park in Tempe made an unusual escape attempt.

The Papago Park camp was so isolated that the American guards considered escape nearly impossible. Up to the challenge, submarine commander Jürgen Wattenberg took his duty seriously. Obtaining a map from the glove compartment of an unguarded truck, he and his men got permission to build a volleyball court. They began to dig a tunnel and got rid of the dirt on the court through holes in their pockets.

By December 23, their 178-foot tunnel was complete, and they were ready to make a break for it. The three-foot-diameter tunnel went under two prison camp fences, a drainage ditch, and a road. The men had even constructed small canoes from canvas and wood for navigation on the Salt River. That evening, Wattenberg had the men in the next compound throw a loud party to cover the noise of their escape. About 9 p.m., Wattenberg, 11 officers, and 13 enlisted men started crawling out in teams of two and three. By 2:30, all were in the clear and on their way.

Twenty-five men got through the tunnel without being discovered and surfaced near the Cross Cut Canal. Their plan was to float down the canal to the Salt River, taking that to the Gila River, then downstream to the Colorado, and down into Mexico.

The men were disappointed to find no water in the canal. They kept on going to the Salt and found it just a mud bog from recent rains. Undaunted, the Germans carried their boats another 20 miles, only to find the Gila River was only a series of large puddles.

On seeing the Gila, Wolfgang Clarus, one of the boat builders, said "Those stupid Americans! They put blue on the map when there's no water in the river!" The guards didn't even know the men were gone until they started straggling back to the camp in small groups that evening. The weather, terrain, and distances were too much for them.

By now, the U.S. Army, the Provost Marshal General's Office, and the FBI were called in. Two of the escapees got close to the border near Sells, Arizona, but Wattenberg was still at large. After a month on the run, Wattenberg was recognized as he slept in the lobby of the Adams Hotel and was arrested on the street. Thus ended the largest escape attempt in America during WWII, foiled by Arizona's "rivers."

mans, who had grown up reading the Old West novels of countryman Karl May, featuring "Old Shatterhand" and his Indian partner Winnetou, were thrilled to be on the locations described in his books.

Japanese Internment

The surprise attack on Pearl Harbor shocked and terrified Americans, particularly on the West Coast, the next perceived target for enemy attack. On February 19, 1942, President Franklin Delano Roosevelt issued Executive Order 9066, authorizing military commanders to create "military areas from which any or all persons may be excluded."

Although worded vaguely, the intent was to make sure that all people of Japanese ancestry were moved away from the Pacific Coast for the duration of the war. Military officers responded quickly, drawing a boundary that covered a huge land mass exclusion area, including the western sections of Washington, Oregon, and California, then starting from the northwest corner of Ari-

zona near Needles, California, and running diagonally south to Wickenburg, through Phoenix, Tempe, and Mesa, through the Superior-Miami-Globe copper mining towns, then east to the New Mexico border.

About 110,000 Japanese and Japanese Americans were moved to "War Relocation Camps" in what were deemed to be more secure areas in several states, including Arkansas, Colorado, Wyoming, California, Idaho, Utah, and Arizona. The detainees were hastily assembled

ABOVE: Memorial at the Poston Japanese Internment Camp commemorates Japanese-Americans who fought for the U.S. in Europe.

BELOW: Thousands of civilian Japanese and Japanese-Americans were imprisoned at the Gila River Japanese Internment Camp south of Phoenix. Courtesy of the Pinal County Historical Society.

and allowed to take only one suitcase of personal belongings each. Many lived for three years in small barracks rooms made of plywood and tarpaper, with communal bathrooms and very little privacy.

In some cases, however, young Japanese Americans were allowed to leave to attend college, and some of any age were allowed to leave to get jobs as long as they were outside the restricted zone. At the same time, Japanese Americans lobbied for and received permission to create the 442nd Regimental Combat Team, an Asian unit made up largely of Japanese Americans, which included those within the camps and those outside the restricted area. This self-sufficient fighting unit fought with exceptional courage in Italy, France, and Germany. It became the most decorated regiment in U.S. military history and included 21 Medal of Honor winners. The unit's motto was "Go For Broke," a gambling term that means to risk everything on one big effort to win big.

Two large desert camps were constructed in Arizona. About 13,000 detainees were sent to the Gila River Camp on the Pima Indian Reservation 30 miles south of Phoenix. Of those, 1,100 were released to join the U.S. military, and 23 from Gila River died in service to their country. Near the Colorado River south of Parker, Arizona, approximately 18,000 were interned, and 24 later lost their lives in World War II. Next to Phoenix and Tucson, the camps were the third and fourth largest communities in Arizona at that time.

In 1988, President Ronald Reagan signed legislation created by Congress that officially apologized to those interned, stating that the government acted based on "race prejudice, war hysteria, and a failure of political leadership." Eventually, the interned Japanese Americans or their heirs received more than $1.6 billion in reparations from the U.S. government.

War Production

Meanwhile on the home front, copper was king in Arizona once again. Miners at Bisbee, Morenci, Globe, Jerome, and all over Arizona began working seven days a week to provide copper for ammunition and other military products. Bisbee had every healthy man and women sign up for emergency duty at the mines.

In addition to mining, many new industries came to Arizona, especially relating to airplanes. Goodyear Aircraft opened a factory southwest of Phoenix at Litchfield Park. Alcoa (Aluminum Company of America) and AiResearch were two other large war plants that opened in Phoenix.

Local citizens were asked to provide spare bedrooms for newly arrived war plant workers. Those in Tucson and Phoenix worked three shifts at the factories, and they shared beds that never got cold because one sleeper was coming home just as another was heading off to work. Restaurants, movie theaters, and even public swimming pools stayed open 24 hours for those who worked the "swing" and "graveyard" shifts.

Arizona's Rosies:
Riveters and Pilots

Arizona had at least three things going for it when it came to defense plants. Senator Carl Hayden made sure the military industry moguls knew about Arizona's isolation from potential bombing or sabotage and, of course, the climate, which meant more hours without costly building heaters.

Since most of the men had gone off to war, manufacturing plants began to hire women. Women also worked as mechanics and truck drivers, and the most fortunate took to the air.

With military airfields all over the state, Arizona also became a leading training ground for the WASPS— Women Airforce Service Pilots. They were based at Yuma, Williams, Marana, Luke, Kingman, and Douglas Airfields, and landed at many other runways across the state. Like their male counterparts, many women sent to Arizona during the war fell in love with the state and made it their lifetime home. One of the WASPS, Byrd Howell Granger, was so fascinated with the area that she became a professor at the University of Arizona, specializing in southwestern history and folklore.

When the war ended, the positive attitudes continued. Arizonans felt they had worked hard and achieved something very good, and they now had the courage to apply that attitude to the building of a new expanding state of Arizona.

FACING: This plaque at the entrance to the Poston Japanese Internment Camp commemorates Japanese American soldiers who lost their lives in battle serving in the U.S. Army.

BELOW: "Rosie the Riveter"—a woman war worker operates a lathe at this Arizona war plant in Globe.

CHAPTER EIGHT
★ POSTWAR BOOM TO THE SPACE AGE

In four short years the war brought a maturation to the West
that in peacetime might have taken generations to accomplish.

—Gerald Nash,
The American West Transformed:
The Impact of the Second World War, 1990

The war was over, but this time the soldiers didn't go home. That is, not to their old hometowns in the East, South, or Midwest. The World War I song "How Ya Gonna Keep 'em Down on the Farm after They've Seen Paree" applied here, too. But this time it was the Southwest and not Paree the soldiers had seen. And they liked what they saw—hundreds and thousands of them liked it so much they made Arizona their new home. From 1945 to 1960, Arizona's population doubled, and the population of Phoenix tripled!

Senator Ernest McFarland made it possible for them to move, but he had help from men like Del Webb, Walter Bimson, and Carl Hayden. Dozens of builders, bankers, and civic leaders wielded the postwar boom as a tool to build Arizona. Not since the arrival of the railroad had the state

changed so much so fast. And it all started with a bill to help veterans.

Several more factors created the new Arizona in the 1950s and '60s, including the Cold War, the

FACING: *Desert Cottonwoods (1944), by Maynard Dixon. Courtesy of Mark Sublette, Medicine Man Gallery, Tucson, Arizona.*
ABOVE: *The Ruptured Duck, insignia on the World War II honorable discharge pin, flies over the memorial park in Bouse.*

Baby Boom, and age-restricted retirement communities. Working together, all the new trends came together to build a completely different modern Arizona, but it was one that still held onto its Old West roots if only for marketing and merchandising purposes. First, though, the soldiers used government funds to make a new home.

THE G.I. BILL OF RIGHTS

World War II created two of the most destructive and constructive things the world had seen to date. Both of them had the power to influence mankind and the earth's future, and they also affected Arizona—the atomic bomb and the G.I. Bill.

The Serviceman's Readjustment Act of 1944, nicknamed the G.I. Bill of Rights (shortened to just G.I. Bill), provided more than $14.5 billion for college or vocational education for returning World War II veterans, as well as home and small business loans to help them get started. By the time the original bill ended in 1956, it is estimated that 7.8 million veterans—almost half of those who served,

used it for a college education or job training, and 2.4 million received Veterans Affairs (VA) home loans.

The most unpredictable aspect of this G.I. college and home boom was connected to the realtor's mantra: location, location, location. One of the best aspects of the G.I. Bill was that it gave the individuals the right to choose where they would go to school and where they would buy their new homes. Senator Carl Hayden and others managed to get about two dozen military facilities as well as defense plants located in Arizona during the war. That meant a large number of servicemen and war workers lived in Arizona, at least for a short time.

It was unpredictable but understandable that they would choose to spend their G.I. Bill money in a warmer climate. They moved away from older, overcrowded, and polluted cities to ones that were building new homes and businesses as fast as they could. Thousands of G.I.s and their wives and very soon their Baby Boomer kids flocked to Arizona's college campuses in Flagstaff, Tempe, and Tucson. The University of Arizona in Tucson tripled its enrollment and had to build Polo Village, a series of metal corrugated Quonset huts near the campus, to house 1,300 veterans (now turned students) and their families.

Two veterans from St. Johns, Arizona, Stewart and Morris (Mo) Udall, were leading basketball players on campus at that time, and in 1947, they helped integrate the cafeteria by inviting a black freshman, Morgan Maxwell Jr., to eat lunch with them inside instead of outside the building. Stewart went on to become Secretary of the Interior under John F. Kennedy; Mo served as a U.S. congressman for 30 years and ran for president in 1976. Mo explains his loss to Jimmy Carter in the primaries in his autobiography, *Too Funny to be President*.

Federal highways put tourists back on the road after World War II. Courtesy of the Arizona Historical Society (MS1255F111_B).

RIGHT: *The stagecoach rides are a popular tourist attraction in Tombstone.*

BELOW: *This vintage passenger car in Parker is now a historic attraction.*

TOWN OF PARKER
EST. 1908

CIVIL RIGHTS FOR VETERANS

The Udalls weren't the only ones helping with integration in postwar Arizona. Mexican Americans and African Americans risked their lives to protect freedom and liberty, and they gained integrity and self-esteem from their wartime accomplishments. Now they had one more mission: they knew they would be returning to segregation and racial discrimination, and they were determined to make some changes.

In 1945, a group of young Hispanic men formed Thunderbird Post #41 of the American Legion, the first of its kind. Men like Ray Martinez and Frank "Pipa" Fuentes quickly threw themselves into the battle to end discrimination in the Phoenix area. One of their first actions was to help desegregate the city public pool in Tempe in 1946. Housing came next. When a veteran was told he couldn't buy a house in a new subdivision, Martinez contacted the developer and pointed out that it was illegal to discriminate when federal money was used in constructing a project.

Other groups organized against injustice as well. The G.I. Forum was founded in Corpus Christi, Texas, in 1948 to address the issue of Veterans Affairs services being denied Hispanics. After achieving success, the group moved on to other issues, such as voting rights, jury selection, integration, and civil rights for all Mexican Americans, not just veterans. A landmark case involved a segregated swimming pool in Winslow, Arizona. The case went to the federal district court, which ruled that it was not equal treatment, and the pool was opened to everyone in 1954. The Winslow decision set a legal precedent that minority groups applied to many other Arizona towns.

African Americans felt the same as Hispanics about

After World War II, farmers began to shift away from traditional crops, like this present-day orchard near Willcox.

their postwar mission against racism. Veteran Tuskegee Airman Lincoln Ragsdale, Morrison Warren, and many other dedicated African Americans worked through the NAACP and the Urban League on issues such as unemployment, substandard housing, inadequate education, and de facto segregation. Like most of the nation, much-needed changes finally came about in the mid-to-late 1960s.

Arizona enrolled more veterans in colleges and training schools than most other states, and even though minorities had to fight for them, Arizona also provided more dream homes than almost anywhere in the country.

BUILDING DESERT SUBURBS

As soon as the war was over, one of the biggest problems facing the United States was a huge housing shortage. From 1941 on, the armed services and supporting organizations had been taking young men and women from their parents' homes and sending them off to Europe or the Pacific Islands. Young men often married their sweethearts just before they shipped out or married them as soon as they came home. More than any other time in history, a large number of young couples needed houses all at once.

In 1947, a New York builder named William Levitt came up with a solution that changed housing and American lifestyles forever. Known as the father of modern suburbia, he built Levittown, the first mass-produced planned community, on Long Island, New York. The idea spread like wildfire, and it became the model for suburbs across the nation.

Taking lessons from Levittown and applying his own special touches, John F. Long built Maryvale in the mid-1950s, paving the way for thousands of veterans to own their own homes. Along with Del Webb, he was one of the giants who built Phoenix from a small farm town into the nation's fifth largest metropolis.

These look-alike starter homes were new and lovely, built in the popular ranch motif with a big picture window, a lawn in front, and a pool in the backyard. It was this style that would become the symbol of urban Arizona. Maryvale set the template for the typical suburban form: separate square miles of cul-de-sac residential streets to slow down traffic, separated by wide avenues with strip malls at the major intersections. Like the hundreds of subdivisions that would follow it (including the one this author grew up in), Maryvale had safe streets, good schools, and new parks supported by lots of civic charity contributed by Long himself.

According to John Talton, journalist and third-generation Phoenician: "With Maryvale, Phoenix began a transition that never ended. The lush, fertile Salt River

Willcox citizens celebrate their mining and ranching past. Courtesy of the Sulphur Springs Valley Historical Society.

Local rodeos like those in Globe were the real thing, not dressed up for tourists. Courtesy of the Gila County Historical Society.

Valley, in which American taxpayers had invested so much to reclaim from the desert, would move from agriculture to suburbia. Power moved from the big farmers and growers to the suburban developers."

Historian Marshall Trimble put it another way when he passed on this old timer's quip: "There's so much building going on, they should change the Arizona state bird from the cactus wren to the construction crane."

The veterans boosted the building industry for several years after the war was over, especially in the Phoenix area where most of the defense plants and military bases were located.

Builders eliminated the desert heat as a deterrent to moving there by installing a fairly new invention on every home—manufactured evaporative coolers. Better roads also made it easier to take a two-hour escape up the Mogollón Rim to Arizona's White Mountains in the summertime.

The Baby Boom continued to keep the builders busy as families grew, succeeded, and moved up to larger homes. But several other political and economic phenomena followed that fed Arizona's growth spurt. The first started as a local reform movement that almost swept an Arizona native into the White House.

THE REPUBLICAN ASCENDENCY

Back in the 1930s, politicians joked that there were three parties in Arizona: the Republicans, the Democrats . . . and the Democrats! In territorial days, Republicans were in the minority, and though their numbers were not so small that they could meet in a phone booth, a railroad Pullman car might fit them all in. Grand Old Party members (Republicans) were usually middle- or upper-class professional men who worked for railroads or mining companies. Many were appointed as territorial officials when there was a Republican president. They also served as army officers. In all cases, they were managers and controllers, not laborers.

The first group of Democrats our jokesters referred to would be of the Southern branch, usually Texas cattlemen or other immigrants who remembered the Civil War, favored States' Rights, and more importantly, chose county rule over territorial, which meant they were anti-federal government.

The second group of Democrats, and the most powerful, was the Tammany Hall type, those who promised jobs for votes, were not averse to kickbacks here and there, and allowed illegal gambling and prostitution if properly controlled. Phoenix more than Tucson had the typical ward healer variety of machine politics whose main goal was to stay in office and reap the rewards. The situation might have stayed that way indefinitely, but the war made drastic changes.

The army was still segregated in 1942, and a riot occurred on Thanksgiving Day that started the reform movement in Phoenix politics. In June 1942, the black soldiers of the 364th Infantry were transferred to Papago Park, where they got much worse treatment than their white counterparts. Their tents had no floors, they received substandard uniforms and boots, and their headquarters and mess hall were tar paper shacks. The chaplain complained of violent racist behavior by two of their white commanding officers, and U.S. Senator John Guffey from Arizona had recommended those officers be transferred.

After several months of punishment and confinement, the men were given a special Thanksgiving dinner, along with all the beer they could drink and passes to go into town. It was the first leave they'd had for more than a month. About a hundred soldiers headed for the African American section of Phoenix and a riot broke out. After three hours of armed fighting, the army used an armored car to get the black soldiers to surrender. Three people died and 11 were wounded, including a 17-year-old black girl who was shot in the hip. Fourteen soldiers received prison terms for inciting a riot, but President Roosevelt set aside the convictions, including one death sentence.

Three days after the riot, military commanders declared Phoenix out of bounds for military personnel, citing rampant prostitution and accompanying social disease problems as the cause. The *Phoenix Republic* agreed that city officials had been ignoring the situation.

Phoenix businessmen were outraged, knowing how much business they stood to lose without the servicemen. Concerned Phoenix citizens called for new, nonpolitical city administrators. Led by the Board of Directors of the Phoenix Chamber of Commerce, a group met with city

Calf-roping competition for working cowboys, their neighbors, and families around Prescott. Courtesy of the Mohave County Historical Society

officials in the Card Room at the Adams Hotel on December 17, 1942. Claiming to speak for the community, the board members demanded the replacement of city manager, police chief, city clerk, and city magistrate. The meeting lasted past midnight. The City Commission was pressured into agreement, and the officials were fired. Three days later, the military ban was lifted.

Once the crisis was over, things went back to business as usual, but seeds were sown for reform. In the Cold War buildup after the war, it was common knowledge that the Pentagon favored efficient cities with clean politics for their bases and civilian production contracts.

the National Municipal League's Model City Charter as their guide. The changes were put to a vote in November 1948 and were accepted by a vote of three to one.

In 1949, the CGC drew up a slate of reform candidates, businessmen, and professionals that included Barry Goldwater and future Supreme Court Justice Sandra Day O'Connor. The candidates were overwhelmingly successful, and as a result, a CGC's slate of candidates was elected easily for the next 10 years. It was the beginning of the "Republican Ascendency" for Arizona that has lasted with few interruptions for almost six decades.

But it was not just the riots or Democratic corruption

ABOVE: *The Wal-a-Pai Court along Route 66 in Kingman benefitted from the post–World War II tourism revival. Courtesy of the Mohave County Historical Society.*

ABOVE RIGHT: *By the 1950s, tourists enjoyed Wild West exaggerations like this 10-gallon curio store in Wickenburg. Courtesy of the Arizona Historical Society (MS1255F125_C).*

FACING: *Don't miss it,* The Thing. *Billboards tout it for many miles in every direction from this roadside curio store and "museum" on Interstate 10 between Benson and Willcox.*

Arizona particularly wanted aeronautics and electronics firms with ties to Washington.

To that end, in October 1946, Phoenix businessman Ray Busey called together a group of prominent citizens, many of the same leaders who were at the Adams Hotel Card Room four years earlier, to form a Charter Government Committee (CGC) to revise the city charter, using

that turned the tide. During the war, many war workers flocked in from the Midwest and Great Plains, particularly from Kansas, to work in the airplane manufacturing and electronics assembly plants. Quite a few were Republicans, but most were of the populist-liberal variety, carryovers from the early 1900s Midwest. Since their arrival coincided with the invention of the evaporative cooler, one old

Arizona Democrat complained, "There weren't no damn Republicans in Arizona until we had air conditioning!"

In addition to the new voting base, newspaper publisher Eugene Pulliam moved to Phoenix from Indiana and purchased the *Phoenix Republic* and the *Phoenix Gazette* in 1946. Through their editorials, the newspapers played a crucial role in reform; it is said that the CGC slate of candidates was always cleared with Pulliam, and it read like a list of the city's social and economic elite. Barry Goldwater went from the Phoenix City Council to become a U.S. senator from 1953 to 1964, when he became the Republican Party candidate for president,

expanded rapidly because of war-related manufacturing plants. An economy based on war production would ordinarily be doomed to failure after the war, but for the first time, a "non-war" kept growth increasing for decades after the armistice.

The Cold War between the United States and the Soviet Union began in 1947 and involved a continuing state of military and economic tension, proxy wars, military coalitions, aid to vulnerable countries, and conventional and nuclear arms races.

This meant that war production did not drop off in Arizona after World War II but continued to advance

then he returned to the Senate from 1969 to 1987. With longtime Senator Carl Hayden as his fellow senator from Arizona, the two packed a lot of political clout to get recognition for Arizona from the 1950s through the 1980s. That came in handy when World War II was followed by a war that was not a war.

COLD WAR HEATS UP ARIZONA MANUFACTURING

In addition to military bases, Arizona's economy

in technology to keep up with the Soviets. Most wartime military bases continued to operate, and they even increased in strength, especially when a ring of Intercontinental Ballistic Missiles (ICBMS) armed with nuclear warheads were placed in 18 underground silos around southern Arizona.

About this time, the state legislature passed tax exemptions for manufacturers working on federal projects. This attracted businesses to the state in spite of its former isolation, particularly avionics, aerospace, missile manufacturing, and the electronics industry.

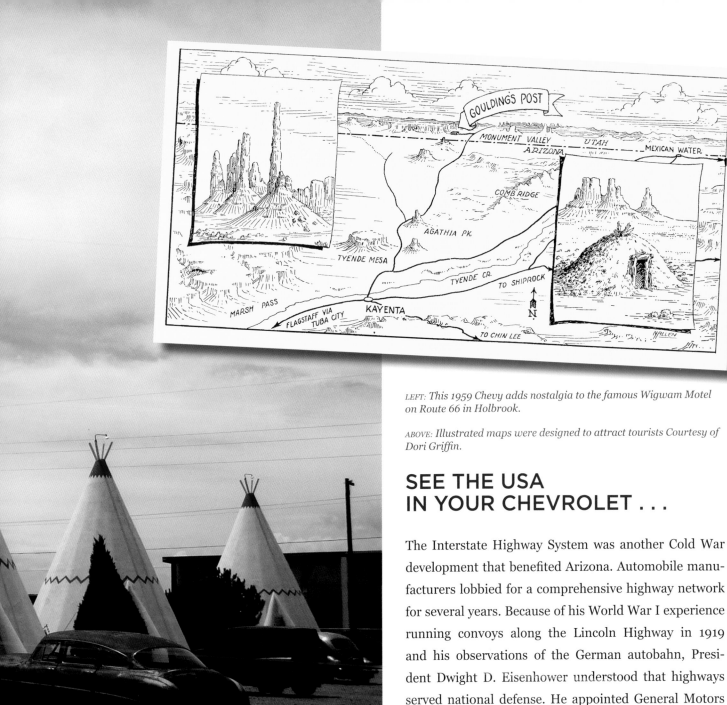

LEFT: *This 1959 Chevy adds nostalgia to the famous Wigwam Motel on Route 66 in Holbrook.*

ABOVE: *Illustrated maps were designed to attract tourists Courtesy of Dori Griffin.*

SEE THE USA
IN YOUR CHEVROLET . . .

The Interstate Highway System was another Cold War development that benefited Arizona. Automobile manufacturers lobbied for a comprehensive highway network for several years. Because of his World War I experience running convoys along the Lincoln Highway in 1919 and his observations of the German autobahn, President Dwight D. Eisenhower understood that highways served national defense. He appointed General Motors CEO Charles E. Wilson as his Secretary of Defense in 1953, and the Federal-Aid Highway Act of 1956 created an interstate highway construction program that would provide military transport routes in case of an emergency or foreign invasion.

But for Arizona, it meant the rebirth of the tourism industry, one of Arizona's economic mainstays since the 1880s, which languished in the 1930s and '40s. When rampant consumerism put TVs in every home in the 1950s, General Motors bombarded viewers with their peppy jingle, "See the USA in your Chevrolet, America is asking you to call." With a new car and a new highway system, Baby Boomer families jumped at the opportunity to show their kids the national park systems, which of course included the Painted Desert, the Petrified Forest, and the Grand Canyon.

As the icing on the tourism cake, publisher Raymond Carlson returned from the war and gave the state highway department engineering journal a miraculous makeover and turned it into *Arizona Highways*, the most beautiful tourism magazine in America. Beginning with Ansel Adams' contributions in 1946, the magazine has become famous for its spectacular photography, and *Arizona Highways* calendars became a favorite Christmas gift for new Arizona residents to send to their friends and relatives

ABOVE: The World's Smallest Museum—pure fun tourism in Superior.

RIGHT: Some scenes never change; still plenty of big sky near Arivaca, south of Tucson.

Back East. It would be hard to imagine how many people decided to move because of those pictures, but it certainly did a lot to reverse the image of Arizona as a desolate wasteland.

RETIREMENT CAPITAL OF THE WORLD

In the 1940s, many companies began to offer retirement programs to their employees. Just as the concept of paid vacations affected the tourism industry in Arizona, now another national business trend influenced an important new economic driver—housing developments. The G.I. Bill allowed a major segment of the population to choose a new place to live, and now that most of them had settled in, builders needed a new group with the economic freedom to relocate.

Social Security and company retirement plans created that new market—retirees, especially professionals and upper management, whose incomes provided generous benefits. Once again, Arizona's climate became a deciding factor for people who could live anywhere they wanted.

Beginning in the 1920s, Florida blossomed as the nation's first retirement area, but a combination of land frauds ("if you believe that, I've got some swampland in Florida I want to sell you") and two major hurricanes in 1926 and 1928 pruned its growth. In spite of these events and more recent hurricanes, Florida is still the favored

FACING: The 1950s TV westerns prompted this outlaw/kid standoff at Colossal Cave. Courtesy of the Colossal Cave Mountain Park.

ABOVE: Westernized ladies in Willcox show off the stylized western wear that became fashionable after World War II. Courtesy of the Mohave County Historical Society.

BELOW: Saguaro cactus furniture is truly an Arizona specialty. Courtesy of the Pinal County Historical Society

spot for those living in the Northeast. On the other hand, Midwesterners, especially from Minnesota, Wisconsin, Ohio, and Indiana, usually choose Arizona.

DEL WEBB BUILDS ARIZONA

In 1927, a 37-year-old California carpenter and avid baseball player named Del Webb contracted typhoid fever and came to Phoenix seeking a cure. Within a year he was working on the woodwork for one of the city's most lavish hotels, the Westward Ho. He started a small construction company that worked mostly on New Deal projects, and by World War II, he had established himself as one of Arizona's largest contractors.

Webb built homes for veterans after the war, but as the market died down, he recognized a good idea when his executives ran it by him. That idea was the brainchild of Ben Schleifer, a Russian émigré who developed Youngtown (northwest of Phoenix) in 1959, most likely the first planned community designed exclusively for seniors.

In quick response, Webb's people developed Sun City, which offered a relatively affluent generation of retirees more active amenities, including a recreation center, golf course, swimming pool, and shopping center. The community was self-contained, and residents were delighted to realize the only vehicle they needed was a golf cart.

Sun City opened on New Year's Day, and more than 200 homes were sold that first weekend. The community grew quickly, and a hospital was built nearby. The success of this new lifestyle attracted national attention, and in 1962, Del Webb was featured on the cover of *Time* magazine. He became the national spokesman for active retirement living, and his legacy manifests itself in hundreds, if not thousands, of Sun City–type retirement communities all over Arizona.

BUSINESS IS BOOMING

By the 1960s, Arizona continued to increase its manufacturing economy, aided greatly by Motorola executive Daniel E. Noble, who spent some time working as a cowboy near Prescott and fell in love with the state. He established the company's first research and electronics center in Phoenix in 1949 to research solid-state technology. This became the headquarters of the Semiconductor Products Sector of Motorola, which eventually separated to become Freescale Semiconductor, headquartered in Austin, Texas, with offices in Chandler and Tempe. Phoenix and Tucson legislators and city officials worked hard to attract industry. Their efforts resulted in General Electric, AiResearch, Sperry Rand, and Hughes Aircraft setting up locations in Arizona in the 1950s and '60s.

CHICANOS AND FARMWORKERS BUILD STRENGTH

Since the first cotton boom in 1918, Mexican farmworkers endured unsanitary living conditions, low pay (if any), inadequate safety conditions, and other degradations. In 1942, the United States and Mexico entered into a series of laws and diplomatic agreements soon to be called the Bracero Program, from the Spanish word *brazo*, or arm. With so many Americans away at war, farmers needed extra hands (or in this case, arms) to harvest crops during the war. Thousands of Mexicans received temporary work contracts and 10 times more entered the country without papers to fill the nation's agricultural needs.

After the war the country's economy boomed and the Bracero Program was extended, finally ending in 1964. By this time, farmers had become dependent on cheap labor, and large numbers of Mexican farmworkers continued to move from crop to crop. Since they were in the country illegally, farmers, especially the large corporate farms that had edged out the family farms, felt no obligation for improving working conditions.

In 1962, César Estrada Chávez, a Mexican American from Yuma whose family lost its farm during the Depression, organized the Farm Workers Association, later known as the United Farm Workers. The union grew quickly and was soon able to provide tens of thousands of farmworkers with health benefits and pensions.

Then in 1969 Chicano leaders in Arizona formed Chicanos Por La Causa, a nonprofit organization that provides impoverished communities with housing, education, job training, health care, and financial assistance. In 1970, La Causa leaders organized a boycott of Phoenix Union High School to protest the school's failure to cope with the high dropout rate of Mexican American students. Tucson also had its share of school walkouts and university protests in this era, and some participants went on to become leaders in local, state, and even national positions of leadership and service.

Arizona changed more in the three decades after World War II than it had since the coming of the railroad. Its geography and climate combined with the G.I. Bill, Cold War, the housing boom, tourism, high-tech industry, and civil rights to became part of the New Southwest while still holding onto its Wild West image and Native American roots. In the years to come, its image, attraction, and economy would shift again.

FACING: These long-eared Oatman friends like the attention . . . and the carrots.

BELOW: December Sky (1940), by Maynard Dixon. Courtesy of Mark Sublette, Medicine Man Gallery, Tucson, Arizona.

CHAPTER NINE
★ MODERN ARIZONA

Senator Barry Goldwater, Senator Carl Hayden, Representative Morris Udall, Secretary of the Interior Stewart Udall and other Arizona leaders teamed up on the creation of the Central Arizona Project, probably the state's most celebrated bipartisan achievement of the 20th century.

—The Arizona Republic

By the 1970s, as America continued to become more homogeneous through mass marketing, media, and manufacturing, Arizona's economy, lifestyle, and politics moved more toward an American norm. However, the state's unique geography, climate, history, and people still involved special adaptations and solutions as well as new opportunities for newcomers, both part-time and permanent.

A MODERN WATER MARVEL: THE CENTRAL ARIZONA PROJECT

In the 1920s, when Governor Hunt refused to sign the Colorado River Compact, farmers and politicians "created" more water for Arizona by adding a series of dams on the Salt River and building the Coolidge Dam on the Gila River. Humorist Will Rogers was the guest of honor at the dedication of Coolidge Dam in 1930. It was a dry year, and the water in the reservoir had only reached a few inches, with natural vegetation sticking up above the water line. Quick on the ad-lib, Rogers quipped, "If this was my lake, I'd mow it!"

FACING: Late Light in the Catalinas (November 1943), by Maynard Dixon, Arizona. Courtesy of Mark Sublette, Medicine Man Gallery, Tucson, Arizona. ABOVE: Built on ancient Indian irrigation canals, the city of Phoenix constructed "Arizona Falls" power station on the Arizona Canal in 1902 and restored it as a working station and public park in 2002.

Arizona's Roosevelt Dam (after Theodore Roosevelt, 1911), Coolidge Dam (after Calvin Coolidge, 1928), and then Hoover Dam (after Herbert Hoover, 1935)—originally Boulder Dam—were all named after presidents, indicating how important federal involvement was to Arizona's vital need for water. The biggest project of all, however, was 70 years in the planning and resulted in one of the largest aqueducts in the history of the world. Since the Colorado River Compact dealt with portioning out water to several states, the United States Bureau of Reclamation advised that a canal be constructed to channel Colorado River water from the northwestern corner of Arizona to Phoenix and Tucson. Since this was a monumental task and reclamation dams east of Phoenix seemed to be a more practical and less expensive solution, the idea went dormant.

It is no mistake that Carl Hayden, whose father ran a flour mill and ferry on the unpredictable Salt River just after Phoenix was founded, would choose to study water law at Stanford. Unfortunately, he had to drop out to run the family business because his father died. None knew more than he did about the importance of the law in dealing with water rights.

After World War II, Senator Hayden began to worry about rapidly increasing water demands. He and others formed the Central Arizona Project (CAP) Association in 1946 to convince Arizonans about the need for the long canal and to urge Congress to fund its construction. After 22 years of lobbying, President Lyndon B. Johnson finally signed the bill authorizing construction of the Central Arizona Project aqueduct.

For the next two decades, construction workers created a modern marvel. The Central Arizona Project cost $3.6 billion to construct, making it the most expensive water system in the United States. It is estimated that it would have cost four times as much to cover the canal. The CAP diverts water from the Colorado River near Parker, Arizona, and runs it through 14 pumping plants along its 366-mile length, raising the water 2,900 feet by the time it reaches Tucson. The canal is one of the world's longest, with the Panama and Suez Canals each being less than half its length.

Completed in 1993, approximately half the 1.5 million acre-feet of water delivered to southern Arizona each year, half of Arizona's total water supply, is used to recharge aquifers in Maricopa, Pinal, and Pima Counties for eventual residential use.

Arizona's Indian tribes, like those all over the United States, have always understood the value of water rights. In 1908, in a landmark case called *Winters v. United States*, the U.S. Supreme Court held that water rights were automatically reserved in the 1888 agreement that created the Fort Belknap Reservation in Montana. The court reasoned that the lands set aside were intended for farming and that water was implicit in making that possible. The ruling, referred to as the "Winters Doctrine," then served as a precedent to provide adequate water for all Indian reservations in the United States. In 1963, a corollary case, *Arizona v. California*, found that tribes whose reservations were created by statute and executive order came under the Winters Doctrine, and more specifically stipulated that the tribes were entitled to sufficient water to irrigate all "practicable irrigable acreage" available on their reservation.

Using these rulings, Arizona Indian tribes along the Central Arizona Project receive approximately half the water delivered from the river. Some of the water is used for agriculture and residential purposes, but some tribes now sell water to non-Indian subdivisions.

FACING: From golf courses to wranglers to the Superstition Mountains east of Apache Junction, water is still Arizona's most valuable resource. Courtesy of Jack Carlson.

LEFT: Parker Dam power-generating plant model at the Lake Havasu City Historical Society Museum.

ARIZONA'S SHIFTING SANDS: SUBSIDENCE AND EARTH FISSURES

Using, and ultimately overusing, groundwater has been a desert way of life since farmers started using electric pumps in the early 1900s; from prehistory to the present, water use has been a major contributor to Arizona's growth. Over long periods of time, millions of gallons of water are pumped out of underground aquifers, and the earth compacts and settles to fill the void. Scientists call the process *subsidence*. When one section of the earth subsides more than surrounding areas, large fissures develop. Fissures begin as cracks or crevices and grow through erosion into gullies or trenches up to 50 feet deep and 10 feet wide, with the central fissure running hundreds of feet into the ground. These giant cracks range from a few hundred feet to as much as eight miles.

Pumping greatly increased in the 1940s, when manufacturing plants like Alcoa and AiResearch needed vast supplies of steam-turbine electrical power to produce aluminum airplane parts. In *Cadillac Desert: The American West and its Disappearing Water*, reclamation historian Marc Reisner concludes that airplane production was the key to victory in World War II, and that the Grand Coulee and Hoover Dams provided the massive electrical power to get the job done. Out in the desert, Phoenix did its part, too.

Burgeoning population growth over the next four decades took its toll, and according to Joe Gelt of the University of Arizona Water Resources Research Center, groundwater withdrawals greatly exceeded natural aquifer recharges by 1984. Water tables in central and southern Arizona dropped drastically.

Outside of Casa Grande and south of Chandler, groundwater levels dropped 500 feet, according to Gelt. In Nevada and New Mexico, subsidence occurs in remote areas, but Arizona's problem is near major agricultural and urban centers, a vast desert triangle with Phoenix, Tucson, and Yuma as its points.

In 1980, Governor Bruce Babbitt formed the Arizona Land Subsidence Committee with representatives from the U.S. Geological Survey and the Bureau of Reclamation to address these concerns. No funding was appropriated to address the problem, however.

Now that the suburbs of Tucson and Phoenix are starting to meet in Florence and Casa Grande, overpumping has become a problem for homeowners. Ground sinks and deep cracks affect water, sewer, gas, and power lines, concrete foundations, highway systems, and even the danger of stumbling into an ever-growing fissure network. Fissures are only known to occur in six of the 50 United States, and Arizona has the dubious honor of recording the largest number of earth fissures caused by groundwater withdrawal.

In order to cope with the problem, the Central Arizona Project has overbuilt its canals, overchutes, and road crossings, and reinforced some areas with steel. While conservation organizations have put out the message that Arizona's groundwater laws protect our valuable water resources for future generations, much less is heard about the more immediate danger presented by subsidence and fissures. If discussed at all, groundwater over-withdrawal is treated like an overdrawn bank account. While this is true in some cases, and the CAP is beginning to recharge Arizona's aquifers, it is not possible to pump water back into them once they collapse.

GOLF, RESORTS, AND WESTERN ART

If Minnesota is "The Land of a Thousand Lakes," then Arizona is definitely "The Land of a Thousand Golf Courses." In the 1950s, tourists swarmed across Arizona, stopping at countless Geronimo, Wagon Wheel, and Sunset Motels across the state with their checklist of must-sees: Grand

RIGHT: The London Bridge spans the Colorado River at Lake Havasu City, above Parker Dam.

BELOW: In order to attract tourists, McCulloch purchased the 1831 London Bridge and rebuilt it in Arizona in 1971.

Canyon, Petrified Forest, Painted Desert, and of course, Tombstone. Westerns were a staple on prime time TV, back when there were only three or four channels to choose from. John Wayne, Dean Martin, and even Ricky Nelson were making western movies at Old Tucson Studios, and Americans were still in love with the Wild West.

But by the 1970s, the nation became more sophisticated. Cool private eyes captured TV audiences, and those who could afford it took Hawaiian vacations, or at least went to golf resorts. Arizona kept up with the trend and began to build large numbers of beautifully designed golf courses as well as topflight resorts to attract the new crowd, and were especially tuned to "snowbirds," who rushed to play golf in December and January, bragging to their friends back home, thus bringing even more players

to what was rapidly becoming the golf capital of the West outside of California.

On the eastern edge of Phoenix, a citrus orchard community called Orangedale sprang up in the early 1880s but changed its name to Scottsdale in 1894 after its founder Captain Winfield Scott (not the general who ran for president in 1852). It then became a haven for health seekers, and Phoenix's first resort, the Ingleside Inn, opened in 1912. Renowned architect Frank Lloyd Wright brought attention to the community when he began to build his winter headquarters, Taliesen West, on the east edge of Scottsdale in 1937.

While Scottsdale catered to Wild West tourists in the 1950s, its motto being "The West's Most Western Town," it vied with Santa Fe, New Mexico, by the 1970s as the

BELOW: Traditional jewelry-making techniques and designs blend with the modern. Courtesy of the Charles King Gallery.

FACING: Modern Native American jewelry experiments with finishes and gemstones. Courtesy of the Charles King Gallery.

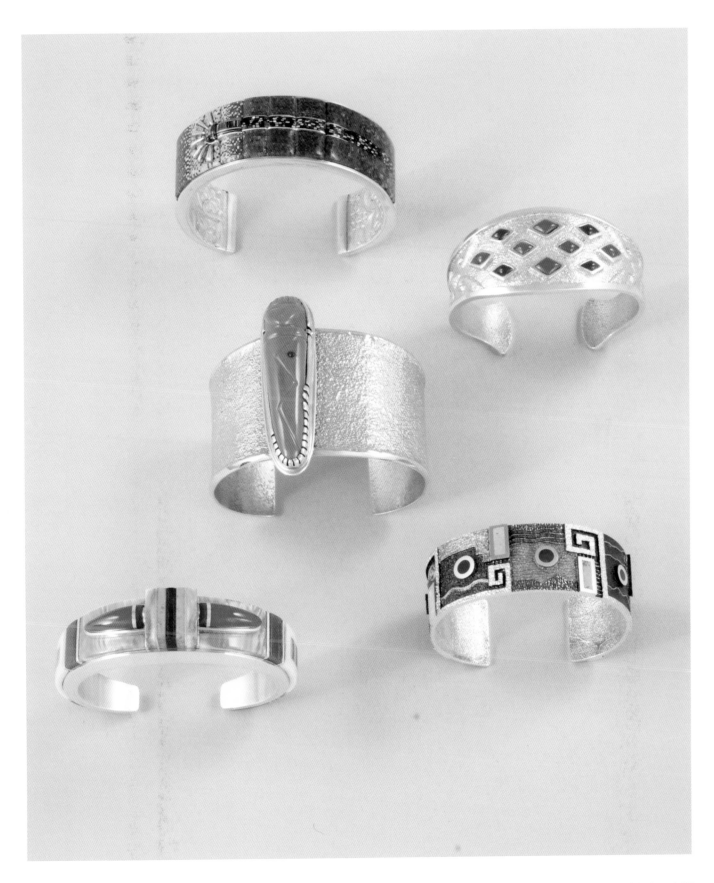

For more than four decades, Scottsdale has been one of the leading centers for Native American art. Courtesy of the Charles King Gallery.

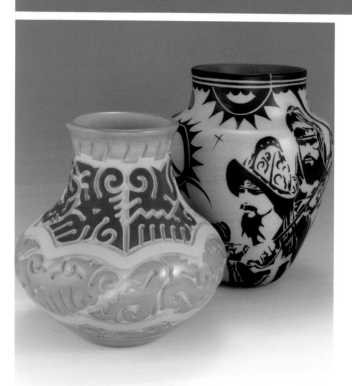

most elite western art center in the country, with dozens of galleries selling Native American pottery, paintings, and jewelry for thousand of dollars per item.

Resort building really took off in Scottsdale, Phoenix, Tucson, and Wickenburg in the 1960s, and more are being built every year. While tourism has adapted to new trends, Arizona's high-tech industry has followed the times as well.

THE BIOTECH INITIATIVE

During World War II, Arizona changed from an extractive to a productive economy. Instead of exporting cotton, citrus, cattle, timber, and minerals, the state began producing war-related products, primarily airplane parts. By the 1960s, high-tech electronics—transistors, circuit boards, and eventually cell phones and computer chips—dominated the scene and remained the lead industry for several decades.

Business leaders, especially in Phoenix, must have realized that success in manufacturing depended in part on understanding the market and getting involved in emerging economic trends. With that kind of foresight, the state began to host biotechnology-based corporations.

Although plant and animal breeding and hybridization are forms of biotechnology that have existed for thousands of years, these days the term refers to technological applications that use biological systems and living organisms to make products for use in health care, agriculture, industry, conservation, and countless other fields.

In recent years, several billion-dollar biotechnology corporations have established facilities in Arizona, producing everything from pharmaceuticals to Homeland Security bioscreening devices. In 2005, *Genetic Engineering and Biotechnology News* reported that Phoenix had recently furthered its "burgeoning biotech initiative" by creating the $46 million Biodesign Institute for bioscience research at Arizona State University. The Translational Genomics Research Institute (TGEN) is one of the first clients to move into the new building, located at Copper Square in downtown Phoenix. TGEN is a nonprofit research institute doing genome-related research in fields that include Alzheimer's, weight loss, cancer, diabetes, and cardiovascular diseases. The International Genomics Consortium, a medical research organization using genome discoveries to identify and develop cures for various forms of cancer, is also based in Biodesign Institute.

MEDICAL CENTERS CATER TO RETIREES

In addition to biotech health care, Arizona has become a leader in traditional medical services as well. It started when Del Webb anticipated the needs of his active retirement communities and built a hospital next to Sun City. As Arizona continued to grow as a retirement destination, developers and health-care professionals recognized age-specific needs. Since the planned communities are designed for clients of above-average means, they have attracted world-class hospitals to the area.

To name just a few, the Mayo Clinic Hospital in Phoenix opened in 1998 and was the first hospital designed and built by the world-renowned Mayo Clinic, which also operates an outpatient clinic in Scottsdale. HealthSouth, one of the nation's largest rehabilitation care providers, operates five rehabilitation hospitals in Arizona, specializing in patients recovering from stroke and neurological, cardiac, and pulmonary disorders. Equally prestigious, the Barrow Neurological Institute in Phoenix is internationally recognized for research and treatment of brain and spinal tumors, cerebrovascular conditions, and neuromuscular disorders.

TELESCOPES AND THE PHOENIX MARS LANDER

Arizona's clear skies have been a perfect location for stargazers. The dwarf planet Pluto was discovered in 1930 by Clyde Tombaugh at Percival Lowell's Flagstaff observatory, established in 1894 and one of the oldest in the United States. Astronomers from all over the world schedule viewing time at the Kitt Peak National Observatory's solar telescope, the Magnum Mirror Telescope on Mount Hopkins near Tubac, the Vatican Advanced Technology Telescope at Mount Graham International Observatory near Safford, the Large Binocular Telescope (one of the world's highest resolution optical telescopes) also on Mount Graham, or any of the other 30-odd observatories around the state. Arizona is considered to have the most world-class telescopes of any state in the United States and the largest concentration of telescopes in the world.

But astronomy is not just practiced from mountaintops. Founded by astronomer Gerard Kuiper at the University of Arizona in 1960, the Lunar and Planetary Laboratory (LPL) combines the disciplines of astronomy, physics, chemistry, geology, geophysics, geochemistry, atmospheric science, and engineering toward the single goal of studying planetary systems.

Over the past 40 years, the LPL has been involved in almost every interplanetary mission to Mars, Saturn, and Jupiter, from building the spacecrafts designing and operating cameras, to designing and operating monitoring and imaging instruments. Most notable is the LPL management of the Phoenix Lander, a robotic spacecraft that landed on Mars in 2008, the first National Aeronautics and Space Administration (NASA) mission to be run by a public university. Although Arizonans now reach into space, they continue to retrieve treasures from deep underground.

Percival Lowell installed his first telescope in Flagstaff in 1894. Courtesy of the Phoenix Public Library.

IT'S STILL A MINING STATE . . .

Since the first pioneers from "The States" came to Arizona to mine its riches, it is only fitting that we should conclude on the same note. Copper mining was a major factor in Arizona's economy into the 1980s, when strikes, environmental and safety regulations, and dropping copper prices caused international mining corporations to close mines in Arizona and shift their focus to mining operations in Chile, Mexico, Africa, and Papua, New Guinea.

Although mining continues at Morenci, Ray, Bagdad, and Miami, the industry is no longer the largest employer or economic driver in the state. However, the Freeport McMoRan Corporation opened a new mine near Safford that will probably be the largest in the state in the next 30 years.

Meanwhile, Augusta Resources estimates that its Rosemont Project in the Santa Rita Mountains will bring almost 3,000 jobs to Arizona. However, as of this writing, the project has been delayed because of significant local opposition to the mine. The Rosemont plan claims to set new higher standards for water conservation and tailing storage, but the project is on hold pending reviews by local, state, and federal authorities.

Another operation on hold, the Resolution Copper deposit near Superior, Arizona, considered potentially the largest copper mine in Arizona, awaits a land swap with the federal government, in addition to protests regarding impact on water quality. The huge deposit, estimated to be 1.34 billion tons, rests more than a mile beneath the surface and would require the latest deep-shaft mining technology; it would be one of the largest copper resources ever mined in North America.

BELOW: *Before it closed down in 1974, the Lavender Pit Mine in Bisbee was one of the largest in the world.*

FACING: *The Copper Corridor group commissioned Jerry Parra's* Skeleton Crew *sculpture at a roadside park in Mammoth.*

ABOVE: *Jerry Parra's*
Skeleton Crew *drill for*
copper in a memorial
park in Mammoth.

LEFT: *The Morenci Mine*
is one of the largest
open pit mines still
in operation today.
Courtesy of Carol Wien.

FACING: *Pouring molten*
copper gives off an almost
neon green glow. Courtesy
of Freeport McMoRan.

NATIVE AMERICANS IN THE TWENTY-FIRST CENTURY

Many things have changed for Arizona's Indian tribes, yet some things remain as they were. Despite concerted attempts, the soldiers and boarding schools did not kill the Indian spirit or culture. Members of Arizona tribes fought in two world wars, and many of the next generations went to college and became professors, chemists, lawyers, nurses, doctors, and every profession imaginable.

Yet many still practice their traditional spiritual beliefs, herd sheep, weave materials, and make jewelry. But artists now combine traditional motifs with the modern, creating their own style. Most have combined the best of both worlds, although there is still much poverty and social struggle in some regions. In the last three decades, Indian gaming casinos have brought much-needed revenues to many tribes, but some are too far from major highways to be profitable. Arizona's tribes are well-represented at the Museum of the American Indian in Washington, D.C., and efforts to preserve Native American cultural traditions continue to grow.

LEFT: *Two generations riding together in the Fourth of July parade in Kayenta.*

BELOW: *Near Dos Cabezas, Longhorn cattle introduced by the Spaniards 300 years ago are making a comeback. Courtesy of Carol Wien.*

Abandoned mine shafts, like the Alma Mine near Prescott, are common throughout the state. Courtesy of Carol Wien.

So there you have it, a broad-brush history of Arizona from prehistory to the present. Although most historians avoid predicting the future, most publishers insist that they try, because readers expect it. While many people are familiar with American philosopher George Santayana's warning, "Those who fail to learn from history are doomed to repeat it," what Mark Twain may have said is much closer to reality: "History doesn't repeat itself, but it does rhyme."

CHAPTER TEN

★ THROUGH THE AGES AND INTO THE FUTURE

Sometimes I hear the still voices of the Desert: they seem to be calling me through the echoes of the Past. I hear, in fancy, the wheels of the ambulance crunching the small broken stones of the malpais, or grating swiftly over the gravel of the smooth white roads of the river-bottoms. I hear the rattle of the ivory rings on the harness of the six-mule team; I see the soldiers marching on ahead; I see my white tent, so inviting after a long day's journey.

But how vain these fancies! Railroad and automobile have annihilated distance, the army life of those years is past and gone, and Arizona, as we knew it, has vanished from the face of the earth.

—Martha Summerhayes, *Vanished Arizona*

So that is Arizona, then and now, painted with a broad brush in red earth, blue sky, and desert sage. It was never like any other state, even in primordial times, as the Grand Canyon will testify. The terrain, climate, and geology all dictated, in one way or another, who would settle here and what they would do to survive and sometimes prosper. While they learned to adapt and sometimes to bend nature to their needs, the land still dictated the boundaries of what happened and what will happen.

ARIZONA: THEN AND NOW

Arizona is rich in prehistory, partially because the sparse population left so much untouched. Its looming cliff dwellings, like those of New Mexico and Colorado, leave traces of ancient civilizations to ponder about their origins. The ancient ones, the ones who came before, are still a mystery. Why did they abandon their cities, and where did they go? Anthropologists and archaeologists are coming closer to the answers, and as usual, it is an

Chollas against Mountains (1945), by Maynard Dixon. Courtesy of Mark Sublette, Medicine Man Gallery, Tucson, Arizona.

overlapping of several items that make up the whole: too many people gathered in one location to support them all, lack of water, epidemics, breakdown of societies, enemy attacks, and other contributing factors yet unknown.

We know they shared one thing in common with us today: the need to control water in a desert climate. The name *Phoenix* was aptly chosen to remind us of those prehistoric canals that gave birth to one of America's largest cities, which prospered with the waters of the Theodore Roosevelt Dam and others, as well as ground-water pumping and, at last, the CAP canal snaking its way across the state, delivering precious water.

But long before that, the Spaniards came to spread their religion, claim the land, grow crops, raise livestock, and scratch for minerals. There were followed by the Anglos, who first saw Arizona only as a wasteland to get through on their way to California—some travelers still do. Then mining began in earnest: gold in the 1850s and '60s, silver in the 1870s, copper in the 1880s and constant even today.

Mining successes, common in a state with so much mineral wealth, brought more miners encroaching on Indian lands, and Native Americans were already caught up in a cycle of vengeance since before the Spaniards. The clash of cultures brought the soldiers, then farmers and cattle ranchers to feed the troops, and later the Indian reservations.

Attempts to erase Indian culture failed, and the railroad brought more Americans, with drastic changes in architecture, fashion, culture, and families. Blended multicultural families diminished; El Camino Real was renamed Main Street; and Arizona became a state.

Massive water projects made the desert bloom with citrus and cotton, and the mines went into overtime production, making a name for the Copper State, producing copper and jobs.

The Wild West became a tourist attraction, marketed by the railroads and later by chambers of commerce in highway towns. Americans rushed to see Arizona's wonders, took snapshots, flirted with cowboys at dude ranches, sent funny postcards, and went home thinking Arizona was just like it was in the movies.

The Depression brought the CCC boys, New Deal building projects, and the usual sidewalks, statues, murals, and guidebooks. But many of the men stayed to make Arizona their home, to become pillars of their communities, and to raise families. Ranch schools came and went, a short-lived phenomenon that still lingers in some places, and the dude ranches reinvented themselves as golf resorts when trends changed.

World War II brought the biggest changes, but Arizona still remained unique. People flooded in to military bases and war production plants as Arizona shifted from an agricultural and mining state to manufacturing. Indian Code Talkers and the Bushmasters played a vital role in victory, then came home to use their G.I. Bill for college and new homes, sparking the building industry.

Tourism returned, and a new economy based on climate began: active retirement communities. Coupled with

FACING: At the Pima County Courthouse fountain in Tucson, a black tile stripe marks the original Spanish presidio wall.

BELOW: Wind snaps the flags in front of the Phippen Museum north of Prescott.

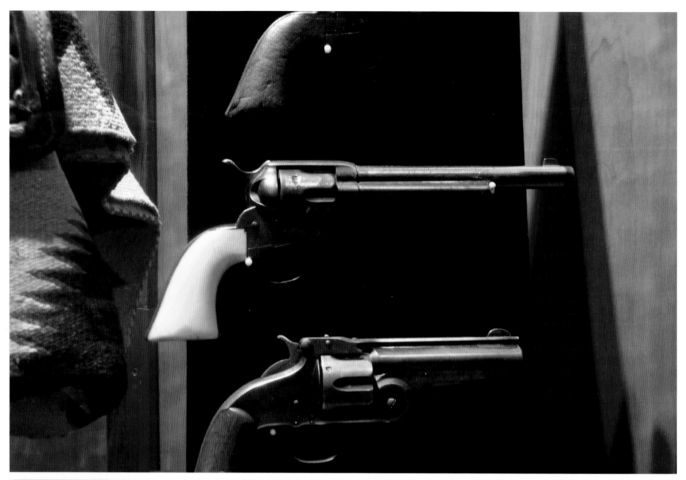

golf resorts that attracted "snowbirds," the detriment that kept Arizona from growing in the nineteenth century—climate—became an asset in the twentieth century.

In the 1950s, Barry Goldwater's charisma changed Arizona from a blue state to a red one. The Cold War kept manufacturing prospering; then it shifted to electronics and finally graduated to biotech industries to keep up with demands. Housing developments continued to spread out, creating concentric rings of bedroom suburbs around Phoenix and Tucson.

Arizona had its share of scandals, from land swindles and bank frauds to an impeached governor, still showing its Wild West lawless character. But we also fostered the United Farm Workers, desegregation, and civil rights. Native Americans experienced some economic prosperity by traditional means and by nontraditional means with casinos and finally some water rights.

And through it all, water remained the most important, immutable characteristic of Arizona's nature, the one that is never conquered or tamed but must always be addressed. From prehistoric canals to Jack Swilling's ditch to the state-changing Roosevelt Dam to the Colorado River Compact and the Central Arizona Project, the history of Arizona is the history of water.

FACING ABOVE: Wyatt Earp's pistol—or at least parts of it—are on display at the Arizona History Museum in Tucson.

FACING BELOW: The Florence 1894 Fourth of July float's banner reads, "Health and Beauty of Arizona: Second to None." Courtesy of the Pinal County Historical Society.

BELOW: Healthseeker Jimmy Turner (seated) is grateful that his whole family loved moving to Arizona in 1951: (left to right) sister Pat, Grandma Winifred Hawley, Grandpa Elihu Turner, mom Mary Turner, and sisters Barb (in front of mom) and Nan at Sabino Canyon east of Tucson.

RIGHT: Oak Creek Canyon provides a cool oasis amid Sedona's red rocks.

OVERLEAF: Sun-frosted saguaros showcase Arizona's panoramic splendor on the north side of the Santa Catalinas near Hwy 77. Courtesy of Jack Dykinga.

WHERE DO WE GO FROM HERE?

Historians hate to predict, but readers request and publishers insist that they do, so here goes. Throughout its history, Arizonans have had to deal with the state's unique terrain, climate, and water supply. Sometimes they adapted and even turned detriments into assets.

So much of Arizona's history is different than other states; even its settlement patterns go against the grain. Throughout American history, the trend has been east to west, along lateral parallels. The descendants of New England Puritans moved west to Ohio, Indiana, and Illinois, while Virginia planters followed their latitudes west to Missouri and then Texas.

On the other hand, Spaniards settled the Southwest from south to north, from Mexico and Cuba up into Florida, Texas, New Mexico, Arizona, and California. Even today, Mexican heritage is much more prevalent in the southern parts of each state than in the northern.

More importantly, English colonists had to cross a difficult life-threatening barrier to reach the New World: the Atlantic Ocean. Once they arrived, not many risked going back, nor could they afford to. In many parts of the East Coast, language froze from the time that immigrants landed here, so that dialects in remote communities still echo Elizabethan England.

On the other hand, Spanish colonists followed the rivers up into the Southwest, and in Arizona they were able to "go with the flow," as the San Pedro and Santa Cruz both flowed unconventionally from south to north. Since those who came into Arizona were not from Europe but rather from a Mexico settled in the early 1500s, they did not leave their culture behind but merely spread the new blended mestizo culture into a southern Arizona terrain that did not differ from northern Mexico.

Most importantly, people traveled back and forth from Arizona to Mexico easily and frequently with no great barriers. Families often sent younger generations north to extend their business, and after a few years, they might return to Mexico for good, being replaced on the frontier by other family members.

These trends continued after the Gadsden Purchase, as mine owners complained that their workers

FACING: This Sulphur Springs Valley view is a rancher's employment benefit. Courtesy of Carol Wien.

LEFT: Arizona is home to hundreds of lizards species, which love to bask in the sunshine.

FACING: The boojum tree (center right) at the Arizona-Sonora Desert Museum west of Tucson grows naturally only on the Baja Peninsula.

ABOVE: Because of its panoramic view, Yaki Point is one of the best places to capture the sunset at the Grand Canyon.

were always leaving the job to go on a pilgrimage or to attend a saints' day festival in Mexico. But the border was fluid then, as it continued to be for decades. Even after the advent of the Border Patrol, guest-worker programs continued the traffic from one country to the other in the 1920s and then for 20 years with the Bracero Program.

Like water flow, centuries'-old patterns are not shifted overnight. As with all of the Southwest, the Latino population—whether from Mexico, the Caribbean, Central or South America—is growing faster than any other culture. This is not just from immigration; it also stems from the growth of *descendiente* families, those who have been in Arizona up to eight generations. Just as the large influx of war-production workers changed the state from

Democrat to Republican after World War II, it is just as possible that the growing Latino population may shift the balance back the other way.

Whether that happens or not is not for a historian to say. But whoever lives here and however they vote, we know one thing for certain—they will have to deal with the age-old question that has plagued desert civilizations since the settlement of ancient Egypt: how can large populations thrive in a land with scarce water supplies?

Subsidence and fissures have already caused irreparable damage to the land, and few efforts are being made to stem the tide. Instead, thousands of homes are being built in areas most affected by the problem. Although most translations of the Pima Indian name *Hohokam* translate as "those who came before," another rendering appears to be "all used up." Could this mean the people were all used up, or that they disappeared because their water was all used up?

If the water problem is addressed promptly and with successful innovations to rival the CAP for its efficiency in replenishing the water table, what then for Arizona? One is tempted to say, "more of the same." Golf course resorts and retirement communities have attracted Midwest-

erners to Arizona for decades and will probably continue to do so, although the next generation may prefer yoga and hiking to golf.

Since Arizona still has huge mineral resources, the mines will continue to operate, providing they address environmental issues. And civic leaders will continue to watch trends to attract business to Arizona. As more Baby Boomers retire, health facilities, especially physical rehabilitation centers, will boom with them.

Whatever happens, Arizona will always be unique. The Grand Canyon will still be grand, saguaros will be just as stately and serene, and Arizona's sunsets will still be the most glorious in the world.

ABOVE: In Arizona's Basin and Range region near Superior, steep roads climb from the desert floor amid giant rock formations.

RIGHT: At the Arizona-Sonoran Desert Museum west of Tucson, an Arizona desert sunset bids farewell to the day.

# BIBLIOGRAPHY

Since Father Ignaz Pfefferkorn wrote *Sonora: A Description of the Province* in the 1760s, millions of pages have been written about Arizona. For detailed reading lists in specific areas, readers are encouraged to peruse the notes in bibliographies of the books listed here. Articles in the *Journal of Arizona History* and *Arizona and the West* are excellent for primary source citations on specific topics. The University of Arizona's website, Southwest Electronic Text, hosts a wonderful selection of primary source materials and full text of rare books at www.library.arizona.edu/exhibits/swetc/projectsa.html

Apache History

Ball, Eve. *An Apache Odyssey: Indeh.* Provo, Utah: Brigham Young University, 1980.

Betzinez, Jason. *I Fought with Geronimo.* Lincoln: University of Nebraska Press, 1959.

Debo, Angie. *Geronimo: The Man, His Time, His Place.* Norman: University of Oklahoma Press, 1976.

Roberts, David. *Once They Moved Like the Wind: Cochise, Geronimo and the Apache Wars.* New York: Simon and Schuster, 1994.

Sweeney, Edwin R. *Cochise: Chiricahua Apache Chief.* Norman: University of Oklahoma Press, 1991.

Thrapp, Dan L. *The Conquest of Apachería.* Norman: University of Oklahoma Press, 1967, 1988.

Utley, Robert M. *A Clash of Cultures.* National Park Service: Washington, D.C., 1977.

Arizona History

Barnes, Will C. *Arizona Place Names.* Tucson: University of Arizona Press, 1960.

Farish, Thomas E. *History of Arizona.* 8 Volumes. Phoenix: Manufacturing Stationers, 1920.

Harris, Richard. *The First 100 Years: A History of Arizona Blacks.* Apache Junction: Relmo Publishers, 1983.

Luckingham, Bradford. *Phoenix: The History of a Southwestern Metropolis.* Tucson: University of Arizona Press, 1989.

Ricketts, Norma B. *The Mormon Battalion: U.S. Army of the West, 1846–1848,* Logan: Utah State University Press, 1996.

Sheridan, Thomas E., *Arizona: A History.* Tucson: University of Arizona Press, 1995.

Sonnichsen, C. L. *Tucson: The Life and Times of an American City.* Norman: University of Oklahoma Press, 1987.

Summerhayes, Martha. *Vanished Arizona: Recollections of the Army Life of a New England Woman.* Lincoln: University of Nebraska Press, 1979.

Thrapp, Dan L., *The Conquest of Apacheria.* Norman: University of Oklahoma Press, 1967.

Trimble, Marshall. *Arizona: A Cavalcade of History.* Tucson: Treasure Chest Publications, 1989.

——. Roadside History of Arizona, Missoula, Montana: Mountain Press Publishing Co., 1986.

Arizona Indigenous People

Dobyns, Henry, and Trudy Griffin-Pierce. *Native Peoples of the Southwest.* Albuquerque: University of New Mexico Press, 2000.

Spicer, Edward. *Cycles of Conquest: The Impact of Spain, Mexico, and the U. S. on the Indians of the Southwest.* Tucson: University of Arizona Press, 1962.

Trennert, Robert A. Jr. *The Phoenix Indian School: Forced Assimilation in Arizona, 1891–1935.* Norman: University of Oklahoma Press, 1988.

Geology and Geography

Chronic, Halka. *Roadside Geology of Arizona.* Missoula, Montana: Mountain Press Publishing Co., 1983.

Walker, Henry P., and Don Bufkin. *Historical Atlas of Arizona.* Norman: University of Oklahoma Press, 1986.

Hispanic Arizona

Bolton, Herbert Eugene. *Coronado: Knight of Pueblos and Plains.* Albuquerque: University of New Mexico, 1990 (originally published in 1949).

———. Rim of Christendom: *A Biography of Eusebio Francisco Kino, Pacific Coast Pioneer.* Tucson: University of Arizona Press, 1984 (originally published in 1936).

Cather, Willa. *Death Comes for the Archbishop.* Lincoln: University of Nebraska Press, 1999.

Kessell, John. *Spain and the Southwest.* Norman: University of Oklahoma Press, 2002.

Officer, James E. *Hispanic Arizona, 1536–1856,* Tucson: University of Arizona Press, 1987.

Pfefferkorn, Ignaz. *Sonora: A Description of the Province.* Foreword by Bernard L. Fontana. Albuquerque: University of New Mexico Press, 1949; Tucson: University of Arizona Press, 1990.

Polzer, *Father Charles. Kino, a Legacy: His Life, His Works, His Missions, His Monuments.* Tucson: Jesuit Fathers of Southern Arizona, 1998.

Sheridan, Thomas E., *Los Tucsonenses: The Mexican Community in Tucson, 1854–1941,* Tucson: University of Arizona Press, 1986.

Weber, David J. *The Mexican frontier, 1821–1846: The American Southwest Under Mexico,* Albuquerque: University of New Mexico Press, 1982.

———. *The Spanish Frontier in North America.* New Haven, Connecticut: Yale University Press, 1992.

Military History

Altshuler, Constance Wynn. *Cavalry Yellow & Infantry Blue: Army Officers in Arizona between 1851 and 1886.* Tucson: Arizona Historical Society, 1991.

———. *Starting with Defiance: Nineteenth Century Arizona Military Posts.* Tucson: Arizona Historical Society, 1991.

Bourke, John G. *An Apache Campaign in the Sierra Madre.* New York, 1886. Reissued by Scribners, 1958.

———. *On the Border with Crook.* New York: Charles Scribner's Sons, 1891; Bison Book, 1971.

Brandes, Ray. *Frontier Military Posts of Arizona.* Globe, Arizona: Dale Stuart King, 1960.

Finch, L. Boyd. *Confederate Pathway to the Pacific: Major Sherod Hunter and Arizona Territory,* C.S.A. Tucson: Arizona Historical Society, 1996.

Masich, Andrew. *The Civil War in Arizona: The Story of the California Volunteers, 1861–1865.* Norman: University of Oklahoma Press, 2006.

Tombstone History

Bailey, Lynn R., ed. *A Tenderfoot in Tombstone: The Private Journal of George Whitwell Parsons—The Turbulent Years: 1880–82.* Tucson: Westernlore Press, 1996.

Carmony, Neil B., ed. *Tombstone's Violent Years, 1880–1882: As Remembered by John Plesent Gray.* Tucson: Trail to Yesterday Books, 1999.

Guinn, Jeff. *The Last Gunfight: The Shootout at the O.K. Corral and How It Changed the West.* New York: Simon & Schuster, 2011.

Marks, Paula Mitchell. *And Die in the West: The Story of the O.K. Corral Gunfight.* New York: William Morrow & Co., 1989.

Tefertiller, Casey. *Wyatt Earp: The Life Behind the Legend.* Hoboken, New Jersey: Wiley & Sons, 1997.

# INDEX